Towards a Critique of Foucault

Economy and Society

Edited by
Economy and Society **editorial board**
Talal Asad   University of Hull
Mike Gane   Loughborough University
Terry Johnson   University of Leicester
Gary Littlejohn   University of Bradford
Ali Rattansi   University of Leicester
Grahame Thompson   Open University
Harold Wolpe   University of Essex
Sami Zubaida   Birkbeck College, University of London

Economy and Society paperbacks

This new series focuses on major issues which have been the subject of debate in the journal *Economy and Society*. Books in the series include:

The Value Dimension
Marx versus Ricardo and Sraffa
Edited by Ben Fine

Economic Calculation and Policy Formation
Edited by Grahame Thompson

Soviet Industrialisation and Soviet Maturity
Edited by Keith Smith

Towards a Critique of Foucault

Edited by
Mike Gane

Routledge & Kegan Paul
London and New York

First published in 1986 by
Routledge & Kegan Paul Ltd
11 New Fetter Lane, London EC4P 4EE

Published in the USA by
Routledge & Kegan Paul Inc
in association with Methuen Inc
29 West 35th Street, New York, NY 10002

Set in 11/12 pt Plantin
by Columns of Reading
and printed in Great Britain
by T.J. Press (Padstow) Ltd
Padstow, Cornwall

Library of Congress Cataloging in
Publication Data

Towards a critique of foucault
(Economy and society Paperbacks)
Bibliography: p.
Includes index.
Contents: Introduction: Michel Foucault
Mike Gane—Foucault's genealogy of the human
sciences   Michael Donnelly—The linguistic fault: the
case of Foucault's Archaeology
Beverley Brown and Mark Cousins—(etc.).
1. Foucault, Michel.   I. Gane, Mike.
II. Series.
B2420.F724T69   1987   194   86-20268

British Library CIP Data also available

ISBN 0-7102-0764-6

Contents

Notes on contributors

Beverley Brown: B.A. London University; PhD. Cambridge University; freelance copy editor 1979-82; Visiting Fellow, Griffith University, Australia 1982-4; currently Lecturer, Centre for Criminology and the Social and Philosophicaly Study of Law, Edinburgh University. Member of the editorial group of *m/f*.

Mark Cousins: Senior Lecturer in Sociology at Thames Polytechnic. Co-author with Athar Hussain, of *Michel Foucault* (Macmillan, 1984).

Peter Dews: B.A. Cambridge University; M.A. Essex University; PhD. Southampton University; currently Visiting Scholar at Middlesex Polytechnic. Editor of *Jurgen Habermas. Autonomy and Solidarity: Interviews*, 1986.

Michael Donnelly: B.A. Harvard University; PhD London. Currently Associate Professor of Sociology and Social Studies, Harvard University. Author of *Managing the Mind, A Study of Medical Psychology in Early Nineteenth Century Britain*.

Mike Gane: B.A. Leicester University; PhD London. Lecturer in Sociology, Loughborough University. Member of the editorial board of *Economy and Society* for which he has written a number of articles on French social theory.

Jeff Minson: lectures in the School of Humanities, Griffith University, Queensland, Australia. He took degrees in psychology and philosophy at the Universities of Strathclyde and Leeds respectively, and did post-graduate research on Benthamism and Social Theory at Cambridge University. He has also published articles in *m/f*; author of *Genealogies of Morals: Nietzsche, Foucault, and the Eccentricity of Ethics* (Macmillan, 1985).

Gary Wickham: B.A. Macquarie University; M.A. Melbourne University; currently teaches social and political theory at Murdoch University.

CHAPTER 1

Introduction: Michel Foucault

Mike Gane

> A nightmare has pursued me since my childhood: I have before
> my eyes a text which I cannot read, or of which only a small
> part is decipherable; I pretend to read it. I know that I am
> inventing it; then the text suddenly blurs entirely. . . .
>
> (Foucault, cited in Major-Poetzl, 1983: 43)

The influence of recent French social theory and philosophy in the
Anglo-Saxon world has been dramatic and far-reaching. The
leaders of this *corps* of philosophically inspired social thinkers
included, most notably, Althusser, Barthes, Derrida, Deleuze,
Lacan, and others. Michel Foucault (1926–84) must be regarded
as one of the most influential of these thinkers. When this
collection was first conceived Foucault was still alive and at the
height of his powers. This collection is now not only a critical
engagement with Foucault's works but also, sadly, a testament to
what is now a completed life's work.

It is hardly likely that Foucault's influence is at an end,
however. Certainly since the beginning of the 1980s there has been
a considerable number of attempts to try to present and assess his
work over a number of fields. There are further essays due to
appear in the near future (two of them by authors of articles in
this collection – Dews and Minson). The pieces assembled here
from the journal *Economy and Society* reveal the level of critical
engagement Foucault's work inspired in a specific sector of social
inquiry.

All the essays which follow are capable of standing in their own
right and do not require a detailed presentation. Before introducing them very briefly it may be useful to offer an introduction to
the writings of Michel Foucault which might serve as a coherent
basis for comprehending the kinds of arguments which follow. It
also seems a good opportunity to present a short biographical
statement. And, in order to balance some of the detailed
discussion and assessment in the individual pieces of this
collection, this introduction will attempt to provide an initial
survey of the kinds of reception Foucault's work has received
elsewhere. These observations should be sufficient to enable the

reader to draw some provisional conclusions as to the nature and value of Foucault's project.

Foucault studied philosophy with Jean Hyppolite at the Lycée Henri IV and then with Hyppolite and Althusser at the Ecole Normale Supérieure where he gained his *licence de philosophie* in 1950 and his *licence de psychologie* in 1952. He taught courses at the ENS until 1954 when he joined the French Department at Uppsala in Sweden. In 1958 he went for a year to the University of Warsaw, and in 1959 for one year to the Institut Français in Hamburg. In 1960 he returned to France to take up the post of head of the Department of Philosophy at the University of Clermont-Ferrand. In 1966, Foucault went to teach in Tunisia, returning to France in 1968 when he took up the position of head of philosophy at the new university campus at Vincennes. He was elected to the chair of the History of Systems of Thought at the Collège de France in 1970, a position which he occupied until his death.

Fortunately Foucault has given some indications of the main influences on his thinking, and these are surely enough to begin to situate the way in which he himself thought about his own intellectual career. Between 1945 and 1955, he remarked, the young intelligentsia in France was dominated by a project to construct a new relation between phenomenology and Marxism (its leading figures being Sartre and Merleau-Ponty). Phenomenology began then to face up to the problem of language structure: 'I remember clearly some lectures in which Merleau-Ponty began speaking of Saussure . . . who was quite unknown . . .'. (Raulet, 1983: 198). When Lacan began to develop a Saussurean linguistic basis for a new reading of Freud . . . 'we had Freudian-structuralist-Marxism'. But there was also another focus – the work of Georges Canguilhem whose students, says Foucault, were neither Marxists, Freudians nor structuralists. 'And here,' says Foucault, 'I am speaking of myself.' The decisive influence was that of Nietzsche whom Foucault read 'by chance' in 1953. Thus, alongside the opposition to phenomenology which came from linguistics and psychoanalysis there is also one which comes from the influence of Nietzsche, via writers like Bataille and Blanchot (in Raulet, 1983: 199).

This (rough) attempt to locate a space relative to influences and to compatriots had its precursor in his inaugural lecture to the Collège de France in December 1970. Then he emphasised his specific debts to Georges Dumézil, Canguilhem, and the 'greatest debt' of all to Hyppolite (in Young, 1981: 73–6). Without specifying any detail Foucault has also mentioned the influence of Bachelard, and it is certainly important to note, as Louis

Althusser, the leading French Marxist philosopher has remarked, 'he (Foucault) was a pupil of mine, and "something" from my writings has passed into his, including certain of my formulations. But . . . under his pen and in his thought even the meanings he gives to formulations he has borrowed from me are transformed into another quite different meanings than my own.' (Althusser, 1969: 257). There is little doubt that Foucault was influenced, but at some distance, by Althusserian Marxism (Ballour, 1971: 189–207). The degree of proximity, of course, may have varied considerably, but when Foucault seemed to be close to the Althusserian project in the 1960s there were some interesting meeting points (see especially the reply to questions from the Cercle d'Epistemologie (Foucault, 1971). On the other hand it is also important to remember that, Derrida, for example, whose work is often highly critical of Foucault, was a pupil of Foucault as his lecture (of 1963) makes clear (Derrida, 1978: ch. 2). It is quite possible then to accept (if we forget the youthful communist phase) Foucault's own insistent assertion that 'I have never been a Freudian, I have never been a Marxist and I have never been a structuralist' (Raulet, 1983: 198). It is also clear that Foucault found it just as difficult to accept the label 'post-modern' or 'post-structuralist' (Raulet, 205) as it was to accept that of 'structuralist'. In fact, he strongly implies that, in the case of structuralism there was a certain justification for the label since there seemed to be a clear problem at issue; in the former case this was far more difficult to justify.

Insofar as critics have tried to pigeonhole Foucault's work the predominant ones have been those of 'structuralist' (e.g. DeGeorge, R. and F. 1972), 'neo-structuralist' (e.g. Wuthnow, *et al.*, 1984), or 'post-structuralist' (Harari, 1979). His work has also been called neo-eclectic, neo-positivist, empiricist, Spinozist, relativist, or phenomenological (for a listing of essays arguing these positions see Corradi, 1977: 160–204 and Clark, 1983: 105–244). Many of the commentaries on Foucault's work (on which see Gane, 1986) try to argue that what makes it particularly valuable is that it successfully bridges the divides between structural and phenomenological approaches (e.g. Dreyfus and Rabinow, 1982), or between structural and historical analyses (Major-Poetzel, 1983), or between Marxist and critical theory (Smart, 1983, and Poster, 1984). Another reason for the wide interest in Foucault's work is its enormous scope, reflected in the discussion of his work amongst anthropologists, historians, sociologists, social administrators, philosophers, literary theorists, etc. It is certainly important to inquire as to whether the apparent dispersion of reading means that Foucault's work is genuinely open to all these possibilities or is being widely misinterpreted. Nevertheless, it is quite clear that there is a very widespread effort to work out some of the implications of Foucault's thought in order to clarify some of the felt limitations of political thought on the left (Marxist and beyond) and, as Dews shows, on the right. One of the principal problems in the attempt to assess his influence is to assess the possibilities of a constructive Foucauldian reworking of social theory.

But there is another strongly emerging point of view, as represented in the following collection by the essay by Peter Dews, and more recently by Perry Anderson (1983), that the work of Foucault has had a mainly pernicious influence on the development of Marxism. Anderson, for instance, argues that Foucault's first phase was one of 'technocratic functionalism' followed by one in the 1970s belonging to 'the neo-anarchist current dominant in much of the French Left, (when he became) a major spokesman of libertarian leftism. . .' (1983: 57). Anderson even finds in Foucault's analyses a cavalier attitude to historical evidence which he relates to the fact that Foucault wished to abolish the possibility of an absolute truth: it is a 'normal and natural licence in a play of signification beyond truth and falsehood' (1983: 48). This kind of comment seems rather woefully distant from Foucault's writing, as if some *cordon sanitaire* should be established around it. There can, however be little doubt that Foucault has already had a profound impact on contemporary Marxism, as can be seen in the way that writers like Nicos Poulantzas (1978) through to Mark Poster (1984) have tried to rewrite some of the basic theoretical propositions of Marxism in Foucauldian terms. Indeed the essays by Minson and Wickham in this collection belong perhaps to this tendency, and indicate some of the issues at stake in such a project. There can however, be little doubt that this is not a project explicitly identified by Foucault himself.

So what exactly are Foucault's projects? In an interview of 1983 he summed up his work in the following way:

> Three domains of genealogy are possible. First, a historical ontology of ourselves in relation to truth through which we constitute ourselves as subjects of knowledge; second, a historical ontology of ourselves in relation to a field of power through which we constitute ourselves as subjects acting on others; third, a historical ontology in relation to ethics through which we constitute ourselves as moral agents.
>
> So three axes are possible for genealogy. All three were present, albeit in a somewhat confused fashion in *Madness and*

Civilisation. The truth axis was studied in *The Birth of the Clinic* and *The Order of Things.* The power axis was studied in *Discipline and Punish,* and the ethical axis in *The History of Sexuality* (1984: 351–4).

In fact, then, Foucault did regard his work as profoundly unified, though marked by a major transition which ultimately he saw linked to the massive upheavals of 1968. As is implied in this summary conspectus, the first works of Foucault are undoubtedly linked to the analyses of knowledge as structured in discursive formations bound to fundamental *epistemes.* A shift of emphasis took place after 1968 towards a recognition that, first, knowledge disciplines were articulated regimes which operated systematic techniques of exclusion and censorship, then second, that the very internal structures were produced as power structures. The objects of analysis at this stage included Foucault's famous consideration of forms of punishment and the 'birth of the prison'. Finally, Foucault began a massive project into the history of sexual morality, conceived as 'the genealogy of desire as an ethical problem' (1984: 356). The range of Foucault's writing, however, is far wider than even this. It includes not only a project on the history of government, but also wide-ranging considerations of literature and art, which are coherently developed alongside and even within the major investigations.

But Foucault's reputation is not simply that of a brilliant wide-ranging critic of Western culture, politics and society, but of an intellectual of great charm and geniality, as all those who were lucky to witness a Foucault interview would recognise. In these situations Foucault, perhaps in contrast to his writings, always seemed to be simple, direct, lucid and coherent, unpretentious, and often very witty. This is evident even when he appeared to be in a certain amount of difficulty. On one occasion, a lecture of 1976, he referred to appearing to others as a 'bit like a whale that leaps to the surface of the water disturbing it momentarily with a tiny jet of spray and lets it be believed, or pretends to believe, or wants to believe, or himself does in fact indeed believe, that down in the depths where no one sees him any more, where he is no longer witnessed nor controlled by anyone, he follows a more profound, coherent and reasoned trajectory. . . .' (1980: 79). In a somewhat enigmatically disenchanted vein he reflected that his previous series of lectures sketching a genealogy of anomaly and related techniques was 'tangled up into an indecipherable, disorganised muddle. In a nutshell, it is inconclusive' (1980: 78).

On the other hand this openness to the recognition of self-disorganisation is complemented by a delight in the apparent 'disorganisation' of the ways in which he has been understood.

> I think I have in fact been situated in most of the squares of the
> political checkerboard, one after another and sometimes
> simultaneously: as anarchist, leftist, ostentatious or disguised
> Marxist, nihilist, explicit or secret anti-Marxist, technocrat in
> the service of Gaullism, new liberal, etc. . . . None of these
> descriptions is important by itself; taken together, on the other
> hand, they mean something. And I must admit that I rather
> like what they mean (1984: 384).

The political dimension of Foucault's project has been something
of a problematic issue. As indeed has been the proposition that
there is an 'unknown' Foucault – Foucault the activist (Mauriac,
1975). As Clare O'Farrell pointed out in a review of Alan
Sheridan's book on Foucault in 1982, Maurice Clavel once
claimed that Foucault was on the barricades with the Trotskyists
on 15 May 1968. Confirmation of Sheridan's assertion that he was
not can be found in a recent interview: 'I wasn't in France at that
time; I only returned several months later' (1984: 385). Foucault
was, however, an active demonstrator and orator as is clear from
Simone de Beauvoir's account of these years (1985: 22); indeed
when Sartre organised an Israeli-Palestinian Conference the office
of *Les Temps modernes* was judged too small and 'Michel Foucault
kindly lent us his big, very well lit, quietly and elegantly furnished
apartment' (de Beauvoir, 1985: 113).

When the Socialist Party came to power in France it was not
long before Foucault became highly critical of its performance:
referring to 'the recent remarks of the President of the National
Assembly to the effect that we must replace the egoist,
individualist, bourgeois model with a new cultural model of
solidarity and sacrifice. . .', he commented: 'I was not very old
when Pétain came to power in France, but this year I recognised
in the words of this socialist the very tones which lulled my
childhood' (Raulet, 1983: 208). The problem is that this kind of
comment might be thought to reflect not only the leftism of
Foucault's thought but also at times its astonishing naiveté. And
then apparent naiveté can harden into a defence of the dictatorship
of the proletariat: 'it may be quite possible that the proletariat will
exert towards the classes over which it has just triumphed a
violent, dictatorial and even bloody power. I can't see what
objection one could make to this' (cited in Major-Poetzl, 1983:
58). In one of his last interviews he stressed that it was not politics
which was at the centre of his concerns but morals, or 'politics as
an ethics' (1984: 375). From having been a member of the French
Communisty Party in his youth, his later involvements seem to

have been non-Party affairs. In an enthusiastic introduction to Deleuze and Guattari's *Anti-Oedipus* he talked of the aim of developing the art of living the non-fascist life and attacked the 'bureaucrats of the revolution' (Deleuze *et al.*, 1977: xii).

It may be useful here to attempt to discuss in a little more detail and substance Foucault's various works and projects. It seems to me possible to suggest that there is thematic unity and there are subgroupings of essays which allow us to see a certain development in Foucault's overall project. The early *Mental Illness and Personality* reworked as *Mental Illness and Psychology* (1962, trans. 1976) obviously accompanies his main doctoral thesis *Madness and Civilization* (1961, trans. 1965). It is clear however that there is a group of essays which apparently tackle literary themes, as well as the book *Raymond Roussel* (1963), written in the years 1962–7, but which attempt in many ways to complement the study of madness. There are many explicit indications of this, for example at the end of *Mental Illness and Psychology* Foucault suggests that psychology can never fully grasp madness, but it can be approached in fiction, 'as in Nerval or Artaud, Nietzsche or Roussel' (1976: 88). The link with fiction alters somewhat in Foucault's suggestion that *The Order of Things* (1966) 'arose out of a passage in Borges' (1970: xv). Unlike *The Birth of the Clinic* (1963) and other works of those years which examined deviation and pathology, *The Order of Things* placed the dominant *episteme* at the centre of the focus of an examination of stages in the evolution of systems of thought in the West since the Renaissance. *The Archaeology of Knowledge* of 1969 represents not a major turning point as some thought at the time but a long methodological summation.

It is after this date that Foucault began to emphasise the relationship between knowledge and power which are the focus in various ways in *Disicpline and Punish* (1975, trans. 1977) and *The History of Sexuality*, vol. 1 (1976, trans. 1978). The latter was a work which seemed in many ways a theoretical and methodological introduction to promised subsequent volumes. As Foucault himself explained later, the promised volumes when they eventually appeared had a rather different objective than first announced (Foucault, 1984: 333–9). A third major axis which had in fact been latent all along had now become important: it was now knowledge, power, and 'the modality of relation to the self'. Thus, in retrospect, whether in the study of madness, illness, criminality, or sexuality, Foucault relates that it was not simply a matter of knowledge and institution (e.g. reason and the asylum, or health and hospital, or norm and prison) but a far more complex threefold interlacing.

> Looking at practices of internment, on the one hand, and
> medical procedures on the other, I tried to analyse the genesis
> of thought as the matter of possible experiences: first, the
> formation of a domain of recognitions which constitute
> themselves as specific knowledge of 'mental illness'; second, the
> organization of a normative system built on a whole technical,
> administrative, juridicial, and medical apparatus whose purpose
> was to isolate and take custody of the insane; and finally, the
> definition of a relation to oneself and to others as possible
> subjects of madness (1984: 336).

It is quite evident that Foucault thus considered his various
projects to be part of a single enterprise.

Foucault also reflected on his methodological procedures at
great length during his career. *Madness and Civilisation* is subtitled
'a history', but *Birth of the Clinic* and *The Order of Things* are
'archaeologies'. But his final works are once more part of a
'History' (of Sexuality). It is interesting to note the comment
towards the end of volume one of the latter: 'the history of the
deployment of sexuality, as it has evolved since the classical age,
can serve as an archaeology of psychoanalysis' (1984b: 130; for a
consideration of Foucault's changing estimations of psychoanalysis
see Forrester (1980)). Foucault goes on to stress that the
archaeology, and genealogy, actually form one side of methodological discussion, which concern the formation of discourses; the
other he suggested is critical, and concerns the consideration of
the regulation of discourses (in Young, 1981: 52–75). Whether or
not he was completely successful in these projects there is little
doubt that Foucault attempted to take an extremely anti-humanist
and anti-structuralist path. His attack on and opposition to
descriptive histories or explanations based on the simple or
complex volitions of acting individual subjects was a sustained and
explicit objective. His interest in Nietzsche seemed to provide one
of the great inspirations of this pursuit. One of his formulations
maintains:

> . . . historical contextualisation needed to be something more
> than the simple relativisation of the phenomenological
> subject. . . . One has to dispense with the constituent subject
> . . . to attain an analysis which can account for the constitution
> of the subject within the historical texture. . . . (In Morris and
> Patton, 1979: 35).

Secondly, Foucault's idea of the critical method hardly led to the
adoption of a simple rationalism, but at some points to a
suggestion that

The essential political problem for the intellectual is not to criticise the ideological contents supposedly linked to science, or to ensure that his own scientific practice is accompanied by a correct ideology, but that of ascertaining a new politics of truth (1980: 133).

If we examine Foucault's claims for the radicality of his conception of history it is clear that most of his important works present a series of historic stages which form the basis for the problems posed. This does, of course, have the advantage of revealing breaks and transitions in a historical process. In fact, the most rewarding aspect of Foucault's work may be said to lie in its ability to reveal new aspects of such series. But although Foucault is willing to consider the problem of functional relations, he is quite insistent that he will not consider legitimate the conceptualisation of society as a whole as a functional entity. He showed little interest in attempting to explain the causes of the transitions, and this has opened him to the charge that 'unable to explain the sudden mutations between the successive epistemes of his early work . . .(he) later resorted to increasing celebration of the role of *chance* as the governor of events' and that this has been accompanied by the insertion of 'methodological principles into an ontology – a panurgic will to power . . . (but) no specific holders of power, nor any specific goals which its exercise serves. . .' (Anderson, 1983: 50–1). Anderson suggests that one of the main reasons for this logic is the Nietzsche-Saussure inspiration of the perspectives which provides no way of thinking the causation of structural historical process.

In fact there is every reason to exercise caution before following Anderson and the attempt to reduce Foucault to either Nietzsche or Saussure. Foucault's own careful specification of the object of his analyses in *The Archaeology of Knowledge* makes clear that it is not a purely linguistic object or a collection of texts, it is, rather, the *archive*, 'the density of discursive practices' which 'do not accumulate endlessly in an amorphous mass, nor are they inscribed in an unbroken linearity, nor do they disappear at the mercy of chance external accidents' (1972: 129). The methodological consequence is monumental rather than documentary. While it is true that Foucault steps back from the science/ideology couple, this is not to avoid the question of evidence as Anderson suggests, but to rethink the question of truth in relation to its mode of production. But the problem of historical causation remains, for it seems that without some specification of the nature of the totality within which the social processes occur Foucault is indeed left only with a principle of immanence: 'Between

techniques of knowledge and strategies of power there is no
exteriority, even if they have specific roles and are linked together
on the basis of their difference' (1984b: 98). This virtual neo-
substantialism is linked to Foucault's descriptive historicism, even
if it is immensely fertile in Foucault's hands.

A second issue can be seen to be related to these questions.
However much Foucault seems to be able to enter into an endless
pursuit of the discontinuities of European social history, and is
able to problematise them in a new way, the fact that he stands
back from an etiological analysis of such displacements has serious
consequences for any strategic conceptions which he might
develop in any of his ongoing practical interventions. There is a
vast gulf between the projects of a cultural, even social, criticism,
and those of a sustained political practice. The irony is that
despite Foucault's emphasis on the strategic elements of power the
moment of strategy in his political vision seems either muted or
absent. His preference for ethics over politics is perhaps a
recognition of it. Nevertheless, a large number of Marxists,
whether of the existentialist or structuralist kind, have found in
Foucault's attempts to rethink political theory a challenge well
worth investigating. It may be worth noting that a writer like
Mark Poster (1984) takes Foucault's challenge to imply a radical
recasting of Marxist concepts, while Edward Said (1984) argues
that it is precisely the concepts used by Marx which should be
installed in Foucault's project if it is to become a weapon in the
struggle for socialism.

But an altogether different level of consideration can be seen in
the critical comments of Perry Anderson noted above. Because
Foucault's conceptualisations are a curious mix of methodological
experimentation and archaeological description freed from the
problem of having to demonstrate and prove theses concerning
social procession, is it contemptuous of questions of the reliability
of evidence and critical self-appraisal? Anderson, it is true, seems
to pose this question from the apparent standpoint of a simple,
absolutist empiricism, whereas Foucault's epistemology, whatever
criticisms can be made of it, is quite conscious of the main
problems at this level. In fact, of the group of French writers
mentioned at the beginning of this introduction, it is Foucault
virtually alone who has attempted to analyse social phenomena
from the position of a critical epistemology. Anderson, for
example, refers to Foucault's 'credulity in the Ship of Fools and
fable of the Great Confinement' (1984: 48), as if Foucault was
indifferent in principle to such questions in his work *Madness and
Civilization*. Anderson's criticisms are taken directly from the
work of Erik Midelfort whose essay (1980) stresses that many

arguments of Foucault's book 'fly in the face of empirical evidence, and that many of its broadest generalisations are over-simplifications' (1980: 259). Midelfort, however, does not try to insinuate that Foucault is not interested in evidence, but that 'in trying to extract or apply Foucault's method, we will have to remain aware of the need to control the force of intuition. . . .' (1980: 259). For Anderson, on the contrary, the whole method and epistemology is vitiated since it appears to abolish the difference between truth and error, the 'central site' of which is evidence itself (1984: 48). If it would be rather easy to show that Anderson's observations seem wide of the mark, and that Midelfort's critical and balanced observations are more typical of the way that Foucault's ideas are being met by historians and social scientists more generally, there is another emerging criticism which turns this on its head by arguing that behind its apparent nihilism (something which Anderson hints at) is 'a new law disguised as beyond politics' (Rose, 1984: 173).

This particular line of criticism is not so much to argue that Foucault has not understood that the 'central site' of truth is located at the level of empirical evidence but that the way in which Foucault has reorganised the Nietzschean project involves him in both distorting the field of problems in the social sciences as well as masking his own objectives. Gillian Rose argues with great force that the nihilism which is central to Foucault can be identified in the specifically depoliticised way in which he has appropriated Nietzsche: by ignoring the fact that Nietzsche's 'thought aims at a new integrity' (1984: 183), a new politics. Rose's complex essay concludes that 'Neither positive nor negative . . . affirmation is without determination or characteristic; it does not represent an encounter with the power of another but an ecstasy of blind laughter or blinding tears, which . . . is simply that old familiar despair' (1984: 207). This can be seen again as another aspect of the problem which arises at the site where Foucault refuses to establish as the basis of his critique a consistent alternative position (either an epistemological support or an 'optimistic' vision of a new social order, or a conception of the relation between the two as can be found in orthodox Marxism). Rose's overall characterisation of Foucault as pessi-mistic nihilist is so at odds with all other readings that one wonders if there is here simply an idiosyncratic viewpoint. In a perceptive review of Rose, Salemohammed (1985) suggests that she has indeed misconstrued Foucault's strategy especially as it concerns philosophy. What is evident is that Rose appears to be unmoved by any appeals to examine the radical charge of Foucault's claims as to the immense damage done in socialist

politics by affirmations of visions of new orders which so often
turn out to be not the negation but, simply, negatives of old
orders.

It is time now, after this wide survey of writing on Foucault, to
come to the essays contained here. They do, as would be
expected, reflect more general tendencies – for example there is a
strong interest taken in Foucault's encounter with Marxism and
politics. But these essays reveal a concern both to present
Foucault's work as itself an important contribution to the
theoretical analysis of history, language and power, and to engage
critically with this contribution. The essays, written at different
levels of difficulty, not only read Foucault but are deeply
interested in how Foucault is read elsewhere, for example in
France itself, and, as the debate between Minson and Wickham
reveals, in Australia where Foucault's work has had considerable
influence.

Michael Donnelly's essay which opens the collection presents,
lucidly, Foucault's basic conception of genealogical method and
looks at the way he attempted to apply it in *Discipline and Punish*.
Donnelly's essay points to some of the apparent difficulties which
Foucault faced especially as they arise out of a project which
appears to privilege historical method, albeit on a new kind. After
examining some of the specific characteristics of the new method,
Donnelly considers its effectiveness against three basic issues faced
by historians: causal versus descriptive analysis of (i) the origins,
(ii) the diffusion and (iii) the functions of social phenomena. In all
these questions Foucault's claim to have made a decisive break
with more or less conventional historical method is not sustained.

Beverley Brown and Mark Cousins, in a tightly written
theoretical consideration of a central Foucault concern, suggest,
again, that although Foucault's own claim that his thoroughgoing
critique of linguistics had broken with the traditional centrality of
the communicating individual subject, this claim can be contested
at critical points. Their investigation focuses in depth on the
argument in *The Archaeology of Knowledge* from which they select
Foucault's discussion of the 'statement' in order to show that it
relies on a hidden acceptance of a whole range of phenomena which
Foucault's explicit project has sought to surmount, particularly
the simple opposition of discourse and institution. But in the gap
between these two orders arises the 'general question of
enunciation for it is here that questions of signs, the subject and
social categories are tied together'. The essay points to unresolved
tensions in Foucault's project.

Peter Dews examines the ways in which *The Archaeology of
Knowledge*, and *Discipline and Punish* in particular have been read

by the French 'new right' philosophers (Glucksmann, Lévy, Clavel, etc.). He shows that while not able to provide unequivocal interpretations of Foucault as a 'new right' thinker, the new right have certainly believed that they have found in Foucault's work a valuable resource and fellow spirit. Dews has shown that because Foucault argues that a theoretical analysis of spontaneous resistance and revolt can be seen as aligning itself inherently within the repressive order against which the revolt is aimed, any serious rapprochement between Foucault and Marxism is unlikely. Dews' essay provides an account of the theoretical background of Foucault's writing in the years after 1970 and of the ambiguities of his positions as seen against the new conjuncture.

The essays by Jeff Minson and Gary Wickham, on the other hand, represent very clearly the way in which Foucault's work has excited the socialist left. Minson takes up the conception of strategy as developed by Foucault in *The Archaeology of Knowledge, Discipline and Punish*, and *History of Sexuality*, and tries to divest it of those elements which most inhibit its radical socialist potential. Wickham, basing himself very largely on Foucault's many interviews, attempts to develop a framework for the analysis of power which might complement and develop the project initiated by Minson, while avoiding some of the specific problems which an unreflected 'use' of Foucault might imply.

By no stretch of the imagination, then, could these essays be called narrow or dogmatic. They could hardly be called irrelevant to the central concerns of the modern debate on history, communication, theory and politics. They are informed, critical and each attempts to make a specific contribution to the debate addressed. It is hoped that the reader will find in them not only a challenge to read Foucault, but also a provocation to think about some new problems and perhaps in a new way.

References

Althusser, L. (1969) *For Marx*, Allen Lane: London.
Anderson, P. (1983) *In the Tracks of Historical Materialism*, NLB: London.
Beauvoir, S. de (1985) *Adieux*, Penguin: Harmondsworth.
Clark, M. (1983) *Michel Foucault: An Annotated Bibliography*, Garland: London.
Corradi, E. (1977) *Filosofia della morte dell'uomo*, Vita e Pensiero: Milan.
DeGeorge, R. and F. (eds) (1972) *The Structuralists*, Doubleday: New York.

Deleuze, G. and **Guattari**, F. (1977) *Anti-Oedipus*, Viking: New York.
Derrida, J. (1978) *Writing and Difference*, RKP: London.
Dreyfus, H. and **Rabinow**, P. (1982) *Michel Foucault*, Harvester: Brighton.
Forrester, J. (1980) 'Michel Foucault and the History of Psychoanalysis', in *History of Science*, vol. 18, pp. 286–301.
Foucault, M. (1976) *Mental Illness and Psychology*, Harper & Row: New York.

Foucault, M. (1967) *Madness and Civilization*, Tavistock: London.
Foucault, M. (1973) *The Birth of the Clinic*, Tavistock: London.
Foucault, M. (1963) *Raymond Roussel*, Gallimard: Paris.
Foucault, M. (1970) *The Order of Things*, Tavistock: London.
Foucault, M. (1971) 'On the Archaeology of the Sciences', in *Theoretical Practice*, nos 3/4, London.
Foucault, M. (1972) *The Archaeology of Knowledge*, Tavistock: London.
Foucault, M. (1977) *Discipline and Punish*, Allen Lane: London.
Foucault, M. (1980) *Power/Knowledge*, Harvester: Brighton.
Foucault, M. (1981) 'The Order of Discourse', in Young, R. (ed.), *Untying the Text*, RKP: London.
Foucault, M. (1984a) *The Foucault Reader*, Pantheon: New York.
Foucault, M. (1984b) *The History of Sexuality*, Volume 1, Penguin: Harmondsworth.
Foucault, M. (1985) 'Archéologie d'une Passion', in *Magazine Littéraire*, no. 221, July–August pp. 100–5.
Gane, M. (1986) 'The Form of Foucault', in *Economy and Society*, vol. 15, no. 1.
Harari, J. (1979) *Textual Strategies*, Cornell University Press.
Major-Poetzl, P. (1983) *Michel Foucault's Archaeology of Western Culture*, Harvester: Brighton.

Mauriac, C. (1975) 'Foucault et Deleuze', in *Figaro littéraire*, 20.xii.75, p. 16.
Morris, M. and Patton, P. (1979) *Michel Foucault*, Feral: Sydney.
Midelfort, H. (1980) 'Madness and Civilization in Early Modern History: a Reappraisal of Michel Foucault', in *After the Reformation* (ed.) Malament, B. Manchester Univ. Press.
O'Farrell, C. (1982) 'Foucault and the Foucauldians', in *Economy and Society*, vol. xi, 449–459.
Poster, M. (1984) *Foucault, Marxism and History*, Polity: Cambridge.
Poulantzas, N. (1978) *State, Power, Socialism*, NLB: London.
Raulet, G. (1983) 'Structuralism and Post-Structuralism: an interview with Michel Foucault', in *Telos*, no. 55, Spring, pp. 195–211.
Rose, G. (1984) *Dialectic of Nihilism*, Blackwell: Oxford.
Said, E. (1984) *The World, the Text and the Critic*, Faber & Faber: London.
Salemohammed, G. (1985) 'The Critic as Prosecutor', in *Economy and Society*, vol. 14, no. 3.
Sheridan, A. (1980) *Michel Foucault*, Tavistock: London.
Smart, B. (1983) *Foucault, Marxism and Critique*, RKP: London.
Wuthnow, R. *et al.* (1984) *Cultural Analysis*, RKP: London.
Young, R. (ed.) (1981) *Untying the Text*, RKP: London.

CHAPTER 2

Foucault's genealogy of the human sciences

Michael Donnelly

Over the last decades Michel Foucault has published a string of important and controversial books about the 'human sciences'. All have been cast in the form of *histories*; that is, they have treated the historic emergence and early development of the respective sciences, particularly in the period around the late-eighteenth and early-nineteenth centuries. Thus Foucault has discussed historic 'discourses' on madness, disease and normality, crime and punishment, sexuality, and much else as well. The books treating these subjects take the form of histories, but they are far indeed from conventionally professional history-writing, particularly as practised in the English-speaking countries. They are also vehemently radical. These two facts have occasioned considerable confusion and misunderstanding around Foucault's books, among enthusiasts and detractors alike, as well as some sound criticism. There is doubtless need for more discussion still before Foucault's work becomes generally accessible.

I want to comment here on two aspects of Foucault's work, and to address to the texts two sets of questions:

1 Why, given his philosophic concerns with the status of the human sciences, are Foucault's investigations historical (or to give them the label he now prefers, 'genealogical')? Why does Foucault have recourse to history as a privileged method? What for that matter is the critical intent which history aids?
2 How can Foucault claim that his genealogies of the human sciences amount to 'writing the history of the present'? How, in other words, can he move from histories of the human sciences to descriptions of their roles in contemporary society? Or to take the most elaborate working-out of this view in *Discipline and Punish*, how can Foucault move from describing the 'birth of the prison' (in an account centred on the early nineteenth century) to describing the mechanisms of contemporary 'disciplinary society'?[1]

The two sets of questions are connected and overlap to some extent, but can be held separate. This is indeed a useful way of approaching and evaluating what has become Foucault's central theme, the notion that power and knowledge form a complex,

what he terms 'pouvoir-savoir', which the human sciences have
helped to constitute, and in which they are still implicated. The
essay offers in conclusion several comments on this notion.

Genealogy

Considering the hostility of historians to much of his work, it is
perhaps surprising Foucault should claim history as his method of
choice. The grounds he gives at the outset are philosophic: history
is a means for cleansing thought of its 'transcendental narcissism';
or, otherwise put, 'the historical sense can evade metaphysics and
become a privileged instrument of [investigation] if it refuses the
certainty of absolutes.'[2] This is by itself not a startling statement.
In its positive spirit it is quite faithful to Comte's programme; and,
more exactly, it follows common procedure in the French tradition
of history of science. It was doubtless through this tradition that
Foucault conceived his first major project, a history of psychiatry.
The study was to trace the constitution of the fundamental
categories of psychiatry, their shifts and turns over time. To
reconstruct the emergence of psychiatry Foucault would describe
how the scientific distinction between 'normal' and 'pathological'
in mental life was developed, against what epistemological
'obstacles', with what subsequent elaborations and so forth.

In the event Foucault produced *Folie et déraison*, a book which
quite spilled beyond the traditional limits of history of science,
and indeed beyond conventional history of all sorts. When the
book appeared its target seemed to be other histories, the conventional histories of psychiatry, against which Foucault's book made
an ironic comment. There were several points of marked difference,
the first a matter of tone. Typically, histories of psychiatry seemed
constructed to vindicate the present, that is, the present state of
the discipline. They read as triumphalist accounts which advanced
progressively upwards across time, from dark ages of superstition,
to Enlightenment, to scientific mastery. The themes recur again
and again: the insane or the mentally disordered have always been
with us; once they suffered utter neglect or harsh persecution — at
all events their real condition was ignored, mistaken or misunder-
stood; then, with the beginnings of the history of psychiatry they
were finally rescued. Psychiatry began to undermine theological
and metaphysical obscurantism, first under the guise of philan-
thropy and humanitarian reform, then more and more as scientific
psychiatry emerged and consolidated itself.

Foucault told a different story indeed, delivered in a different
tone. Far from triumphalist, it induces scepticism about the present
and seems to celebrate a period long before the advent of modern

science. It works an inversion of valuations. The point is, Foucault claimed to do this precisely with history as a weapon. To undermine histories constructed (apparently) in the service of the present, Foucault as he later described his procedures turned back himself to historical researches in order to represent the past otherwise, if not 'as it really was', then nonetheless in such a way as to reveal the distortions or illusions introduced or sustained by conventional histories. To this end he deployed several techniques:

1 making the past unfamiliar. Instead of treating the past as prologue, as part of an easily comprehensible, continuous series of events unfolding into the present, he tried to establish its radical otherness, its difference. Consider, for instance, the marvellous and richly imagined evocation of the 'ships of fools' which introduces *Madness and Civilisation*:

> they did exist, these boats that conveyed their insane cargo from town to town. Madmen then led an easy wandering existence. The towns drove them outside their limits; they were allowed to wander in the open countryside, when not entrusted to a group of merchants and pilgrims . . . Often the cities of Europe must have seen these 'ships of fools' approaching their harbors.[3]

The very strangeness of the image arrests the reader. Or recall likewise his portrait of the great philanthropic reformers of the late-eighteenth and early-nineteenth centuries, a portrait which reproduces their humanitarian sentiments but within a strange, untidy and diverse (to modern eyes doubtless contradictory) tangle of views. The foreignness of this tangle of views which Foucault tried to recover interrupts any easy identification by modern readers with these historical subjects.

2 highlighting breaks or discontinuities in the historical record, a tactic for which Foucault became notorious after the publication of *The Order of Things*. The target here is historicism in several of its senses, particularly the tendency in historical writing (as Foucault reads it) to suppress 'novelty' within an apparently continuous flow of events, as if new events could and must be accounted for as the result of a series of antecedent (ie, chronologically prior) circumstances and events. Foucault on the contrary emphasized *dis*continuities, in part as a rhetorical device, in order to erect safeguards as he put it against mystifying concepts like 'progress', 'human nature', and the like. What his histories record is typically a complex, radically contingent, frequently surprising course of events.

3 making the basic concepts and categories of the human sciences problematic. Foucault has tried to query the 'obvious-

ness' of basic categories by studying the circumstances in which
they emerged or were produced. To this end he can claim to have
made in *Madness and Civilisation* a strong demonstration in an
apparently unpromising or unfavourable case. The category
'madness' is conventionally taken for granted as an historical-
anthropological universal. 'Madness' may be better or worse
understood, but the category itself seems to refer undoubtedly
to a universal experience. Foucault is led to suggest, on the
contrary, that there is no original, univocal fact or experience of
'madness'.[4] The object itself has changed, historically, in startling
and often dramatic ways: far from being universal, it is radically
contingent. Hence psychiatry is not to be understood as the first
scientific approach to understanding an eternal problem; in a
strong sense, on Foucault's view, early psychiatry helped to
constitute the object 'madness' which it then developed to treat.
The 'objects' of other human sciences betray similar, historically
contingent beginnings. On Foucault's view historical objects,
including the array of apparent attributes of 'human nature' or
the knowing subject, have no essence; the essences attributed
to them do not inhere intrinsically, but on the contrary are
constructed and cobbled together from foreign, diverse
elements.

This conclusion is already implied within *Madness and Civilisation*. For if Foucault has demonstrated that 'madness' has been
variously and contingently constructed as an object, then likewise so has its obverse, 'reason'. Indeed this is the larger theme
of the book. Reason has been constructed historically by a series
of exclusions. But the identity — the collective *we* which then
experiences *our* history — thus constituted is forever marked by
its origins. Against its universal pretensions Foucault tries to
demonstrate its parochial and partial origins: the point is meant
to be telling, in the same way as one says: 'History (as the privileged form of consciousness) is the western myth'.[5]

From here it is but a step to the statement: 'as the archaeology
of our thought easily shows, man is an invention of recent date.
And one perhaps nearing its end.' This perhaps seems less now
than before a bombastic slogan, rather than a view Foucault has
tried to develop and elaborate at some length. It is, despite
appearances, intended as a 'neutral' statement, that our structures of experience and indeed the place of man in the process
of knowing are artifacts of the modern period, not eternal
features of a knowing subject who strides through a general
history of science or of 'man's attempt to know'.[6]

'Genealogy is gray, meticulous, and patiently documentary.' This is Foucault's own description of the recourse to history, and of its neutral, positivist stance. The description doubtless sits uneasily with readers' impressions of reading Foucault; in the event the rhetorical flourishes and the literary flair so evident in his prose are not at all incidental to the popularity of his texts. As for his arguments, they do nonetheless work atop documentation, not perhaps with the carefully justified choice of sources that professional historians might expect, but with an unquestionably imaginative and wide-ranging sweep through the 'archive'. In this respect Foucault's use of history — his reconstruction of the emergence and of the conditions of possibility of the various human sciences — might well have a salutary effect; or, otherwise put, Foucault's works provide salutary demonstrations of the possibilities for 'genealogy' in the history of the human sciences.

The politics of discourse

The 'gray, meticulous' historical reconstruction is, however, only one partial way to represent the enterprise; and not a good way to capture its animus. The term 'genealogy' is obviously chosen to echo Nietzsche, and Foucault borrows a good deal of Nietzsche's reputation to enhance criticism with polemics. It has become clearer and clearer across Foucault's works that his criticism has a wider intent than slow reconstruction in the historiography of the human sciences. At the beginning of his *Discipline and Punish* Foucault puts the question to himself, why, now, write a history of the prison? 'Simply because I am interested in the past? No, if one means by that writing a history of the past in terms of the present. Yes, if one means writing the history of the present.' The meaning of this in itself is not immediately clear; but it follows close upon a long allusion to prison revolts in recent years (ie, the early 1970s) which were the springs of Foucault's reflections. The revolts were not a stimulus to Foucault's historical curiosity; his purposes were rather more immediate. *Discipline and Punish* is hence written self-consciously 'in a field of power relations and political struggle'; the book again and again 'brings us back to the present' and thrusts itself into what Foucault calls 'the overall political issue around the prison'.[7] This is obviously not a matter of historiographical debates on the prison.

What exactly is Foucault claiming to do here? What arguments does *Discipline and Punish* (like his previous works cast in the form of history) muster for an intervention into the contemporary situation? How can a book subtitled 'The birth of the prison' be construed as 'history of the present'?

The easiest answer to these questions is to say Foucault is an

ideologue, and hence drawn like other parties to a dispute to
marshall arguments of all sorts, including appeals to the past.
Discipline and Punish is therefore a book in search of a 'usable
past' for partisans — a past or a myth of the past useful in contemporary struggles against the prison because it undermines or
debunks the ideological justifications of the other side. There is no
question the book has or can be made to have this effect, just as
Madness and Civilisation was once brought to bear prominently
in ideological debates over modern psychiatry.

But this considerably misjudges and underestimates a book
which ought to be read more seriously than as or in the manner of
a radical exposé. Foucault's purpose is indeed more serious, and
his arguments have more weight. Regardless of whether they
succeed, the arguments are substantial and not in a weak sense
rhetorical.

How then does Foucault construct an historical argument which
is critical and more broadly politically pertinent? The argument is
quite complicated, and can best be considered first in its different
stages, then on the different levels where it works.

The book begins, dramatically, with a pair of images, one
describing with gruesome detail the public torture and execution
of a regicide in 1757; the other the timetable of a reformatory
from 1837, carefully detailing the daily penal regimen of its
inmates. The two images are dated precisely, and with enough
details filled in to establish their remarkable historical difference:
they are emblematic for two styles of punishment, separated by
less than a century but hardly to be compared, apparently a world
apart. By this contrast of images Foucault opens his question,
how was such a transformation in punishment possible?

The argument falls into a number of stages, treating:
1 the old style, the criminal trial and punishment under the
ancien régime;
2 the programme for penal reform advanced by Idéologues and
other reformers during the Revolution, and anticipated by their
Enlightenment predecessors;
3 contemporary practices of 'discipline' as a technique for
training and managing bodies (techniques developed in monas-
teries, military units, schools);
4 why the prison became virtually the sole means of punishment;
5 how prisons actually developed and functioned in early- and
mid-nineteenth-century France.

There are several things noteworthy about this order of exposition, which is quite carefully arranged. Section 3, on 'discipline',
seems a great digression, although it is in fact the organising centre

and principle of the book. Having discussed penal matters, and at some length treated a series of proposals for penal reform on the very eve of the transformation he is trying to account for, Foucault suddenly drops the topic and shifts to discussing 'discipline' (which on the face of it is not at all concerned with punishment) through examples as far afield as monastic regimens, the teaching of hand-writing in royal schools and the military drill: all techniques working to train 'the body'. It is only after a lengthy excursus that Foucault turns back to punishment; or rather, to close the digres-sion he tries to argue precisely that discipline was the new style of punishment.

The order of exposition also displays interesting shifts in the level of Foucault's argument. Section 3, again, is central. The first two sections are not significantly different from standard or conventional histories of punishment: they offer an account of prevailing practices and the legal principles apparently or in theory underlying them; a description of strains, tensions, problems in the legal system; a look at proposals for reform or adjustment to bring the system into line or to correct abuses, and so on. What normally follows, after exposition of the different ideas or proposals for reform, is some account of the politics of reform: what groups were involved, how they perceived the situation, what was the balance of forces, what in the end was the momentum to carry through or block one or other programme, and so forth. In place of the expected narrative here, Foucault shifts to talking of 'discipline', an as yet rather vague cultural form which he discovers in quite varied social contexts. He thus side-steps the crucial stage in conventional accounts, where the text typically moves from the reformers' ideas to explain how they were or were not, or to some extent were, put into practice. The implication is clear; the reformers' ideas were not decisive, indeed they are not even parti-cularly apt for rendering the style of the new punishment, which owed more to 'discipline'. Hence the reformers were not agents of 'reform', and Foucault's historical reconstructions reveal a quite different and more complex 'genealogy' of the new style.

The way section 3 ends is equally of interest. Having digressed from punishment at the beginning, then argued discipline was the new punishment, at the end Foucault turns quite away from 'the birth of the prison' to describe a general diffusion of discipline subsequently, over the next century and a half. This announces the broader theme of a book which ceases to talk of prisons in the institutional sense at all. Discipline, which enters the discussion as the crucial (cultural) element in the birth of the prison (an institution of exclusion and segregation) has spilled well beyond the limits, and now is everywhere in 'carceral society'. Here is

Foucault on contemporary society: 'Is it surprising that prisons resemble factories, schools, barracks, hospitals, which all resemble prisons?'[8] Whatever one's opinion of the sketch of disciplinary society, it must be clear Foucault did not get there by the patient work of historical reconstruction. Another sort of argument is plainly at work.

There is yet another shift in levels. Having answered his question why the prison became a means, *the* means, of punishment, Foucault then turns to describe the actual functioning of prisons. There is a shift in levels because Foucault first answers the question why prisons? by constructing a general 'diagram' of disciplinary punishment as a technique or mechanism: Bentham's design of the Panopticon assumes the ideal form of this diagram. Foucault quickly acknowledges that the Panopticon itself was never actually put up. This seems to raise a distinction between the diagram of disciplinary punishment and its realisation, or between panopticism and the practices of actual prisons. It is not clear given Foucault's purposes this problem need arise; it does so, however, since Foucault tries to comment toward the end of the book on how prisons actually functioned in nineteenth-century France. Here Foucault produces an interesting but straightforwardly functionalist account of prisons, which seems quite at odds with his methods elsewhere. If one imagines that the diagram of disciplinary punishment supplies the purposes or the plan prisons are built to carry out or realise, then prisons are failures. They don't work, if this means realising in practice the apparent promise of the design. Foucault, however, turns the 'failure' of the prison actually to discipline and normalise its inmates into part of its definition and function. There is a corresponding shift or slide in how Foucault uses his terms: from crystallising a highly refined machine for surveillance and normalising discipline (the image of the 'prison' which is the centrepiece of the book), the 'prison' becomes in the end a mechanism for *producing* or supervising the production of delinquents, in politically safe circumstances. Hence the ostensible 'failure' of the prison is part of the explanation for its endurance and survival as an institution. I am here not concerned with the merits of this argument, but with its form which is again not genealogical.

These shifts in the level of discussion raise several issues for Foucault's politically inspired 'history of the present'. There are three varieties of argument in *Discipline and Punish* I wish to distinguish among, and to examine in turn:

1 the *genealogical* analysis which re-traces 'the birth of the prison'; or as Foucault also puts it which constructs a 'history of the modern soul and of a new power to judge' (these are the

object and the means of punishment through discipline);

2 the *evolutionary* or *diffusionist* account (for want of better terms) of how discipline 'was destined to spread throughout the social body', via the 'indefinitely generalizable mechanism of panopticism';[9]

3 the *functionalist* description of the nineteenth-century prison in France.

Of these arguments the 'genealogical' is most responsible for discharging the formal historical burden of the book, to describe the birth of the prison; the other arguments are more pertinent to 'history of the present', and hence to the avowed political purposes of the text.

1 Here, as elsewhere, the genealogical argument is descriptive. It eschews large-scale causal theories, indeed tries to undermine such explanations by the patient reconstruction of a conjuncture. It re-traces different elements (with their different 'times' and dynamics) present in a conjuncture, but without implying any necessity or uniform covariation. Foucault collects a large set of such elements pertinent to the birth of the prison, each reconstructed and described in turn:

— changes in judicial practices and in the rationales for punishment

— changes in the pattern of offences, especially an increase in crimes against property.[10]

— the extension and generalisation of 'disciplinary methods', a process Foucault describes in phrases typical of genealogy:

> The 'invention' of this new political anatomy must not be seen as a sudden discovery. It is rather a multiplicity of often minor processes, of different origin and scattered location, which overlap, repeat, or imitate one another, support one another, distinguish themselves from one another according to their domain of application, converge and gradually produce the blueprint of a general method.[11]

— the 'accumulation of men and the accumulation of capital', which Foucault evokes in these terms:

> If the economic take-off of the West began with the techniques that made possible the accumulation of capital, it might perhaps be said that the methods for administering the accumulation of men made possible a political take-off in relation to the traditional, ritual, costly, violent forms of power, which soon fell into disuse and were superseded by a subtle, calculated technology of subjection. In fact, the two

processes — the accumulation of men and the accumulation
of capital — cannot be separated; it would not have been
possible to solve the problem of the accumulation of men
without the growth of an apparatus of production capable of
both sustaining them and using them; conversely, the techniques that make the cumulative multiplicity of men useful
accelerated the accumulation of capital.[12]

And the list of elements could easily be extended.

There is no point to search for causal arguments here (even if
Foucault's language occasionally lapses into causal expressions),
since the enterprise is different. It may not satisfy a certain
longing for explanations, but this is exactly Foucault's intent, to
starve that longing, and provide only 'documentation'. It is true
that the documents (historical representations) are arrayed this
way and that, plainly for polemical ends. Foucault's defence to
this charge is simple, that he is producing *an* account; others may
do likewise, and it is dishonest or disingenuous to claim that
anyone can or ought to do more. This is not the place to examine
such claims.

The greatest merit of Foucault's genealogy, on my reading at
least, is to develop the central notion 'discipline' itself, in particular
as he describes the practices or mechanisms of discipline as forms
of *pouvoir-savoir* (power-knowledge). This is a real advance. At
the same time it is unclear exactly what role the prison or penitentiary plays in the larger story of discipline. Doubtless 'discipline'
informs or inscribes itself in the form of the prison; but need the
prison play a central or exemplary part in an account of disciplinary
mechanisms? Might one better choose another institution as the
exemplary instance of 'discipline'?

There is a serious point here, for if the prison were not the
central instance (in one sense or another) of discipline, then it
would be hard for Foucault once he generalises the notion of
discipline throughout the social body to call the result *carceral*
society. It is not just a question of labels, but of what place the
prison properly holds in an account of discipline and the emergence of the human sciences; this is a major, and only partly
answered, question for Foucault's argument.[13]

2 The argument about 'diffusion' is more complicated to deal
with. In part the problem is a slackness in Foucault's writing.
He describes the disciplinary mechanisms (in particular panopticism) in highly rarefied terms — indeed in a way quite at odds
with the documentary aspect of his genealogy. The genealogy
is concerned with the historic constitution of discipline and a

set of disciplinary practices, on the threshold of the human
sciences. The broader argument refers to nothing so fixed, or
fixable. 'Discipline' in the generalised form of panopticism is
rather as Foucault has it, 'a figure of political technology that
may and must be detached from any specific use'. It is a 'schema
. . . destined to spread throughout the social body'. 'It programmes,
at the level of an elementary and easily transferable mechanism,
the basic functioning of a society penetrated through and through
with disciplinary mechanisms' — apparently because discipline is
'indefinitely generalizable'.[14] And so, carried by such phrases,
from 'the birth of the prison' Foucault easily reaches the present,
as if simply by 'the logical culmination of . . .' or 'a natural extension of . . .'

> Is it surprising that the cellular prison, with its regular chrono-
> logies, forced labour, its authorities of surveillance and
> registration, its experts in normality, who continue and multiply
> the functions of the judge, should have become the modern
> instrument of penality? Is it surprising that prisons resemble
> factories, schools, barracks, hospitals, which all resemble
> prisons?[15]

The obvious problem with this last statement is that it works by
analogies, and only by analogies. They are, perhaps, plausible ones
in this respect or that, but hardly the basis for the argument they
must bear. What Foucault does not ask is how this diffusion
occurred; nor does he ask what supported and continues to support
it. As compared with the careful reconstruction of 'discipline' and
disciplinary practices in the early-nineteenth century, everything
after is drawn slapdash, in a rush to the present; indeed the whole
intervening period is more or less flattened-out.

This is, perhaps, a curious lapse for a practitioner of genealogy.
Why after all should genealogy cease? Once the human sciences are
constituted, what then shapes their development? Foucault
provides a genealogy of the emergence and constitution of the
human sciences and their objects; in *Discipline and Punish* he
leaves it at that, as if once constituted, the sciences with their
programmes and techniques seem to hold sway and perpetuate
themselves. The simple question is, what produces this continuity
of discipline? Foucault assumes or asserts it, without the means to
demonstrate it. He comes ironically close to the perils of the
argument from origins — as if to understand an object one need
discover its pristine origins, and hence the key to or germ of its
subsequent development — which is precisely the fallacy genealogy
is contrived to correct.

Foucault seems here to lose his historical sense and succumb to a simple dichotomous conception of past/present, as if the two emblematic images with which the book begins sufficed. This difficulty is obviously not Foucault's alone. It is likewise, just to turn to other accounts of the history of punishment, the difficulty inherent in Durkheim's 'two laws of penal evolution' — to which, incidentally, Foucault's argument bears a strong resemblance. What organises Durkheim's conception are the end-points of what he describes as evolutionary processes; in fact the 'processes' are not at all specified. Rather Durkheim sets out a striking, qualitative contrast between two states or situations which don't differ in degree but in kind. He then suggests that one state or situation *tends* to evolve toward the next. It is only the progressive or advanced 'modern' end-point, however, which retrospectively gives this evolutionary process any meaning. The 'laws' therefore don't really describe developments but rather hint at their (putative) telos, which is itself a term already contained in the prior dichotomy.

In Foucault's case this lapse may be inadvertently a vestige of his earlier investigations, which were organised as 'archaeologies'. Particularly in *The Order of Things* he was concerned to reconstruct the 'episteme' which underlay the possibilities of knowing over an epoch. The book marked sharp mutations or discontinuities between the episteme of one epoch and that of another, but within an epoch Foucault stressed the regularity and continuity of discourse. It is important to recall that Foucault then dated the modern episteme (and hence the moment of emergence of the human sciences) from the beginning of the nineteenth century; the periodisation is the same as recurs in *Discipline and Punish*.

Now there are great differences in method and aim between archaeology and genealogy, which are properly the subject of an essay in itself and cannot be treated here. But there are also unmistakable and worrying similarities. Consider what Foucault writes about the late-eighteenth century 'humanization' of the criminal, the recovery of the criminal as an 'abnormal individual'. This was a new departure, with apparently long and dramatic consequences:

> The constant division between the normal and the abnormal,
> to which every individual is subjected, *brings us back to our*
> *own time*, by applying the binary branding and exile of the
> leper to quite different objects . . . All the mechanisms of power
> which, *even today*, are disposed around the abnormal individual,
> to brand him and to alter him, are composed of those two
> *forms from which they distantly derive.*[16]

The jumps forward to the present are only casually suggested here; and there is the adverb 'distantly' acknowledging the past. But the passage as a whole, and indeed much of *Discipline and Punish*, read as if on Foucault's view the years around 1800 marked a threshold, the initiation of a new epoch in power relations, etc. Once across the threshold it is as if one could begin talking about the characteristics of the epoch unfolding ahead.

There is possibly a parallel here with the design of Foucault's earlier 'archaeological' studies. Note, for instance, the conclusion to *The Birth of the Clinic*:

> In the last years of the eighteenth century, European culture outlined a structure that has not yet been unraveled; we are only just beginning to disentangle a few of the threads, which are still so unknown to us that we immediately assume them to be either marvellously new or absolutely archaic, whereas for two hundred years (not less, yet not much more) they have constituted the dark, but firm web of our experience.[17]

Here the distance or difference of past (post-1800) and present, so far as this 'structure of experience' is concerned, disappears. Indeed as Foucault hints it is only because the present is now changing that it is possible to understand what the continuum from past-to-present has been; the present in these terms is not different from the past, it is its continuation:

> Medicine made its appearance as a clinical science in conditions which define, together with its historical possibility, the domain of its experience and the structure of its rationality. They form its concrete a priori, which it is now possible to uncover, *perhaps because a new experience of disease is coming into being* that will make possible a historical and critical understanding of the old experience.[18]

Here, strangely, it is possible to understand the 'birth' of a structure because (perhaps because) of its imminent demise. The figures of 'birth' and 'death' plainly provide, however, no means of understanding how or why the structure endures in the meanwhile. For the purposes of archaeology, which tried to describe retrospectively certain evident regularities in, e.g., medical perceptions, this is not a difficulty. For writing 'the history of the present', where the argument flows forward in time from the birth of the prison to the diffusion of discipline, it is a difficulty indeed. What has happened in the meanwhile is important — for genealogy it is the only way of approaching 'the present'.

In two crucial respects the diffusionist argument remains, on my reading at least, indeterminate. First, in so far as it depends on the notion of 'diagram' or 'programme' it risks lapsing into the difficulties of thinking in traditional/modern terms — the difficulties which come with circumventing history by positing a simple dichotomy to represent past/present. This is not the same as the complaint by historians that Foucault gets it all wrong by oversimplifying history and reducing its real complexity to ideal schemata. This complaint asks instead for detailed social histories of prisons, criminal justice practices, etc. Foucault in fact welcomes such social histories; he is at pains to explain that his own work is not meant to supplant such studies, for the simple reason that he is asking different questions and pursuing different objectives than social historians. The problem with the diagram of panopticism is not that it fails to represent the empirically rich and variable character of actual prison practices, it is not intended to do so. For what it is intended to do, in Foucault's discussion of the emergence of disciplinary mechanisms, it is necessary and fully appropriate. The problem comes, on my view, where Foucault extends the notion, and has it stand in as the conception of a new 'political anatomy of the body social'. The diagram is at best a *figure* to represent a novel feature of the 'modern epoch', but not a guide to the mechanisms or conditions of existence of the epoch — if indeed it is useful to speak at all in such terms.

Where Foucault does turn, secondly, to discuss the mechanisms or the practices of the new political anatomy, the so-called microphysics and technologies of power, he encounters further difficulties. The conception of power itself is intriguing, particularly where Foucault suggests that alongside the centralisation of State power, there has occurred a parallel and necessary 'development of power techniques oriented toward individuals and intended to rule them in a continuous and permanent way'.[19] Discipline is the key element in this second development; indeed in its ideal, generalised, diagrammatic form 'it programmes, at the level of an elementary and easily transferable mechanism, *the basic functioning of a society* penetrated through and through with disciplinary mechanisms'.[20] As far as investigating these mechanisms goes Foucault has produced a number of exemplary studies, which doubtless he and others will supplement with future researches. This is important and very promising work. But it remains at a rudimentary stage. And hence when Foucault speaks of summing up the effects of a whole web or network of these disciplinary mechanisms, he has gone well beyond the limits of any of his researches. To speak of 'disciplinary *society*' he must obviously do so. What he does not address, however, is the question how these mechanisms are or could be coordinated. There are, on Foucault's account, myriad sites of discipline — a great array of disciplinary practices. It is a virtue of Foucault's researches that they again and again try to locate the specific effects of these different practices. But if these mechanisms are to work in concert, to programme 'the basic functioning of a society', what is it that renders them coherent or consistent? What produces a uniform *pattern* of discipline such that the results can be summed up as a form of political rationality, or rule over individuals? Foucault rejects the notion that there is any calculating class of human agents behind the scenes pulling the disciplinary strings. But what impersonal force then allows Foucault to talk of discipline univocally, as a strategy by which whole peoples can be ordered? If the answer comes back, it is the general diagram which programmes or informs specific practices here, there and everywhere else, that simply transfers the problem without resolving it. This is not to suggest that Foucault's notion of 'disciplinary society' is utterly unfounded: it is rather premature and still inchoate. What would ground it better are still more, and more contemporary, studies similar to the exemplary genealogies Foucault has already provided.

3 The 'functionalist' strain of argument is probably the closest in the book to what one finds in conventional histories of punishment, not that it isn't ingenious and original in certain respects. The question of origins with which much of the book has been concerned more or less drops away; after describing the genesis, Foucault turns to examine independently the function of the prison. Here the account is familiar, since the prison evolves functionally or is used instrumentally as a tactic in a familiar field of social struggles. Foucault begins to speak, for the first time in any elaborate way, of the 'asymmetries of disciplinary subjection', which is a rather gingerly way of broaching the problem of class structure. This cautious beginning announces the theme that prisons actually functioned (or function, one doesn't know which to write) as a tactic of, or in the interests of, class domination. They are a tactic for controlling illegality, precisely by producing it; ie, by producing a group of delinquents in and around prisons who can be constituted as a 'dangerous class' outside the boundaries of and refused by the respectable working class. Under appropriate police and prison surveillance and supervision this criminal sub-class are then tolerated and allowed to work as law-breakers. At the margins, and cut off from the mass of the popular classes, they then commit a 'politically or economically less dangerous form of illegality' which the bourgeois order can both contain and stigmatize.

If this is intended as a description of nineteenth-century prisons, there is a good deal to say for it. But the argument supporting it would have to be considerably developed. There are at least two problems. It is not clear, first, how to square this account of the prison with all that has gone before in *Discipline and Punish*. How, if the second account remains straightforwardly functionalist, does the whole previous discussion of discipline remain pertinent? Is the mechanism of the new functional prison disciplinary? In what sense: vis-à-vis its inmates or only in a broader sense that it serves to help discipline a whole non-criminal populace? How does discipline take on a 'class' character, so that discipline not merely produces competent individuals adjusted to norms, but reproduces conditions of 'the new class power'? And so forth.

Secondly, if the prison is used tactically in social struggles, who or what calculates the possible effects of tactics? Foucault doesn't and need not speak of human agents calculating this or that effect; the way he speaks of tactics does still require him, however, to deal one way or another with the question of calculation. For the moment he has side-stepped it. As before, none of these is an insoluble or insuperable problem; the comments here are simply a means of showing where the argument ought to be clarified, or developed further.

> There is no power relation without the correlative constitution
> of a field of knowledge, nor any knowledge that does not
> presuppose and constitute at the same time power relations
> (*Discipline and Punish*, p. 27).

What, finally, do these remarks imply about Foucault's larger concern with 'pouvoir-savoir'? What do they imply about the avowed political purposes of his work?

The notion 'power-knowledge' seems undoubtedly significant for his genealogies of the human sciences. It has directed his enquiries, and it is through his attention to the apparent minutiae of disciplinary practices (the early forms of power-knowledge) that he has constructed his argument about both the emergence of the human sciences and the origins of a new political 'technology' focused on the individual. On both counts the notion has led to important new conceptions — of knowledge, of power, and of their connections.

More narrowly the notion has also proved serviceable in recent accounts of current penal and criminal justice practices. This was of course a direct purpose of Foucault's project in *Discipline and Punish*, and it has produced quick results. His phrase 'administration of punishment' — evoking the whole array of powers, psychological, educational and medical, which are involved along with judges and the police in modern criminal matters — effectively summarises a view emerging on several fronts. Foucault, however, names rather than accounts for this character of modern punishment; so far as he attempts to explain modern penology, he is if anything less successful than Parsons, who had already noted the 'medicalisation' of the instruments of social control in *The Social System* of the early 1950s.

With regard to his larger purposes — to establish a discourse on new forms or technologies of power and political rationality — where he is most ambitious, Foucault is doubtless least successful. The notion of 'disciplinary' or 'carceral society', based on a grand extension and diffusion of what the prison in his argument originally crystallised, remains more evocative than demonstrable. There is even the risk that Foucault's careless use of slogans about power-knowledge and the role of intellectuals in the contemporary period may reduce the real force of his historical researches. The researches are undoubtedly important in reconstructing the emergence of the human sciences, and their early development. What is (as yet) not established is the connection between the *genealogy* of the human sciences and an analysis of power-knowledge in *contemporary* mechanisms of discipline.

Notes

1. *Surveiller et punir. Naissance de la prison* (1975). Translated as *Discipline and Punish: The Birth of the Prison*, by A. Sheridan (London, 1977).
2. 'Nietzsche, Genealogy, History', in ed. D. F. Bouchard, *Language, Counter-memory, Practice* (Ithaca, New York, 1977), pp. 152–3.
3. *Madness and Civilisation: A History of Insanity in the Age of Reason*, tr. by R. Howard (New York, 1965), p. 8. The original book, of which the English translation is an abridgement, was titled *Folie et déraison. Histoire de la folie à l'age classique* (Paris, 1961).
4. Ibid., pp. 58 and 115.
5. This is an argument elaborated in Vincent Descombes, *Modern French Philosophy* (Cambridge, 1980), pp. 109–17.
6. *The Order of Things: An Archaeology of the Human Sciences* (New York, 1971), p. 387.
7. *Discipline and Punish*, pp. 31, 306.
8. Ibid., p. 228.
9. Ibid., p. 207.
10. See ibid., p. 77.
11. Ibid., p. 138.
12. Ibid., pp. 220–1.
13. See ibid., p. 249.
14. Ibid., pp. 205–7.
15. Ibid., pp. 227–8.
16. Ibid., pp. 199–200 (emphasis added).
17. *The Birth of the Clinic: An Archaeology of Medical Perception* (New York, 1973), p. 199.
18. Ibid., p. xv (emphasis added).

19. 'Omnes et Singulatim: Towards a Criticism of "Political Reason" ', in ed. S. M. McMurrin, *The Tanner Lectures on Human Values*, vol. 2 (Cambridge, 1981), p. 227.
20. *Discipline and Punish*, p. 209 (emphasis added).

CHAPTER 3

The linguistic fault: the case of Foucault's archaeology

B. Brown and M. Cousins

Abstract

It is argued that the concept of discursive formation presented by Foucault provides the means whereby conventional treatments of 'discourse' can be criticized. These would include historical, linguistic and epistemological forms of investigation. But it is also argued that Foucault does not sufficiently displace linguistic categories. As a result his account of the theoretical problems of 'conditions of existence' of discourses cannot be sustained.

Specifications of discourse

The Archaeology of Knowledge (AK) provides an ambitious challenge to the means by which knowledges are traditionally analysed in the human sciences. The declared object of contestation is what Foucault calls the History of Ideas, but his strictures fall equally upon the way in which sociology or historical materialism can function to reduce these knowledges to something else.[1] In this sense AK functions as a criticism of such procedures, arguing against their flattening of those knowledges into the expression or representation of other social relations, of the historical development of those social relations or of the human subject whether that be considered as free or imprisoned. By contrast Foucault seeks to specify a realm, that of discursive formations, and to insist upon the specificity of their material character and hence the necessity of concepts for its analysis.

This insistence is to be satisfied by the proposal of a general means of the analysis of discourses, that of an archaeology. What is to be investigated is the 'totality of all effective statements (whether spoken or written) in their dispersion as events and in the occurrence that is proper to them'. A discourse is not expressed in statements; it is a group of statements. Central to this enterprise is the identification of regularities of statements by means of which it is possible to speak of a discursive formation, and at the same time the identification of statements themselves. For if state-

ments are the elements of a discursive formation the definition of
their character becomes decisive. It is here that Foucault is at his
most insistent that his concept of a discursive formation and a
statement be derived neither from the categories of linguistics nor
from the categories of logic. A statement is not a formulation which
is either a sentence or a proposition and thus a discursive formation
is not simply a series of sentences or propositions. For the question
which an archaeology asks is: 'how is it that one particular statement appeared rather than another' and thus a 'statement is
always an event that neither the language (*langue*) nor the meaning
can quite exhaust'. And yet it is here that certain ambiguities
emerge. For while Foucault has clearly marked out the necessity
for concepts which break from linguistic or logical categories, we
will maintain that his definition of the statement remains crucially
ambiguous both in respect to linguistics and to 'language'. Moreover we will argue that the text fails in its claim to be able to
identify and stabilise discursive practices as definite discursive
formations. This problem will be exemplified by demonstrating
the oscillation of the conception of 'conditions of existence' and
of the articulation of discursive formations to institutional sites
and other social practices.

We will argue that as a consequence of failing to produce a definition of the statement which is adequately differentiated from
categories of language, Foucault is ultimately thrown back upon a
distinction between discourse and its conditions which mirrors a
conventional distinction between language and its institutional
context. We will argue that the problem is concealed but not
resolved by the attempt to stitch together statements and institutions by means of a general concept of discursive formation. There
are two sorts of problem here. We accept that it is possible to
identify a discourse as an effect of a particular form of analysis;
we also accept that it is possible to indicate discursive organisation
using concepts to be found in or to be developed from AK. But we
do not accept that it is possible to individualise and unify discursive
formations as a general form of positivity possessing a total regularity and definite limits.

The archaeology is a task which emerges as a result of the
contestation of the presuppositions and effects of the History of
Ideas. There is no singular and cardinal error which is denounced
but the History of Ideas is considered as a body of writing which
continually and inescapably returns to certain philosophical tropes,
such as genesis, continuity and totality. To this are usually added
the themes of author and consciousness. Each of these singly or in
combination serves to organise and unify formulations or a corpus
of formulations. But above all this is the persistence of methods of

interpretation by which it is established what the documents really mean, what is concealed or revealed by them. Conversely, archaeological analysis sets its face against any form of interpretation. It refuses to treat discourses as the sign of something else, be it unconscious wishes or the development of capitalism. It is this which prompts Foucault to write of an archaeology, for he does not propose to treat discourses as documents to be interpreted, he does not seek for what is behind the document, the reality which is more or less revealed or represented by certain traces. Rather, he treats those traces as describable elements of discursive formations. An archaeology is no longer organised by specifying the theme of the distribution and History of Ideas. It is rather concerned with specifying discourses in their individuality. This has decisive consequences. For that theme entails two problems, the originality and regularity of ideas.[2] The problem of originality is usually seen as the problem of accounting for points of discontinuity within a larger frame of development. Clearly, this in turn raises questions of the criteria to be adopted in respect to analysing time (what is to count as 'before') and of the criteria to be adopted in respect to measuring the resemblance of formulations (what is to count as the same or different formulations). Foucault rejects the two conventional answers to these two questions. He rejects the use of the calendar as a means of establishing the originality of a statement on the grounds that the temporal hierarchy which it produces assumes the very continuity of discourses which he is at pains to disrupt. That is to say, that the specification of a discourse through calendrical time already assumes that the answer to the second question shall be that the identity or difference of formulations shall reside in their semantic or propositional similarity. For it is only on that condition that the traditional theories of antecedents and descendants in the history of ideas can be sustained. Foucault is concerned with the regularity of statements, and even with the question of time, but he resolutely refuses to conceive them in these terms.

These two questions are usually linked through the category of 'history', questions which Foucault is determined to separate. Firstly, the question of the time of the discourse; this will undoubtedly be one of its elements, but it will not be part of a general continuum of time, of a homogeneous calendrical tunnel called history, capable at any moment of revealing itself in an essential section. Secondly, there is the question of the link between discourses and other events whose connection is normally conceived to be unproblematic because they happen 'in' history at the same 'time'. Now, Foucault does not deny that the discourse of the Analysis of Wealth is connected to the monetary events of the

seventeenth and eighteenth centuries. But he does deny that it is
the expression of, or representation of, those events. That is to say,
there is no *general* form of the connection between a discourse (and
indeed its transformation) and a general class of 'external' events
which could function as a totality, either in the form of the 'real'
or as a cause. There are two quite different problems involved here.
One concerns the status which is accorded to 'events' which are
conceived as external to the discourse. Some general theories of the
social always already unify those external events by attributing to
them fixed and general characteristics (as the real, material life,
history, practice, etc.) by which they will then function as the
extra- or non-discursive. Since Discourse and the Non-Discursive
are thus conceived as general realms, whatever form of connection
is advanced, its form will also be general. All such positions require
epistemological justification (see Hindess and Hirst, 1977, Ch. 1).
Foucault's argument rests upon no such general position. He makes
no distribution of phenomena into two classes of being, Discourse
and the Non-Discursive. For him the question is always the identity
of particular discursive formations. What falls outside a particular
discursive formation merely falls outside it. It does not thereby join
the ranks of a general form of being, the Non-Discursive. Since no
general relation may exist between 'external events' and discourse,
a second problem can be freed from its grip. This is to investigate
what in particular external events (which may of course include
other discourses) can be given as an object of particular discourses,
of what the connection between a discourse and those events can
consist and of what forms and limits that connection will take.
Indeed, one of the purposes of archaeological investigation is to
show what in 'external' events can be given as an object of a discourse, of what the connections between a discourse and 'external
events' can consist and of what forms and limits that connection
will take. But there will be no general degree, form or mechanism
at work. It will depend upon the organisation of the discourse.
Those external events will always be discursively organised, and it
is to the discourse rather than to the 'events' that analysis of the
principle of organisation must be directed.[3]

So far the term 'archaeology' has been used simply to register
Foucault's differentiation of his work from that of the History of
Ideas; the differentiation has been largely negative. Positively,
archaeology is the general description of what he refers to as the
archive. This is the most general category of an archaeology, and it
describes the general horizon within which investigations can take
place. It is not to be confused with an historian's concept of an
archive, as the materials awaiting interpretation. Nor is it a library
of libraries, a repository for the corpus of all formulations ever

made. Rather, it defines the position from which any investigation
confronts the great series of formulations. As such it is that which
governs the connection of discourses, their appearance, their transformation and their disappearance. It orders the form in which
formulations are grouped as that which is given to us. This 'complex
volume of discourses' Foucault calls the Historical A Priori, which
might seem an unlikely term from one so sceptical of the category
'historical', and so hostile to the analytic deployment of a prioris.
But each term serves to cancel out the philosophical weight of the
other. That the a priori is 'historical' entails that the a priori is concerned not with truth but with formulations made, their organisation and their mutability. But it is not 'history' which organises
this; it is the a priori, and this a priori is the product of the inter-
connection, and possibility of the relations, between discourses and
the shape which their relations will take.

The way in which discourses will be organised and formulations
will appear will be according to a system of formation which will
govern a particular discourse. It is this which enables one not only
to identify but also to unify a group of formulations as a discursive
formation. For it is the characterisation of a group of formulations
by the regularity of a practice. But before an exposition of this is
possible it is necessary for ease of exposition to reverse the order
of presentation. Up to now Foucault's concepts have been presented in reverse order in order to show how the concepts of a
high level of abstraction (which are in truth not elaborated to any
great degree) function partly as a set of criticisms of the History of
Ideas and whatever else shares its presuppositions. If one now
reverses the procedure and continues by outlining Foucault's
conception of a discursive formation and his conception of a
statement it can be seen that their development also takes the
form of a criticism, this time of the dangers of attempting to
conceptualise discourses by reference to linguistic or epistemological criteria.

Archaeological analysis is directed towards the individuation and
description of discursive formations. A discursive formation is a
necessary concept if, as Foucault accepts, the answer to the question
'how is it that one particular statement appeared rather than
another' is to be attempted by reference to something which will
organise statements, distribute them and determine their appearance
in such a way that one may speak of a distinct individuality. It then
becomes imperative to ask of what its individuality may consist.
Naturally for such a demonstration Foucault has already laid upon
himself the self-denying ordinance that it will not be attempted by
reference to the conventional individuations or unifications of
groups of formulations. It will not consist of an author, oeuvre or

text, nor of a tradition, nor of an evolution, nor of a geist. Nor will it consist in a genre, nor of disciplines. And most importantly, it will not be unified by reference to an origin in which everything is always already said but never quite heard. Not that all these categories are to be equally and permanently banished, but they are placed under a suspended sentence for the duration of the investigation.

Through a retrospective examination of his own work, chiefly *Madness and Civilisation, The Birth of the Clinic* and *The Order of Things*, Foucault examines four possible ways in which statements might be unified as a group. They might form a group if, whatever their differences in form and place in time, they referred to the same object; they might form a group if they are linked by a certain common mode of stating; they might form a group if they were governed by a constant set of concepts; lastly, they might form a group if they are linked by a common theme or common programme of employment. Each of these possibilities is rejected as yielding a possible formulation in terms of the analyses carried out in that earlier work.[4] Objects of discourses are not singular; the 'style' or mode of statements slides away from any definition; concepts form neither a permanent nor coherent system; in respect to 'themes' what was discovered was that a discourse could permit the strategic possibilities of different themes, and that different discourses could support the same theme. Where a principle of unity had been sought only the fact of dispersion had been found.

But it is this very fact that Foucault then takes as central to the definition of a discursive formation, that the dispersion is not as it were merely the negation of a unity, but was itself capable of being conceived as a *system* of dispersion. 'Whenever one can describe between a number of statements, such a system of dispersion, whenever between objects, types of statements, concepts or thematic choices one can define a regularity (an order, correlations, positions, functionings, transformations) we will say that we are dealing with a discursive formation.' Three points should be noticed here. Firstly, that a discursive formation is being individuated by reference to different levels at which statements can exist. Secondly, not only do the different levels display regularities but there are regularities *between* the different levels. Thirdly, that the individuality of the discourse is related to conditions of existence that do not normally come within the class of the discursive; each of the levels entails definite social agents, practices, sites and statuses as their conditions of emergence, existence and transformation. Nor are these conditions of existence merely enabling conditions, accidental supports of the discourse. The relations within the levels and between the levels do not constitute the inside of the discourse, which is then merely held up by external supports; 'if there really is a unity it does not lie in the visible horizontal coherence of the elements formed; it resides well anterior to their formation, in the system that makes possible and governs their formation' (AK: p. 69). While conditionality cannot be identified with any general realm such as the non-discursive, clearly there is an ambiguity between possibility and government here. The system of dispersion for Foucault can be specified in respect of the conditions of regularity, emergence and transformation of discourses as a discursive practice of the system of formation. 'To define a system of formation in its specific individuality is therefore to characterise a discourse or a group of statements by the regularity of a practice' (AK: p. 69).[5]

These ambiguities can only be explored by examing what is perhaps the central category of AK, the statement. As a concept it is designed to provide the means of specifying the elements of a discursive formation in a way which decisively breaks from the normal means of characterising discourse — that of linguistics, of logic (or epistemology) or of a Marxist account of 'discourse'. This last category is not directly confronted but we append it in order to differentiate it from the purposes to which Foucault puts the category. As such we contrast the position of Foucault with that of an Althusserian position represented by Pecheux.

In *Les Verités de la Palice*, a sustained and original attack upon traditional semantics and the inadequacy of Marxist work within linguistics, Pecheux is concerned to avoid the positions both of Marr and of Stalin.[6] That is to say, he agrees with Stalin in denying that language is part of the superstructure but he disagrees with Stalin that language is 'of all the people unique for society and common to all its members'. In this he holds that Stalin, like the young Marx, repeated a traditional error of linguistics in identifying language as the communication of a sense between persons, a position which crucially obstructs theoretical advances and closes off important arenas of ideological struggle. This appears to place Pecheux in a paradox. On the one hand, language is indifferent to class struggle, on the other hand, class struggle is not indifferent to language. The resolution of the paradox for Pecheux lies in the elaboration of a theory of discourse, that is the production of sense, which is independent of language (the proper object of a scientific linguistics) and which properly is articulated to that instance known as ideology, as conceived in Althusser's work (Althusser, 1971).

For Althusser the ideological level is one site of the condition of the reproduction/transformation of capitalist relations. They are located materially in a complex set of related Ideological State Apparatuses. Thus in concrete terms the ideological level may be said to exist in the form of ideological formations which may be thought of as 'moments' of the Ideological State Apparatuses. The form of connection between these constitutive elements of the ideological level is said to be complex because they are uneven and are ranged in a hierarchy. Thus within any conjuncture the ideological level exists materially as a structure of uneven and hierarchically arranged elements which, according to the doctrine of structural causality, will form the complex whole in dominance of the ideological formation of a social formation. It has always remained unclear, however, how this can provide the means of specifying the place and limits of a particular ideological formation. Bluntly, what is the relation between the 'moments' of the Ideological State Apparatuses and the institutional sites referred to in their definition?

But nevertheless it is Pecheux's argument that discursive formations can be derived from each of these ideological formations, as that region of ideological formations in which subjects are hailed by words, expressions or propositions by which action subjects experience them as making sense. Pecheux emphatically denies that there is any general problem of meaning that could be captured by a semantics. For there is literally no meaning or sense (nor even any polysemy) which predates the sense which words, expressions and propositions have in specific discourses. They take their sense from the ideological formation of which they constitute the discursive element. Thus a discursive formation is whatever can and should be said within an ideological formation, be it in the form of a speech, a sermon, a pamphlet or a conversation. The sophistication of Pecheux's attempt to extend Althusser's theory of ideology and its attendant weaknesses will not be dealt with here, but the project for a theory of discursive formations will merely be contrasted with Foucault.[7]

Like Foucault, Pecheux is concerned to wean the analysis of discourse from traditional linguistic categories. Like Foucault he thus denies the pertinence of any general theory of meaning for that analysis. Like Foucault he is concerned to demonstrate that discursive formations have definite conditions. But he is quite unlike Foucault in respect to two central matters. Firstly, for Pecheux discursive formations are merely a region of ideological formations which are themselves distributed by the ideological level and in the last instance by the economic.[8] This is not so in Foucault, for while discursive formations are not in a 'vacuum', have definite institutional sites and supports, and are articulated to other practices, this distribution is not made according to any concept of the social totality. Secondly, Pecheux, in accordance with Althusser's theses on the mechanisms of ideology, makes the inter-

pellation of subjects the singular mechanism of discursive formations. Now while Foucault does have a concept of the positions
which subjects can take up within a discourse it is not as an interpellation of the subject whose effect is to induce the illusion that
it is the author and origin of its experience and its meaning.
Rather, the discourse is the site of the dispersion of the subject
and the system in which the discontinuity of the subject with itself
can be registered. The category of the subject as the effect of
interpellation is displaced in Foucault's concept of the discursive
formation. This is not to say that there may not be a residual
problem of the subject in AK, but that the problem will not take
the form of interpellation of the subject within ideology. The
means of individualising discursive formations for Pecheux will be
through the differentiation of the way in which subjects are hailed
by Ideological State Apparatuses at the level of words, expressions
and propositions. Clearly for Foucault the means of the individualisation of discursive formations will be radically different.
What is it?

Signs and statements

The individuality of a discursive formation[9] lies in the fact that it
governs a group of statements. It is of Foucault's definition of the
statement that an account must be given. Up to now, and indeed
in Foucault's text, the terms 'statement' and 'formulation' have
been used interchangeably. This is misleading for the term 'formulation' seems to belong to the domains of linguistics or of logic.
And it is precisely these domains that Foucault is insistent upon
vacating in approaching the problem of the statement. The term
'statement' is also misleading if it is allowed to suggest itself as a
unit, different from a formulation but capable of being stabilised
as a definite entity. It is part of Foucault's insistence that the
statement is not a thing, an elementary particle of a discursive formation. For while a discursive formation cannot be individualised
save by reference to a group of statements, at the same time a
statement cannot be specified save by reference to the discursive
formation within which it appears. They are simultaneous and not
successive modes of specification. We will argue that Foucault does
not succeed in resolving these problems, that is of the difference
of the statement from objects specified by linguistics or logic and
of the mutually identifying relation between the discursive formation and the statement. But it is worth pointing to the necessity of
the problem for Foucault. It follows from the general outline of
the task of an archaeology, to treat knowledges not as ideas but as

discursive formations and to treat not of Discourse as language or
as a general instance but of discourses. As such neither an epistemological analysis which extracted the conceptual system of a discourse, nor a linguistic analysis which attempted certain supra-
sentential groupings would be relevant. One does not have to
question the validity of this enterprise to question its success.

At the most general level Foucault is dealing with signs, interpreted in their evident sense, that is any series of signs, figures,
marks or traces.[10] This is simply assumed as the positive condition
of the discursive in general. A statement is the mode of existence,
the specific materiality that these signs have in a discursive formation, that is to say that which permits them to be more than just
those signs (AK: p. 108). As such the statement is not a thing or a
unit but a function, what Foucault calls the enunciative function,
a function which bears upon signs. It puts a series of signs into the
specific form of existence required by discursive formations.

This function distributes series of signs into four forms of relation, that is, with the four levels of a discursive formation. The first
is that of reference. This type of reference is not conceived according
to a logicist programme of reference to empirical objects, facts or
states of affairs, but is to objects of the discourse, that is to say, the
laws of possibility or rules of existence of what can appear, be described or referred to in the discourse. These objects or 'spaces of
differentiation' as they are sometimes called, are what the signs
must refer to in order that they function as statements. Secondly,
the signs will function as a statement by bearing a relation to a
subject. This does not mean recourse is being made to human persons either as the authors, speakers or actors in the conventional
sense as the origin of formulations. Rather, it designates a position
of the subject, a controlled space from which the signs may function
as a statement in their enunciation. Thirdly, the sign will function
as a statement by being related to an associated domain, a coexistence with other statements which can work to formulate a series
of concepts. Lastly, the sign will function as a statement by taking
up what Foucault calls a material repeatability. This materiality is
problematic, for the same statement can recognise different enunci-
ations of it, while on the other hand identical forms can exist as
different statements. Its materiality consists in its status, in an
institutional sense, and this defines the possibilities of use and persistence of use.[11]

This definition of a statement is designed to provide a specification of the elements of a discursive formation which is appropriate
to the designation of such a formation as itself a set of levels,
composed of objects, enunciative modalities, concepts and strategies. This is performed by the fact that the statement is a function

and can bear upon signs in ways that are consistent with the levels of a discursive formation. In this sense the enunciative function is essentially empty. It consists in the possibility of relation between signs and those discursive levels. It is a possibility, which is realised by the particularity of a statement. Statements are themselves then essentially relational. Thus the analysis of discursive functions is the description of statements in the sense that such a description is the demonstration of the enunciative function in operation.

The objects, subject positions, concepts and strategies which are the terms of analysis of a discursive formation are also the range on which an enunciative function maps a group of signs in the production of statements (AK: p. 115).[12] This is to insist that discursive formations, enunciative functions and statements are not ontologically distinct classes of being. To analyse the discursive formation is at the same time to specify the operation of the enunciative function and to describe the statement. The specification of the discursive formation on the one hand and the specification of the statement on the other work towards a common identification although they pose different questions. The description of the identity of the statement will reveal the way in which signs are produced as a statement and will involve reference to conditions of existence of the levels onto which the signs are mapped. The analysis of a discursive formation will show the way in which series of statements are regulated by a system of dispersion. But the concept of the statement permits Foucault to distance himself from other modes of specifying discourse and its units and to reject them as inadequate to the concept of a discursive formation which he has outlined. The chief areas of differentiation he makes are those of linguistics and logic: he is able to deny that the statement is a sentence, that unit specified by linguistics. Hence the analysis of a discursive formation will not be the problem of the analysis of discourse as it is often specified by linguistics, that is, of the supra-sentential units. This must be so on the grounds that the statement is not a unit, but more importantly it is not so because the same sentence can be the support of different statements. Moreover, there are statements that cannot be isolated as sentences. Conventional series, say a book balance, a graph or a genealogical table can all support a statement but cannot be isolated as sentences. Nor by extension can the statement be what is usually called a speech act, a formulation which is individuated by reference to the way in which an act is embodied in it and the way in which both action and formulation support each other. Again this is because the statement cannot be a unit, but more precisely it is because a speech act may from the point of view of a discursive formation consist in several statements. Lastly, Foucault denies that a statement can be identified with a proposition, where the proposition is considered as a unit of epistemological analysis. He considers that the criterion for identifying and differentiating propositions is according to their meaning, where meaning is defined by reference. That the proposition and the statement are not co-existent is because the formulations 'no one heard' and 'it is true no one heard' will function as a single proposition, but as separate statements. Moreover, the fact that a proposition is 'meaningless' in no way excludes it from functioning as a statement.

However this distance which he establishes between the statement on the one hand and sentences, speech acts and propositions on the other is not a simple question of their not being equivalent. There is an asymmetrical relation between these orders. Firstly, speech acts and propositions *can* be statements. That is to say, they can be the accidental substance of possible statements insofar as they are the forms which those statements take under definite discursive conditions, in which signs will be distributed as sentences, speech acts or propositions. But secondly, in some sense statements are actually always the condition of existence of sentences or propositions. This fact is concealed by linguistics or by logic which treats sentences or propositions as exhibiting general features which can define all possible sentences or propositions. Yet ultimately, Foucault argues, the ideal entities of sentence and proposition are derived from, as they are exemplified by, actual sentences and propositions which are in fact signs distributed as statements in the form of sentences and propositions. This ought to entail a critique of linguistics and logic as modes of specification of entities which always and necessarily occlude the discursive conditions of its entities. But in fact Foucault treats the problem in a more cautious but also more haphazard fashion.[13] He merely declares that sentences and propositions exist at a different level of existence from the statement. As a consequence of this there exists a continuing thread of ambiguity in AK about the relation between language and statements.

This can be illustrated by reference to the objects which are excluded from being statements. As has been seen, it is denied that sentences, propositions and speech acts can define the statement. But it is admitted that statements may take the form of sentences, propositions and speech acts. The problem is what limits or supports the types of entities which can provide the 'accidental substance'. Could the statements not take the form of intentions, actions or values or other objects of a humanist sociology? It is clear why Foucault's general position would exclude these. But it is not clear why he should accept, say, the speech act as a possible form of a statement. That is to say, the categories of sentences, propositions and speech acts are denied the status of entities which can define the statement but are promoted as phenomena, a realm of stable things which can support statements, while at the same time he argues that the theoretical means whereby sentences, propositions and speech acts are isolated can only operate by blinding themselves to the discursive conditions of their entities. This contradiction returns that ambiguity in the argument which is symptomatic of the general confusion concerning the relation between language and the statements.

The problem may be stated as follows. The resources upon which statements draw is a realm of signs, what Foucault calls either a natural or an artificial language. Little attention is given to the theoretical specification of this realm. It is whatever can function as signs, a limitless realm of discursivity, the general semiotic field. But the systematicity of semiological systems is never referred to, there are simply signs. Foucault's disregard here is not simply an overlooking of semiological problems in favour of his own concerns. For it plays a definite role in the relation between signs and statements. As has been shown, there is an intermediate stage between signs and statements, that is, units of a group of signs which can function as the possible forms of statements. The only two which Foucault mentions are the sentence and the proposition. They are dealt with in order to deny their equivalence or correspondence to the statement but to admit that they can appear as its accidental form. In this way, Foucault appears to have detached himself from the dominance of categories of linguistics and logic. But in fact he is always dragged back to it. For the disengagement has been made in an arbitrary fashion.

There are two reasons for this, and they both bear upon his practical limitation of the forms that statements may take to sentences and propositions. Firstly, it is clear that if statements are a function which bear upon signs, and if the field of the sign is that of semiological systems in general, the possible forms of statements could not in any way be limited to sentences or propositions. Pictorial representations or bodily movements equally support statements. The restriction to sentences and propositions is thus arbitrary in respect to other semiological systems. Foucault could perhaps easily accept this. But this leads also to the problem that since statements are a function which bears upon signs, it is difficult to defend the categories of the sentence and the proposition as a possible form of statement at all. For neither of them as such are particularly relevant to groups of signs or to statements. The fact that they are powerful conventional categories should not justify the assumption, which Foucault makes, that statements can take the form of sentences or propositions. This is not to say that accidentally what is called a sentence could never support a statement. But it is to say that the accident of the correspondence between a sentence and a statement is much more accidental than Foucault assumes. Thus his statement, 'Whenever there is a grammatically isolable sentence one can recognise the existence of an independent statement' (AK: p. 81) must be decisively rejected. The qualifications which Foucault does make in respect to the relation between sentences, propositions and statements is insufficiently radical and this insufficiency is what protects Foucault from directing a necessary attention to semiological systems in general. This insufficiency also protects Foucault from dealing with the problem of the production of sense by semiological systems. For while of course he is indifferent to problems of meaning in general, he simply assumes that 'signs' have meaning, and indeed his use of 'signs' seems to suggest that there is some meaning of signs independent of their discursive employment, even while a discourse invests them with that 'something more'. This is not as it were to accuse Foucault from the point of view of an insistence upon the pertinence of semiology. Rather it is that his sleight of hand protects him from the criticisms which can be directed against the concept of semiological systems. In the absence of this attention to problems of the sign, the categories of sentence and proposition are accorded, in respect to the analysis of discursive formations, an arbitrary privilege, at the very moment when Foucault denies that this is the case.[14]

One defence of this might be that since the field of Foucault's analysis has been in general the development of the human sciences or that since 'modern' discourses are likely to be written and spoken, this privilege either does not matter or in fact corresponds to the weight of evidential matter which archaeological analysis will confront. There are two replies to this. As AK recognises, the specification of discursive formations, even if they refer to the forms of investigation Foucault had already performed, are in no way limited to them. But more importantly it does have theoretical effects upon the concept of a discursive formation. The separation of the statement from linguistic categories by being in respect to sentences and propositions rather than by being done in respect to the sign in general, produces a separation of the statement from 'language' that remains curiously parasitic upon it. The statement or the enunciative function is placed at the limit of language, eccentric to its rules of combination but always somehow hollowed out by it. One has only to reflect upon the very dependence of the category of enunciation in the text upon linguistic phenomena even while recognising the distance it bears to any conventional linguistics. As a consequence of this slippage, the problem of analysing discursive formations, the account of why one statement rather

than another appears, is directed to a separation from the problems
of language. But again to insist upon the non-correspondence of
language and statements is not to answer the larger question of the
relation between signs and statements.

Foucault can, even if in a fumbled manner, continue to assert
that statements are neither the same as linguistic units nor are they
like language. He thus recognises that in respect to the infinite possibility of the combinatory of linguistic units the analysis of statements reveals a comparative rarity. And the rules for the generation
of possible statements do not take the form of a combinatory
which can generate all possible statements of a discursive formation,
because such a conception would make a discursive formation
either an infinite series or a totality given in the rules of combination. The 'rules' governing the appearance of statements cannot
take this form at all, for it would be inconsistent with the statement being a function. As such the appearance of statements has
to be accounted for, in part by reference to the levels of the
discursive formation, of the objects, subject positions, enunciative
modalities and the strategies of the discourse. Nor can the appearance of statements be made equivalent to or coextensive with all
the formulations which are or have been made, and which might
be said to constitute the historian's ideal archive. This is again
because statements are not equivalent to formulations, but also
because statements will be relatively rare compared with actual
formulations just as they are compared with the possible formulations opened up by language. The analysis of statements and their
systems of dispersion attempts to specify something which is
neither conventionally 'visible' nor 'hidden'. It is not visible
because the enunciative function is effaced in its operation and
can only be described by simultaneously working at the level of
the discursive formation and of the statement. On the other hand
it is not hidden in the sense that it is reconstructed as something
behind the repository of formulations, or can be extracted as the
essence of formulations. But to point to the rarity of statements is
still not to come closer to identifying the principle of regularity.

In fact the problem of regularity is dealt with in an equally
negative fashion. It is argued that the History of Ideas cannot provide any concept for conceiving the problem of regularity for it
poses the regular in terms of the deviant. The regularity refers to
an index of frequency or likelihood, and its opposite is the
irregular formation, be that considered as unusual, pathological,
archaic or prophetic. The kind of regularity with which archaeological analysis is concerned is not this but the effective field of
appearance of statements, and it must reject therefore the conventional mode of the History of Ideas. Not least it must reject it

because the History of Ideas does not in its treatment of formulations specify the level of the statement but is trapped by the
linguistic analogy of formulations and the logical equivalence of
propositions that it discovers in its archive. This cannot afford an
archaeology with any purchase on the analysis of discursive
formations. For a quite new discursive practice may be supported
by formulations that remain linguistically analogous or logically
equivalent. To say 'the species evolves' is to say nothing in the
specification of a discursive formation in which the formulation
might appear.

Regularity must then refer to the level of the statement, and as
was indicated before, cannot take the form of a communality of
statements governed by consistency, for a discursive formation is
a system of dispersion. Nor can it take the form of a generative
system of statements, for there is no deep structure of a discursive
formation. For Foucault what is at stake in what governs the
appearance of statements must be stated at the level of the enunciative function since that is what statements are related to. But
those rules which produce the 'discursive homogeneity' which must
be an enunciative homogeneity cannot be formalised. Yet 'certain
groups of statements put these rules into operation in their most
general and widely applicable form . . . One can thus describe a tree
of enunciative derivation . . . at its base are statements that put into
operation rules of formation in their most extended form; at its
summit and after a number of branchings, are the statements that
put into operation the same regularity, but one more delicately
articulated, more clearly delimited and localised in its extension'.
(AK: p. 147). The problem is that the tree of Jesse has more conditions than arboreal science dreams of.

Archaeology will place at 'the root, as governing statements,
those that concern the derivations of observable statements and the
field of possible objects, those that prescribe the forms of description and the perceptual codes that it can use, those that reveal the
most general possibilities of characterisation, and thus open up a
whole domain of concepts to be constructed and lastly, those that
while constituting a strategic choice, leave room for the greatest
possibilities' (AK: p. 147). Clearly then the regularity of statements
is not a deduction from axioms, nor the germination of a general
idea, and were it to be so, a discursive formation could not admit,
as Foucault insists that it can, divisions and 'contradictions'.

But when all that is allowed as a persuasive critique of the linguistic and philosophical presuppositions of the History of Ideas,
and as an insistence upon the way in which the investigation of a
discursive formation must respect its different levels and its differentiated character the question must remain. What are these

rules and how do they function? It is perhaps worthwhile recalling why an answer has to be given at all. It is because without the regularity of statements it would be impossible to cohere a discursive formation into a definite identity, even while stressing that this 'identity' is composed of divisions and differentiations. But this loads the concept of rule with so many disqualifications that it is difficult to see how Foucault's tree of derivation can permit the specification of a regularity. It is not so many things that it is difficult to see what it is. This difficulty is compounded by the fact that the rule functions in three different ways. The first refers to the possibility of a discursive formation, the way in which the conditions of existence of a discursive formation can relate to each other in such a way as to function as a rule, that which can support a discursive practice. This practice then secondly relays a regularity to a group of statements which thirdly are related as a regime of derivation. Possibility, regulation and regularity all tend to be run together in the service of protecting the discursive formation. It begins to seem that it is the very concept of a discursive formation which is at risk, given the failure to state its necessary theoretical supports, that is, the statement and the regularity of statements, with any coherent consistency.

For a crucial gap has opened up. It was declared that discursive formations could be individuated by means of specifying the regularities which constitute the effective field of appearance of statements. But, having denied that statements can be unified by linguistic properties, AK thus has to deny that the 'rules' at stake can be any sort of combinatory on the one hand or that the type of regularity could be any sort of statistical regularity of formulations on the other. The various types of regulation and regularity which are alluded to are quite ad hoc and differentiated. They merely paper over the gap left by the denial of linguistic analogies of rules. We are not contesting that denial but indicating the disastrous consequences for the attempt to individuate a discursive formation. These problems merely increase when the problem of conditionality is addressed.

The status of speaking

The existence of statements depends upon their capacity to be mapped onto the levels of a discursive formation, which must then in some sense function as the conditions of a statement. To be a statement is to refer to objects, to take a particular form of enunciative modality, to specify one concept rather than another and to take a certain form which is capable of repetition. Since a group of signs can be constituted as a statement only if it fulfils one or more modalities of existence of the discursive formation, the action of differentiation (or system of dispersion) is assigned to the various levels of the discursive formation. In which case the relation between statements is always referred back to the relations at the level of or between the levels of a discursive formation; despite the allusion to the possibility of relating statements to each other, of regularities of statements as such, the fact is that comparisons between statements will always be made in terms of their accumulation around the levels of a discursive formation. Thus although there are echoes of a Kantian transcendental argument in that the conditions of referring to an object are also the conditions of existence of the object, this escapes any real transcendentalism since the pragmatically audacious reduction of reference to existence necessarily precludes the possibility of a correspondence. There is simply no means of speaking of a relation between statements independently of their relation to the levels of a discursive formation. And thus to speak of a coexistence of statements is a pleonasm.

Hence the 'conditions' which the statement has to fulfill in order to exist are merely that those objects, subject positions, concepts and strategies to which they distribute signs, do themselves exist. But these levels of the discursive formation themselves have conditions of existence in the form of their conditions of emergence. This raises the problem of the relation between on the one hand signs and on the other hand the various institutional sites of the conditions of emergence of discursive formation. There is here a gap, and the analysis of the various enunciative functions in AK is to a large extent determined by the problems and embarrassment of this gap. It is in this gap and the attempts to bridge it that Foucault can be spied resorting to categories which have been vehemently rejected in other parts of the text.

We will consider the case of the category of the 'subject', a category which Foucault is normally held to denounce in its humanist manifestations and to escape in its anti-humanist necessities. But of course it is impossible to banish all traces of a category by fiat. For here is no simple case of residual traces lingering nostalgically in exile, for Foucault compels his gentle reader, especially in the postscript, to watch the 'disappearance' of the subject with the maudlin attention of Sir Bedevere craning ever more insistently as King Arthur's speck vanishes over the horizon. Rather it is to mark the way in which the subject is required to paper the split between signs and the conditions of emergence/existence of the levels of the discursive formation. The gap is opened precisely by Foucault's failure to consider, other than as a positive resource, signs in the sense of their analysis by semiology. The subject, through the relay of certain covert categories, is thus required as the bridge between

unproblematic signs and definite institutions. Of course this charge
cannot be read off from the text and cannot be read save against
the direction of the argument. It can only be established by demonstration.

Any invocation of the subject in AK is flatly declared to be
incompatible with and dismissive of any category of the individual
person who comes armed with intentions and memories, and
mounted upon a social context. Nor is it to be confused with a
perceiving, knowing, or speaking subject. Nor as the necessary
bearer of imaginary relations which support the ideological
instance. In short, neither a sovereign nor an enslaved subject. On
the one hand all humanist conceptions of the subject are rejected
because they require that discourse be treated as a representative
expression of that subject, a means of communication between
human subjects in a linguistic anthropology. On the other hand
anti-humanist conceptions of the subject are equally rejected
because they work to unify discourse by reference to a stable and
unitary subject-form, such that the totality of practice can exist as
a society rather than as a poached baby elephant.

Foucault can dispense with both humanist and anti-humanist
conceptions of the subject because he is not concerned to support
either a general concept of the human or the social. But this is not
to say that the category of the subject does not continue to have
residual effects. Where this problem does arise is through the
general question of enunciation for it is here that questions of signs,
the subject and social categories are tied together. It will be recalled
that this question is put in terms quite other than those of formal
linguistics, and in fact is raised as three different questions. Firstly,
that of the statement as an enunciative function, which means the
distribution of signs to the levels of a discursive formation. This has
already been dealt with.

Secondly, there is the enunciative modality, a level of the discursive formation, which consists essentially of three questions:
Who is speaking? Where is it being spoken from? What is the relation
between the speaker and what is being spoken of? The first question
concerns the necessary forms of recognition of particular forms of
agency as a status. There are no general forms of recognition and
hence it is always a question of particular statuses and their con-
struction/recognition.

A professional status, for example, will be a bundle of different
forms of recognition. Some of them are more crucially definitive
than others but do not by that fact determine the others. This raises
the question of the sources of the forms of recognition which is
best answered by reference to the second question; the site from
which statements issue. For Foucault this is an institutional field

from which the discourse derives both its legitimate course and its point of application. The problem is that this runs together the materiality of forms of recognition and the materiality of discursive practice together with some material form of institutions. This is clearly done in order to underline the insistence that the discursive formation is not separable from institutions. Reference to institutions is understandably concerned to disrupt distinctions between the internality and externality of a discursive formation and even more of distinctions between the discursive and the non-discursive as if they were different classes of phenomena.

But all this does is to displace an already existing problem which is an implicit distinction between institutional moments of the discursive formation and the institutional sites of their incidence. And in its turn this can be traced back to the problematic relation between statements and the enunciative function. Elements of institutions function as part of the discursive formation viewed from the point of its levels. But these same elements, appear to function as conditions of the discursive formation when viewed from the point of the statement. This contradiction is attributable to the way in which the definition of the statement, as has been argued, is parasitic upon concepts of language. Insofar as it has been argued that the statement is ultimately tied to a privilege of the sentence and the proposition this must tend to render institutions *external*. Insofar as the statement is the enunciative function, elements of institutions become *internal* to the discursive formation. Hence there is an instability in the reference to institutions. In the first case institutions are external and it is impossible to conceive of elements of institutions save as general conditions; in this case the levels of the discursive formation are then threatened with decomposition into those levels which generate a regularity and those which become conditions. In the second case elements of institutions are incorporated within the discursive formation but this then threatens to decompose institutions into the discursive and the non-discursive, but with no principles of differentiation save that of reference back to statements conceived as units of meaning in language, sentences and propositions. So in fact the second is simply a more complicated version of the first.

The last question of the elements of the enunciative modality — what is the relation between the speaker and what is being spoken — concerns the relation of this authorised status, together with its institutional site, to the objects of discourse. This is a magnificent perversion by Foucault of the relation famously known as subject and object, by which he seeks to escape from posing a philosophical question. He is not concerned with a general question of the relation of knowledge, but of a particular 'knowledge'. Nor is he concerned with the epistemological subject of 'knowledge' but with a particular type of subject position, institutionally fixed. Nor is he concerned with a general mechanism of knowledge but rather with particular mechanisms whereby the object can be registered. All this functions as a useful cannibalisation of traditional categories and extends into the possibilities of conceiving of forms of perception, experience and reasoning which are intelligible only by reference to the discursive formation within which they appear rather than as some epistemological or cognitive a priori. But these important possibilities are severely limited in AK by the fact that both subjects and objects are subjected to the oscillation which has been established between the cleavage in the conceptualisation both of institutions and statements. This cleavage appears to be overcome in the enunciative modality only by welding the categories of status, of institutional site and of 'knowing' together. This is only possible on condition that they are linked by something which can have a status, be in a place and 'know'. And this is only plausible on condition that these are linked through the category of speaking — who speaks, from where and of what. The subject of philosophy has been expelled only to admit the subject of sociology and the subject of language.

This can be developed by reference to analogous problems, this time in respect to the question of the statement. One of the elements of a statement is that it possesses a particular relation to a subject. Since the statement is an enunciative function and is supposedly distinguished from categories of sentence and proposition, it is held to necessitate an element of positionality in respect to its source. The enunciative function distributes signs to the level of the discursive formation in the manner which is proper to their existence; statements do not have the function of stating or communicating anything but rather have the function of supporting a practice. Hence statements must be capable of supporting enunciative modalities.

Since a statement is different from a linguistic category its form of relating to a subject cannot for example take the form of a grammatical category. In that the subject of a sentence is external to the linguistic unit it designates an exterior point of reference. The asymmetry between grammatical subjects and the subject of the statement can be marked out in the following ways. A statement which does not contain a first-person grammatical form nevertheless has a subject position. Moreover different statements of the same grammatical form do not thereby have the same relation to the subject of a statement, while identical sentences can have different subjects of statement.

In terms of grammar, the subject of the sentence is exterior to the sentence, and in the case of the first-person singular, is identical to the author. Is then the subject of the statement as opposed to the sentence always the author (i.e. the subject of enunciation) no matter what the subject of the sentence is? But what could 'author' mean? Who is the subject of enunciation when an actor speaks a part? The author as the subject of enunciation is not the author of copyright law. Foucault uses the novel to remind us that the different kinds of enunciation within the novel presuppose different subjects of enunciation. There are different relations between the subject of enunciation and the énoncé.[15] This distinction between the author and the subject of enunciation/statement is a general characteristic of statements.

The consequence of this is that there is a radical non-correspondence between the subject of enunciation/statement and the continuity of persons. Yet Foucault moves from an indifference to persons to the rather different task of framing an increasingly stringent set of conditions of individuation, not in terms of authorship, it is true, but in terms of a more differentiated set of relations attached to the subject of a statement.

There are two criticisms to be made of this position. Foucault uses the concept of the subject of enunciation in order to differentiate the relation which a subject bears to a statement from that of a grammatical subject or from an author, where author is conceived either in the sense known to publishers or in the sense of producer of the formulation. But he fails to deal with the consequences of the fact that the concept of the subject of enunciation is itself internal to lingusitics and as such incapable of being severed from the concept of the énoncé. It is a form of positionality that cannot be considered independent of natural language and thus which cannot be presumed to define the possible positions which relate signs to the levels of a discourse. Put baldly, Fouçault never considers what a non-linguistic enunciation would be.

Secondly, the characterisation of the subject of a statement relies upon an elision between the means of individualising the spaces of the subject of enunciation and the filling of them by individuals. There is no requirement to deal with the problem of the positionality of the subject of enunciation in terms of mobility of individuals. For linguistics individuals as such need not come into the problem, even if it does require reference to the category of the subject as a means of registering variations. But where for linguistics the subject of enunciation is a position given by an operation, for Foucault it is defined in terms of the activity of that operation. It is this which allows Foucault to mistake subject positions of a statement with individual capacities to fill them, 'in determining what position can and must be occupied by an individual if he is to be the subject of it' (AK: p. 96).[16]

We have attempted in both the account of the institutional com-
ponents of the enunciative modality and the way in which signs are
distributed in a relation to a subject to work from the peripheries
to the coordinates of the discursive formation. On the one hand it
can be seen how the question of status and the institutional sites
is drawn into the regularity of the discursive formation by the utilisation of the relay of the subject; on the other hand, the subject
of language, its positionality as conceived by the category of the
subject of enunciation, is drawn towards that relay by converting
the question of positionality into the question of the classes of
individuals and their capacities to fill those positions. The subject
of language and the subject of sociology have been expelled only
to admit the individual, subject of philosophy.

Conclusion

We have sought to demonstrate that in AK the residual categories
and concepts of language operate in different ways. The dismissal
of theories of the sign is attended by a dismissal of any general
theory of meaning, be that construed in concepts of reference, use,
semantics or ideology. Indeed the capacity of any general theory of
discourse is denied by arguing that they must all be blind to the
discursive conditions of the production of their basic units; they
are as it were post-statemental rationalisations capable of forma-
lising groups of formulations but never of identifying the conditions of that formalisation. They are exemplified for Foucault
in the procedures of linguistic and epistemological analysis whose
rules of combination and reference mistake the field of their operation for global levels of existence. But for all this dismissal of
general theories of the sign a fundamental contradiction is set up
by assuming a general domain of the sign as the unconditional
resource for the constitution of statements.

What is proffered is a declared but quite incomplete rejection of
general problems of semiology and meaning together with the
promise that the concept of the statement shall both avoid these
areas and go on to account for them. Against this one could pet-
tishly insist that some of the claims advanced on behalf of the concept of the statement are already established theses in the rejected
'sciences' of logic and linguistics.[17] More directly it has been argued
that despite the claim to dismiss categories of language, certain linguistic categories are accorded an arbitrary privilege. For what
could the subject of enunciation be, indeed, what could enunciation itself be, if not still conjugated and declined through a linguistic medium?

The other linguistic category so privileged is the sentence. The conventional entity is left to exercise an unexamined capacity to characterise groups of signs. This capacity is twofold: firstly, that the sentence is privileged as a support of statements; secondly, that linguistic entities have a privilege in respect to organising signs. Nor is this privilege a mere slip of the tongue which can be repaired by adding botanical tables and laundry lists as groups of signs capable of supporting statements. For these other, any other, groups of signs are still considered as resembling sentences (by which it is *not* meant that they can simply be rewritten as sentences). It means that they will be considered both in terms of their singularity, as *a* sign and in their form of connection, as a series of signs, as exhibiting a sentential form. At an immediate level this limits the types of candidates which are entertained, a limit far narrower than semiology imposes in its attention to styles of dress, cuisine, film or technical instruments. And clearly it would function as an obstacle if the concept of the statement were to be developed in investigations of political and administrative practices, as Foucault contends is possible.

Such a possibility would be limited by the consequences of Foucault's arbitrary (if conventional) delineation of what shall count as a sign. For one of those consequences is that 'institutions' and more generally the conditions of existence of a discourse are cast in a place of externality. Of course we recognise that this is a regrettable consequence which much of AK seeks to efface. To consolidate the institution and conditionality with the non-discursive would be to return to the most banal of sociologies. But it remains a problem for Foucault as it does for any employment of the term 'discourse' which takes the realm of signs for granted. It can never be sufficient to delimit a sphere of signs as the effective range of discourse and then to attempt to escape the ill effects of such a position by simultaneously repudiating any conventional theories of representation. It can be seen that this is no recommendation of semiology, but rather an insistence upon the need to open up the consideration of other types of signs in a way which would not distinguish the question of their systematicity from the question of their 'supports'. The question of Foucault's own concept of 'material repeatability' is one which bears upon this and which could be elaborated (see note 11).

We are also aware that Foucault's attempt to individualise specific discursive formations is part of his attempt to displace general questions of orders of meaning. Our insistence upon the requirement to deal with the problem of the concept of the sign is in no sense a return to these general questions; it is rather a purgative required by the inadequacy of the displacement. Nevertheless certain parallel problems have been raised with respect to the unity of those discursive formations. These relate partly to Foucault's demand that it consists in the 'regularity of a practice' by which he seeks to demonstrate that the different levels of a discursive formation work together. This demand requires, as has been argued, a homogenisation of different types of conditions of that 'regularity of a practice'. Regularity, regulation, possibility, government, derivation, enabling conditions, mutuality of effect are all run together in the term 'condition of existence' to threaten a new generality.

This suggests that such unity (or unification of levels) is neither possible nor desirable in the analysis of discourses. The objects, subjects, concepts and strategies simply need not display that definitive cohesion-in-dispersion that Foucault would require. And it is not an accident that where such unity is sought for, the otherwise rejected forms of unification return. For the 'systems of formation', the locus of appearance (categorically or historically) of a discourse from its conditions threatens to reduce the discursive formation to the regime of its origin and to promote the subject as the knot which binds together objects, institutions, status and style.

The resurgence of the category of the subject in AK arises then both out of the incomplete excision of the concepts of natural language and from the demand for a unification of levels of a discourse as a *formation*, that is, as an entity with definite limits. But these criticisms, although damaging to the declared project of AK do not disqualify the project of identifying forms of discursive organisation, nor of performing that through the levels Foucault advances. But there will be no requirement that those levels be *unified* as a discursive formation. If it is argued that Foucault's more recent work is not subject to these criticisms that is largely because the same problems have not been pursued. Clearly the intrusion of the project of 'genealogy' cannot be conceived as the simple extension of an archaeology into fields of the ethical and the administrative. The notorious problems which exist in those works surrounding the questions of historical reference, the concept of strategy and the category of the body suggest that problems of AK have not been solved while its possibilities have not been exploited.

Notes

1. The 'History of Ideas' is used here to indicate not just a scholarly discipline but a presupposition: 'ideas' form an order of motivated representations whose distribution (appearance, persistence, mutation) in time forms a coherent object of investigation. Calabashes, microscopes, wafers, falling apples, displaced bathwater can all be made to yield their tithe of ideahood. It should

also be noted that Foucault's critique of the History of Ideas operates as an analogue to the sorts of critiques of classical theories of representation which have become conventional in contemporary theories of discourse. However, by directing this line of attack against the History of Ideas, Foucault is able to perform a persuasive demonstration of the pervasiveness of such presuppositions. He can thus shift the focus away from the area of concepts of language and representation as such and towards the functions they serve in historical research.

2. See for example, Chapter 1 of Lovejoy (1936).

3. We admit bluntly that AK is a contradictory text in respect to this problem. It is not difficult to attribute to it a different and more conventional position and it is to be found especially on pp. 44—46. The set of social relations, termed 'primary relations', is admitted and said to be independent of 'all discourse or objects of discourse' and specifiable in their own right. This gesture towards a common appeal in historical or social investigation may seem to turn Foucault away from the radicalism of his rejection of epistemological conceptions of social relations. But his example of what can count as that which can be studied in its 'own right', that is independent of all discourse, cannot be taken seriously. For it is the relations which existed 'between the bourgeois family and the functioning of judicial authorities and categories'. Leaving aside the enchanting prospect of non-discursive categories, it is of course Foucault and his collaborators whose investigation of that phenomenon 'in its own right' proved decisively a rather contrary case. Indeed the transparent inefficiency of Foucault's deference justifies us in not considering his division into 'primary' and 'secondary' social relations at any length.

4. Thus *Madness and Civilisation* was an attempt to delineate madness as an object, *The Birth of the Clinic* to find a certain pervasive style, *The Order of Things* to found a system of permanent and coherent concepts on the one hand, and also to designate certain groupings of concepts at a level of compatibility which would produce options and hence strategic options. It is also true that in presenting those works in a polemical and schematic way in AK Foucault underplays the elements of discontinuity and differentiation that are already at work in the earlier texts and the extent to which they are not directed solely to those forms of unity: *The Birth of the Clinic* is in effect as much concerned with delineating objects of discourse as with 'style', precisely because the objects of discourse are constituted in part through enunciative modalities.

5. As will be argued, the question of 'regularity' is crucially weak and ambiguous. Archaeology's claim is to answer the question of 'why this statement rather than that' appeared, and thus central to the answer are the problems of the regularity and individuality of a discursive formation. This clearly raises questions of *conditions* of emergence of statements. But the relation between regularity and conditionality remains opaque: if regularities are constitutive of a discourse then to add a notion of conditionality is empty. If on the other hand they are merely regulative and effectively selective then the productivity of statements resides elsewhere. J. P. Minson has formalised two sets of equivalences by which the text proliferates this confusion: on the one hand an equivalence between the law-like regularities in a discourse and the conditions of emergence of a discourse; on the other hand an equivalence is made between the conditions of possibility of statements, the fact of their systematic emergence and the co-existence of statements (Minson, forthcoming, Ch. 6).

6. See Stalin (1972), first published in Pravda, June 20 1950.

7. This consists largely of two elements. The first is to refine the concept of the subject as it appears in Althusser so that it can respect the distinction which

psychoanalysis draws between the ego and the subject in such a way that the proposed mechanism of interpellation cannot be accused of confusing them. The second is to derive from Lacan's work on metaphor and the unconscious a theory of the production of sense which breaks from linguistic theories of semantics. There is no space to deal with these important issues but we would argue that the first point still does not escape the problems posed by Hirst (1976). Nor is it easy to see how the second point, whose very premises derive from linguistics, can fulfill the tasks assigned to them, nor if they could where it would leave the residual category of 'language'.

8. Ultimately, Pecheux like Althusser, remains relatively indifferent to the necessary distinction (in their theory) between an ideological/discursive formation in particular and the ideological/discursive space in general. This has two sources: the first which is mentioned above is the failure to relate the 'moments' of the ideological level to the institutional spaces of the ISAs. Unless that were to be resolved, the Althusserian concept of an ideological formation could not be advanced. The second source is one which obscures the necessity for resolving the first. It is the singularity and ubiquity of the *mechanism* of ideology, the hailing of subjects. It is this which permits the Althusserian remarks on the subject to remain both at the level of abstract generality and at the same time to proliferate examples from the quotidian particularity by which sociological lovers of 'everyday life' are suavely lured. At this point it is not Althusser's 'strangeness' which permitted a certain sociological assimilation of the ISAs paper, it is his 'familiarity'.

9. AK offers a proliferation of different terminologies which are in fact consistently differentiated from each other in the text. As a general principle it is wise to remember that such differences do not signify entities to be related to each other, but the same entities viewed from different directions of the analysis. Thus 'discursive formation' is used to signify that body of different levels, the objects, subjects, concepts and strategies of a single formation, while 'discursive practice' refers to those same levels conceived as working together, operating under a form of regularity which draws the different levels into a unity. 'Discourse' is reserved by Foucault — though not consistently by us — to designate a discursive formation viewed from the point of view of the groupings of its statements rather than its levels.

10. Foucault gives no clear account of parts of his position and much of this section should be treated as a theoretical reconstruction rather than as an exposition. In particular, we stress the necessity of a relation between the statement and signs which Foucault's own exposition would tend to shy away from for reasons which will become clear.

11. Materiality is the correlate of strategy in a discursive formation. What is involved in both cases is the persistence (and limits) of the identity of statements through degrees of variation. The question of 'strategy' raises this problem in the form of the 'same' statement appearing in a series of statements which can represent alternative or incompatible themes. But this is in fact only a particular instance of the identity of statements as they are circulated and re-circulated. The 'repeatability' of statements is certainly not an ideal content to which formulations refer; nor is it that unique occasion of its enunciation. Its repeatability is said to be material insofar as it is inseparable from the institutional conditions of circulation, its inscription and reinscription. Thus it concerns certain physical forms of inscription but only insofar as these themselves are implicated in forms of authorisation: it is thus not so much a question of machines or things as of apparatuses. An apt illustration is in the analytic distinction which is drawn between film and cinema.

12. While in general, of course, analogies from mathematics should be treated

with extreme caution especially in the social sciences, Foucault's use of the term 'function' is considerably less inconsistent with mathematics than is usual. Reference to this serves to underline the *relational* character of the statement, that mapping of elements from one set (the domain, which is here the group of signs) onto the range (here the levels of a discursive formation). It is also worth noting that these relations may be one-one or many-one: an object of a discursive formation may be mapped onto by one or more groups of signs, which provides that degree of flexibility required with respect to signs. But the fact that there can be one and only one member of the range for such a mapping would make any attempt to develop the analogy ill-advised.

13. Indeed, the extremely peremptory mode of conceiving the problem of the sign can be seen in Foucault's reasons why discourses are irreducible to language (*langue*) and speech. It is, for him, that discourses 'do more than use signs to designate things' (AK: p. 49), a somewhat cavalier treatment of signs.

14. We have sought to demonstrate that in Foucault's text the concept of the statement is dependent upon the use of 'signs' and that the concentration of analysis upon the sentence and the proposition is both a diversion from and a concealment of this. If this is so it places the text in an embarrassment, the unwanted return of the 'sign' and the theoretical problems it brings in its train, which in fact leaves Paris for Geneva. Our argument is simply that this be confronted, and its implication would be that it would then have what would undoubtedly be regarded as the uncongenial task of dealing with, rather than dismissing, the arguments of Derrida. For a statement of the impossibility of the necessary coincidence of signs and meaning, see M. Cousins (1978).

15. See Benveniste (1966) pp. 225—288.

16. One consequence of this would be to destroy the possibility of non-human occupancy of subject positions which Foucault's analysis opened up.

17. For instance, Frege's 'logical' account of meaning not only places sense alongside reference but argues that the 'reference of a term is determined by its sense, inasmuch as its reference consists of that set of individuals which satisfy a set of conditions which must be fulfilled if the term is to be used in the correct sense'. (Gaukroger 1979: 18).

References

Althusser, L. (1971) 'Ideology and ideological state apparatuses' *Lenin and Philosophy*, New Left Books, London.
Benveniste, E. (1966) *Problemes de linguistique generale*, Paris.
Brown, B. (1979) 'The universe of discourse', *Oxford Literary Review*, Autumn issue.
Cousins, M. (1978) 'The logic of deconstruction', *Oxford Literary Review*, Summer issue.
Gaukroger, S. (1979) *Explanatory Structures*, Harvester Press, Brighton.

Hindess, B. and Hirst, P. Q. (1977) *Modes of Production and Social Formation*, Macmillan, London.
Hirst, P. Q. (1978) 'Althusser and the theory of ideology', *Economy and Society*, Vol. 5 no. 4.
Lovejoy, A. O. (1936) *The Great Chain of Being*, London.
Minson, J. P. forthcoming *Social Relations and the Sovereignty of Ethics*.
Pecheux, M. (1976) *Les Verites de la Palice*, Maspero, Paris.
Stalin, J. (1972) *Problems in Linguistics*, Peking.

CHAPTER 4

The *Nouvelle Philosophie* and Foucault

Peter Dews

Abstract

The first part of this chapter gives an account of some of the intellectual and political background to the characteristic positions of the *Nouvelle Philosophie,* and details the presentation of these positions in the work of André Glucksmann. The important influence of Foucault on the *Nouvelle Philosophie* is then discussed. Foucault's interpretation of his own earlier work and his present manner of posing the question of power are critically analysed, and found to be defective in a way which allows room for the exploitation of his results by the *Nouvelle Philosophie.* This partial convergence is illustrated by a comparison between Lardreau and Jambet's *L'Ange* and Foucault's recent discussions of sexuality. The chapter concludes with a brief location of the *Nouvelle Philosophie* in the context of intellectual developments outside France.

In June of 1976 the literary weekly *Les Nouvelles Littéraires* published a dossier edited by one Bernard-Henri Lévy, philosophy teacher, journalist, and *directeur de collections* at a major Parisian publishing house. It consisted of articles presenting the views of a number of young, and for the most part unknown, intellectuals, interspersed with interviews or exchanges of letters with well-known figures such as Lévi-Strauss and Roland Barthes. In this way the impression was created that the *imprimatur* of the philosophico-literary establishment had been granted to the 'new movement' which the dossier purported to herald. In fact the texts thus assembled were remarkably disparate, the real, unspoken connection between them being the fact that all but one of the young authors represented had recently published or was about to publish in one of the series edited by Lévy for *Grasset.* Lévy's introduction on page one of the dossier gave the reader to understand that something original and exciting was happening in French thought, and a number of theoretical points of reference were indicated: Foucault, Lacan, Heidegger, Nietzsche. Marx was conspicuous by his absence. The title of the dossier: *Les Nouveaux Philosophes.*[1]

Reaction was not immediate. A trickle of articles in the weekly press expressed interest in the 'new gurus', and in the autumn there were radio interviews under the title 'The Lost Generation'. But it was not until the spring of the following year that the *Nouvelle Philosophie* truly became media property, with the publication of *Les Maîtres Penseurs* (The Master Thinkers) by André Glucksmann, best known in England for his critique of Althusser (Glucksmann, 1977a), and of Lévy's *La Barbarie à Visage Humain* (Barbarism with a Human Face), a banal patchwork of ideas culled from the writings of his associates which immediately became a best-seller. Appearances on television and public debates were accompanied by a flood of press interviews, many in magazines (*Lui, Paris-Match . . .*) not normally noted for their interest in philosophical questions. Some members of the group even went for drinks with the President at the Elysée Palace. In fact the *Nouveaux Philosophes* occupied from the beginning a characteristic position of bad faith, depicting themselves as a persecuted and censored minority, as 'dissidents', while exploiting to the full the resources of the bourgeois media. Given this barrage of publicity the French public was soon to grasp the essentials — that a group of young intellectuals, for the most part veterans of May '68 and former leftist militants, had discovered the works of Solzhenitzyn and concluded that Marxism leads inevitably to concentration camps. The single word 'Gulag', which in Solzhenitsyn bears all the weight of a terrible historical reality, started on a rapid degeneration through the stage of pseudo-concept to that of slogan. By the autumn of 1977 reports were appearing in the international press, many betraying evident pleasure, like the *Time Magazine* cover-story under the title 'Marx is Dead', at the discovery (at long last!) of a group of young, handsome and militantly anti-Marxist French intellectuals.[2]

It would be a little too easy, however, to dismiss the *Nouvelle Philosophie* as purely a product of the media, as part of the ideological rearmament of imperialism,[3] or even to see its emergence, as certain commentators did at the time, as a right-wing conspiracy to sabotage the chances of the Left in the 1978 elections (in the event the parties of the left effectively sabotaged themselves). Although most of the charges brought against the *Nouveaux Philosophes* have more than an element of truth, including the charge that their 'philosophy' is not very good, they also have the disadvantage of portraying the *Nouvelle Philosophie* as a manipulated product of the present, while neglecting the continuities between its attitudes and practices and more general post-'68 developments. As Jacques Rancière, one of its

most intelligent critics, has pointed out, the *Nouvelle Philosophie*
did not *invent* the Parisian intellectual star-system, the use of
'politics' to spice up literary theories or academic courses, or the
practice of exchanging complimentary book-reviews, which has
reached epidemic proportions with Lévy and his associates.
Similarly, although the *Nouveaux Philosophes* were among the
first to openly and violently proclaim their anti-Marxism, they
were preceded by a whole generation of thinkers (Baudrillard,
Deleuze, Foucault and others) whose work was already a long way
from being Marxist. If Hegel's dictum that 'philosophy is its own
time comprehended in thought' required confirmation, it could
be found in the developments of the last decade in France. The
theoretical effort of the thinkers just mentioned can be understood to a large extent as an attempt to 'make sense' of May '68
and its aftermath, based on the conviction that what happened
in '68 — the development of diverse forms of 'cultural' revolt —
was, in Foucault's words, 'profoundly anti-Marxist'. It is misleading to represent the *Nouvelle Philosophie*, as certain reports
have done, as the first challenge to a monolithic hegemony on the
French left.

The most that can be argued is that the *Nouvelle Philosophie*
legitimated and helped to accelerate the surprisingly rapid
emergence of a new orthodoxy on the French intellectual left. It is
as though all the necessary elements had long been held in
suspension, but required the *succès de scandale* of the *Nouvelle
Philosophie* to be precipitated into a new 'Parisian consensus'.
Among the major doctrines of this new consensus would be the
following: that Marxism is in some way responsible for the terror
of the Soviet camps; that the state is the central source of social
and political oppression, and that therefore any politics directed
towards the seizure of state power is dangerous and vain; that
science always operates within and reinforces relations of power
or, to raise the stakes a little, that 'reason' is inherently totalitarian;
that since any political ideology will eventually be used to justify
crimes against humanity, the only 'safe' form of political action is
a militant defence of human rights. These themes allow of
permutations (Marxist doctrine glorifies the state, totalitarianism
equals the scientists in power . . .) but the underlying principle
will be clear. It consists in a 180-degree reversal from the anti-
humanist severity of the 'high structuralism' of the mid-sixties
(Althusser is the major reference here) to various forms of
romanticism and individualism, in which 'science' and any
totalising movement of reflection are denounced in the name of
the spontaneous, the immediate and the particular. The major
stages in this highly compressed replay of the transition from
classicism to romanticism can be followed in that faithful mirror

of Parisian fashion, *Tel Quel* magazine: 1966—8, *rapprochement* with the P.C.F. and strong influence of Althusser; after '68, the long detour through 'Maoism' which transforms into an abandonment of historical materialism; 1976, disillusionment with China and beginning of a realignment of theoretical 'pluralism of the text' with political pluralism; 1977, enthusiastic treble-issue on the United States, where, as we learn, 'the state is free of repressive structures'; 1978, emergence of an ideology of 'dissidence' and discovery that Christianity and literature (ideally combined in Solzhenitsyn) are the true bastions against totalitarianism and the 'political view of the world'. In many respects *Tel Quel* is now a reactionary publication (Philippe Sollers, its editor, has announced in an article in *Le Monde* that 'capitalism is ten times less repressive than socialism'), or at least one which has 'no enemies on the right'. Sympathetic to religious thought, and with all the complex theoretical machinery of *sémanalyse* now left far behind, it has opened its pages to such frankly right-wing commentators as Eugène Ionesco and Jean-François Revel.[4] But *Tel Quel* is an extreme example. In general the new *'post-gauchiste'* consensus is in favour of the struggles of feminists, regionalists, ecologists, the 'psychiatrised' and imprisoned, as long as these struggles are not defined in terms of any overall strategy, or supported by any global analysis. Rebellion counts for more than results.

A history of political militantism has become an almost indispensible trademark for a New Philosopher.[5] Not only does it provide denunciations of Marxism with the authenticity of disillusionment, it serves as a source of moral authority for present political pronouncements, and continues to provide their work with a vague aura of leftism. It has become a publicity cliché to represent the *Nouvelle Philosophie* as the emergence, nearly a decade after the event, of the true voice of May '68. In fact a glance at the history and politics of the organisation to which many of the *Nouveaux Philosophes* belonged makes clear that, even as militants, they were already a long way from Marxism. This organisation was the *Gauche Prolétarienne*, the most important of the Maoist groups, which, by the inventiveness of its political practice, rallied the support of a number of prominent left-wing intellectuals (in 1970 Sartre agreed to take over the editorship of their paper, *La Cause du Peuple*, in defiance of a government ban). It was born in the aftermath of May '68 from a fusion between elements of the *Movement du 22 Mars*, the leading student movement of the events, which modelled itself on the Marcuse-tinged radical anti-authoritarianism of the German SDS, and the *Union de la Jennesse Communiste (Marxiste-Léniniste)*, which emerged from a split in the autumn of 1966 among the

Althusserians at the *Ecole Normale Supérieure* on the question of the Cultural Revolution in China.

The *Gauche Prolétarienne* bore the marks of this double heritage. Transferring the anti-authoritarianism of the *22-Mars* from the faculty to the factory, it preached a doctrine of spontaneous rebellion against the hierarchy and discipline of the workplace. The sequestration of a boss, the jamming of a production line, a wildcat strike against unfair treatment were seen as the basis of a struggle against 'fascism in the factory', and as a means of circumventing the 'repressive apparatus' of the trade-unions. The GP was not afraid of the label 'populist', or to accept the comparison between these forms of action and the most 'primitive' era of the workers' movement. Indeed their positions entailed a conscious break with the entire Leninist tradition stemming from *What is to be Done?* which assumes that socialist consciousness must be imported into the working class from without. For the GP, on the contrary, all political criteria were subordinated to the immediate experience of oppression and revolt. If the trade-union delegate is perceived by the workers as just another boss, he *is* another boss; a rebellion of small-shopkeepers must be unconditionally supported despite the fact that at elections they vote solidly Gaullist.[6] The counterpart of this spontaneism was an attack on the 'fetishism of knowledge' and a rejection of 'academic' and 'authoritarian' Marxism, of both sophisticated structuralist and semiotic remakes and the ossified thought of the P.C. This attack, however, as more conventional Maoists noted with chagrin, was not accompanied by an attempt to elaborate an 'authentic' Marxism, but tended to slide — a movement consummated by the *Nouveaux Philosophes* — into an attack on Marxism as such. This was inevitable given the GP's political perspectives, since theory no longer had any function to serve. May '68 had shown that when the masses are in movement they are perfectly capable of thinking and speaking for themselves; the worker does not need Marxism to tell her/him when to revolt. The role of the intellectual, therefore, is not to produce theory, but to erase her/himself as intellectual in the service of the people. In place of a 'theory', however, the GP did possess what could be termed a 'guiding political fantasy'. May '68 had marked a qualitative upturn in the class struggle in France, which meant that the bourgeoisie could not longer take its order for granted, but was obliged continually and forcibly to re-establish it. As a result the French state was undergoing a process of internal fascisization 'from above', against which the GP attempted to reactivate the mythology of the French Resistance. Trade union delegates and foremen were labelled 'collaborators', the GP proclaimed itself the kernel of the 'New Partisans'.[7] In other countries this kind of 'analysis' lead eventually to terrorism

(Baader-Meinhof, Red Brigades). The GP teetered on the brink. In 1972 a minor official was kidnapped following the shooting of a young Maoist worker by a factory guard at *Renault.* The official was soon released, however, and shortly afterwards the GP opted for self-dissolution.

In the early seventies the vision which informed the political practice of the *Gauche Prolétarienne* was reflected in a number of 'transitional philosophies' which foreshadow the *Nouvelle Philosophie,* and in which 'Maoism' is revealed in the process of becoming an anti-Marxism. A good example of the genre is Jean-Paul Dollé's *Désir de Revolution* (1975), whose title well indicates the fateful slide from object to subject which was then taking place. Dollé employs a Lacanian conception of the relation between science, truth and desire to transform the fissure between science and critique which has marked the history of Marxism into an irreducible conflict. For Dollé the aim of the revolution is to realise radical autonomy, to effect a transformation of human relations which will 'make it possible for everyone to say "I" '. But this entails that the desire for revolution must itself be an act of radical autonomy, that 'the cause of the revolution is the revolution itself'. In Lacanian terms, the object of desire is desired — in an endless circularity — because it is desirable; the *object* of desire is not the *cause* of desire. Any theory therefore, including Marxism, which presents the rebellion against exploitation as sociologically or historically explicable, is already a form of recuperation. It allows the possessors of 'scientific knowledge', who invariably coincide with the leaders of the party, to counter the immediate impulse of the masses to rebel with a pedagogy of the mechanisms of the capitalist system and its ultimate collapse. For Dollé, however, exploitation is not the *result* of the capitalist system; it is rather my failure to rebel against exploitation which allows the perpetuation of capitalism. An absolute dichotomy is supposed between rebellion and recuperation, which entails that only the immediacy of revolt, the 'coincidence of politics and life', offers an escape from the cycle of oppression.

Within this perspective, the question to be put to science is no longer the question of the objective truth at which it aims, but the question of the 'truth' of the desire by which it is animated. If Marxism is 'true', it is not because it represents a science of capitalist society, but because Marx wrote from the point of view of the oppressed. For Dollé what is important in *Capital* is not the theory of value, but the history of the struggles for the shortening of the working day. Similarly the greatness of Lenin consists in the 'madness' of his proposal of the April Theses, against the accepted wisdom of the Bolshevik Party. His failure resulted from his 'scientific fideism', his conception of the Party as the possessor of revolutionary truth, since the 'mad will to designate and possess the truth', formulated in the ordered discourse of science, is linked with the desire for a totalitarian ordering of society. Thus Dollé is driven to the conclusion that Marxism, if it is not to be dangerous, can express no more than what the proletariat already knows. Its sole function consists in a 'systematisation' of the desires of the masses, and in a lifting of the prohibitions that prevent their expression. In fact there is nothing left at the end of this demolition except the single Maoist slogan that 'Rebellion is justified'.

About the time of the publication of Dollé's book, Sartre began a series of discussions with the Maoist leader Pierre Victor and the journalist Philippe Gavi which were published in 1974 under the title *On a Raison de se Révolter*. A comparison between the two books reveals very similar ideas being expressed in two different vocabularies. The pattern of Lacanian concepts used by Dollé translates without difficulty into the Sartrean notions of serialisation, group, practical thinking, freedom. Sartre and his comrades suggest that a revolt against oppression cannot be explained as the result of a chain of cause and effect — it represents an expression of freedom which is irreducible to its preconditions. The danger of 'authoritarian Marxism' is that it neglects this truth, displacing the aim of struggle away from the immediate agent of oppression (the boss) towards an anonymous system of production of surplus value. It places us on the terrain of the enemy capitalism, the terrain of abstractions. Even movements with broad social and economic objectives, however, are rooted in the primary experience of revolt, since it is here that the domination of 'serialised' thought is broken and the masses begin to make concrete their spontaneous desire for justice. The danger of political parties, illustrated by the degeneration of the Communist Party, is that they will forget these origins and produce a kind of 'frozen' morality to which the masses sacrifice their creative autonomy. 'What needs to be developed in people', says Sartre, 'is not the respect of an *order* which claims to be revolutionary, but the spirit of revolt against every order' (Gavi, *et al.* 1974, 48). The *Nouvelle Philosophie*, with its replacement of the political opposition of Left and Right with that between power and resistance or Marxism and dissidence, does not seem far away.

The publication in 1975 of André Glucksmann's *La Cuisinière et le Mangeur d'Hommes* (The Cook and the Man-Eater) marked the inevitable resolution of the Maoists' contradiction-laden attitude to Marxism in favour of an outright hostility, and in many ways set the stage for the coming of the *Nouvelle Philosophie* a year later. Glucksmann was himself a former leader of the *Gauche Prolétarienne*, and his book was perhaps the first violent attack on Marxism to gain currency as coming 'from the left'. Leaning heavily on the testimony of former camp-inmates, and in particular on Solzhenitsyn's *Gulag Archipelago*, Glucksman argues bluntly that the concentration camps of Stalin's Russia were just as much Marxist as Treblinka was Nazi. Marxism represents the 'political science of the century', a formidable instrument for the seizure and maintenance of state power. This seizure does not benefit the oppressed however. Marxism is not the banner of the masses, but the science of the intellectuals and party elite with their plans for progress and modernisation, plans which entail the exclusion and confinement of the vagabonds, poets and rebels who resist the implementation of the new, 'rational' social order. What for the Maoists represented the last hope of Marxism, its capacity to act as a genuine expression of popular rebellion, now becomes for Glucksmann its ultimate danger. In the Soviet Union men could be made to sign their own death warrants for the sake of socialism and the revolution, while in the West the Marxism of the intelligentsia for decades rendered it deaf and blind to the horror of what was happening in the East.

This attempt to label Marxism unambiguously as a discourse of power leads Glucksmann to play off the concept of the proletariat against what he calls the '*plebs*', in a manner which recalls the G P's attempts to mobilise immigrants, students, young peasants and workers of a peasant background against the organised body of workers supposedly subjugated by the 'social-fascism' of the trade-unions. The proletariat becomes a theoretical fiction, the myth of a revolutionary working class, from which all 'lumpen' elements have been excluded, on behalf of which the possessors of Marxist science seize power. This 'dictatorship of the proletariat' is then turned against all those — peasants, artists, Christian believers — in fact the majority of the population, who offer even if only passive resistance to the encroaching power of the state. This stubborn resistance, the refusal to collaborate with the trickery of power, is the principle virtue of the *plebs*. Thus Glucksmann's vision of society resolves into a simplistic dichotomy of dominators (the wielders of state power, whether philosophers, kings, jacobins or Marxists) and dominated. This dichotomy even extends into the domain of knowledge. On the side of the bosses is to be found 'scientific' knowledge (*savoir*), from which inevitably flows an exercise of mastery and oppression (for Glucksmann the Nazi concentration camps represented 'the advance post of industrialised scientific Europe'). On the side of the *plebs* is to be found the immediacy of a knowledge (*connaissance*) which springs from the realities of suffering and resistance, and which Glucksmann equates with the wisdom of the peasant Spirodon in Solzhenitsyn's *The First Circle*. This rudimentary epistemology explains why Marxism, if it did not actually 'produce' the Gulag (Glucksmann has more recently modified this conclusion), at least rendered us systematically deaf and blind to its horrors. For to 'explain' the Gulag in Marxist terms is to remain within the circle of power. An analysis of post-revolutionary Russia which accounts for the development of Stalinism in terms of social and economic factors — vestiges of Tsarism, low level of the productive forces — will tend to attribute responsibility for the 'failure' of the revolution to the people (the thesis of the 'backwardness' of the peasantry is there in Lenin), rather than to the party chiefs and the doctrine which inspired them. Thus Glucksmann sees it as part of his task to demonstrate the fallacies of Medvedev's Marxist reply to Solzhenitsyn, with its reliance on the thesis of backwardness, while arguing in a newspaper article that Solzhenitsyn's political positions (support for regionalism, ecological awareness) are less reactionary than they may seem. In general for Glucksmann any discourse which comes 'from below' is automatically 'to the left' of one which comes 'from above': who would dare to suggest that Brezhnev is 'to the left' of Solzhenitsyn? The general aim, therefore, is to transform what Foucault would term the 'regime of truth' which controls our view of the Soviet Union. The reality of a regime is revealed not by 'sociological' analysis, but in the fate of its victims. (This irrationalist view is one which Glucksmann already held as a militant of *La Cause du Peuple*. The criteria of the political scientists notwithstanding, the USA *is* fascist if George Jackson, writing from prison, *calls* it fascist.[8]) Accordingly Solzhenitzyn, the Christian and 'reactionary', reveals the truth papered over by a hundred learned left-wing dissertations. Marxism is morally disqualified from speaking of the Gulag: it is rather now the case that 'Kolyma necessarily represents a point of view on Marxism' (Glucksmann, 1975, 41). This valorisation of immediate experience to the point of 'revelation' (the religious connotations are intended) has now flourished into the fashionable Parisian discourse on the 'failure of the human sciences'. This discourse is bolstered by the assumption, also present in Glucksmann, and which amounts to a form of moral blackmail, that to seek an explanation of suffering is already to have rendered oneself complicit: 'one cannot tell from a tortured body whether its torture was "socialist" or "capitalist"' (Glucksmann, 1977b, 75).

In his review of *La Cuisinière*, Jacques Rancière has endorsed the idea that Glucksmann's position was long implied by the logic of post-'68 *gauchisme* (Rancière, 1975). Although he proclaims a violent rejection of Marxism, Glucksmann carries at least one of its illusions to the limit. His concept of the *plebs* is equally devoid of contradiction as the proletariat of the Marxist theoretician, while offering the additional advantage of representing an unsullied innocence, a pure will to resistance which cannot threaten to produce in its turn structures, strategies and organisations with their own inevitable effects of power. The *post-gauchiste* intellectual can thus realise the *gauchiste* dream of a fusion without remainder of his own discourse with the language of the masses, all the more so when these masses are no longer the inhabitants of *bidonvilles*, but the camp-inmates of far-away Russia. Yet in Glucksmann this leads to a number of disturbing consequences. Not the least of these is an ambiguous aesthetic of rebellion, in which the 'subversive' potential of the work of art and the natural goodness of the *plebs* merge in the wounds which the inmates inflict on themselves in protest against conditions. These pages in Glucksmann's book mark the return of an ethic of rebellion in which the moral value of the act, in an always unequal battle against power, becomes all important, and its efficacy counts for nothing. Furthermore, in attempting to label Marxism as solely a discourse of power Glucksmann involves himself in obvious dishonesty. Not only is he obliged to avoid the question of the value-as-knowledge of Marxist texts, but also their contestatory value. Yet, as Rancière points out, her Marxism did not render Rosa Luxembourg noticeably blind to the abuses of the Bolshevik dictatorship, nor does it dampen the militancy of the considerable section of the East European dissidents who still claim adherence to the ideals of socialism (this is a fact which the *Nouvelle Philosophie* in general, with its ideology of Marxism *versus* dissidence, prefers to forget). When Glucksmann suggests that the Marxist consensus after the coup in Chile was that Allende should have slowed down in order not to provoke the bourgeoisie, the bad faith of the exercise becomes plain.

In Glucksmann's latest book, *Les Maîtres Penseurs*, the manicheanism which consigned Marxism to the realm of darkness is pushed one stage further. Glucksmann steps back from his local examination of Marxism and the Gulag to trace the shaping influence of nineteenth-century German philosophy on the modern world. The book is flashily packaged like a *Série Noire* detective novel (yellow lettering on a black background, with the heads of the four villains — Fichte, Hegel, Marx and Nietzsche — lined up along the back cover) as if to emphasize its status as a kind of metaphysical thriller. The crime in question is the expansion of a practice of domination and control founded in the institutions of the modern state. And the chain of suspicion leads back from the petty bureaucrats and dictators of the present day, via Marx and Nietzsche, to the fountainhead of German Idealism.

For Glucksmann the 'fatality' begins with Fichte, with the attempt, inspired by his enthusiasm for the French Revolution, to transfer the 'Copernican revolution' of Kant in philosophy from the natural to the social world. Glucksmann suggests a homology between the demonstration of the absolute autonomy of reason dreamed of by German Idealism and the desire of the revolutionary to reconstruct society from zero. Indeed this is more than a homology, since for the Master Thinkers this autonomy must be made concrete in the institutions of a state in which reason and liberty will be as one. To this end philosophy now proclaims itself a science; under its tutelage the complex tissue of human affairs — art, history, religion, life and death — will be placed on the dissecting table of the 'human sciences', which emerge within the horizon of a global theory of social transformation (Glucksmann mocks Althusser's naïveté in supposing that the idea of 'revolutionary science' begins with Marx). The mixture of theory and practice may vary: for Fichte the building of the rational state requires a pedagogy founded in his *Doctrine of Science*, while for Marx in 1848 the exploited class discovers from its own situation the purpose of its revolutionary activity. But, throughout these oscillations, the pursuit of the grand marriage of Science and Revolution continues. The revolutionaries need the arm of theory, otherwise they would never believe a total transformation of society possible, while the savants need the revolution in order to 'realise' their philosophy, to provide them with a vantage point from which to measure out the landscape of history. Both are obsessed by the illusion that, beyond all particular forms of knowledge and means of social change, can be found a point zero around which Reason can make the human world revolve.

Glucksmann's vision of the rational state, which promises freedom yet brings only tyranny, is couched in terms borrowed from Foucault's description of the Panopticon in *Surveiller et Punir* (Foucault, 1975, 197–229). The state installs a regime of 'high surveillance', observing and assessing the actions of its subjects according to a political grid which it imposes. Just as the Panopticon continues to function, to give the impression of visibility, even when the guard is absent from the central tower, so the fact that his state is capped by an hereditary monarch, who may be a paranoiac or a congenital idiot, is taken by Hegel as evidence for the excellence of its construction. For the Master Thinkers only those nations are 'historical' which possess such a state. Thus the persistent anti-semitism of their writings can be explained in terms of an intellectual discomfort, faced with a people which appears to thrive without one. The jew becomes the symbol of a stubborn particularity, of that spontaneity and immediacy which must be abandoned as we enter the 'universality' of the Panopticon-state. The eternal vagabond eludes the unfolding schemas of reason and history.

Against this nightmare of transparency Glucksmann again mobilises his concept of the *plebs*, whose 'naturalness' the Master Thinkers (and their followers) see as a blank page on which beautiful characters can be written. Glucksmann interprets this naturalness differently, in terms of secular forms of cultural and moral resistance, a complex system of bulwarks and strategies which have made livable a position of subordination. The crime of the Master Thinkers is their wish to erase these traditional forms of resistance and replace them with a unified decisive battle. The Hegelian dialectic of master and slave is repeated throughout their work; it is only a confrontation with the absolute master, death or the juggernaut of Capital, which can educate the slave into self-consciousness. For Glucksmann, on the contrary, it is global struggles which are recuperative, which lead from one domination to another, while only local and partial struggles are truly subversive. To adopt the perspective of global confrontation is already to have adopted the viewpoint of the master. Thus Marx is accused — wrongly — of describing the system of factory discipline from the point of view of Capital, as if this domination were ever perfect, while neglecting the spontaneous forms of resistance of the workers.

As Dominique Lecourt has pointed out, with this conception of the traditional opposition of the pleb, the idea that 'all resistance is rooted in a past of resistances' (Glucksmann, 1977b, 172) Glucksmann rejoins one of the most revered themes of the counter-revolution, of a Burke or De Maistre: the outrage of the revolution is that it cuts through the living tissue of institutions which have the sanction of the centuries. For Glucksmann the danger of the revolutionary is his desire 'to reduce society, with all its traditions, diversity, its homosexuals, opium-smokers, drug-takers, poets, to a blank page on which to write the poem of the science of the collective happiness of men' (cited in Lecourt, 1978, 64). Yet this absolute dichotomy of planned innovation and tradition drives him to absurd conclusions. A literacy programme becomes a sinister method of forcing the *plebs* 'to unlearn what the state does not have the privilege of teaching' (Glucksmann, 1977b, 172), while Marx's critique of the division of labour is suspected of being a ploy to reduce all to homogeneity before the steam-roller *cogito* of the Master Thinker. The duplicity involved here, characteristic of the *Nouveaux Philosophes,* operates by means of a chain of negatives. Glucksmann will not state outright that private ownership of the means of production is desirable, merely that the idea of the community of producers is a pretext for the reinforcement of the state. Likewise he will not say that Capital is a good thing, but that there is no such thing as Capital since, as everyone can see, there are only different individual capitals. In fact Glucksmann's quarrel is no longer with this or that social system. The underlying vision of the book, its conception of the relation between knowledge and power, has slid from Foucaldian onto Heideggerian foundations. Glucksmann's fairytale of the Master Thinkers is none other than Heidegger's story of the imperialism of the *cogito* and the 'deployment of the unconditional domination of Metaphysics'. It is simply that where Heidegger sees the planetary expansion of technology, Glucksmann sees the expansion of the state. But if 'all modern domination is metaphysical', as Glucksmann assures us, the idea of political resistance becomes meaningless. In a world in which everything becomes calculable and predictable, resistance can take the ethical forms of laughter and paradox, but never result in a counter-project of comprehension and transformation.

In general relations between the *Nouveaux Philosophes* and the leading philosophers of the previous generation have been less than amiable. Deleuze and Guattari, authors of *L'Anti-Oedipe*, are accused by Lévy of fomenting a new fascism, while Jean-François Lyotard, another 'philosopher of desire', is subjected to a savage attack in Lardreau and Jambet's *L'Ange*. Althusser, for most of the *Nouveaux Philosophes* a now-distant station on the way, suffers the double stigma both of being a Marxist and, even worse, of having attempted to establish that Marxism is a science. The two great exceptions to this hostility are Lacan and Foucault. There is nothing mysterious about this in the case of Lacan, who has never claimed to be a Marxist, who expressed no sympathy for post-'68 *gauchisme,* and who has explicitly mocked the idea of 'sexual liberation' in the name of a very traditional Freudian pessimism. Since 1970, with the development of the theory of the 'four discourses' (among them the 'discourse of the master', cornerstone of the *Nouvelle Philosophie*) Lacanism has taken an explicitly anti-Marxist turn. In the case of Foucault the situation is more complex. Not only does the *Nouvelle Philosophie* claim inspiration from his work, as it does with Lacan, but Foucault himself has in certain respects shared the same intellectual and political trajectory as the militants who have become the *Nouveaux Philosophes*. On his own account, it was the explosion of May '68 and after — the development of localised struggles in the school, the prison, the psychiatric hospital — which made it possible for him to take up explicitly the problem of the interrelation of power and knowledge. The 'genealogies' which he has since produced may be seen as a highly sophisticated realisation of the project of an 'interruption' of the discourse of the human sciences, embedded in the hierarchies of the academy, which the Maoists sought to bring into conjunction with shopfloor actions against the 'despotism of the factory'. Furthermore these genealo-

gies aim to reveal a secret of origins, occluded by the official
histories of knowledge, in which the birth of this discourse and of
this despotism are intimately linked. To this must be added
Foucault's own militant activity, as co-founder of the GIP (Group
for Information on Prisons) following a hunger-strike which began
among leftist detainees in 1971, as supporter of the 'counter-
information' paper *Libération,* and as one of the leading intellectuals who participated in actions mounted by *Secours Rouge,* the
'democratic front' animated by the *Gauche Prolétarienne* (an old
photo shows Sartre, Foucault and Glucksmann together on a
street demonstration). Although in discussion with the Maoists
Foucault always prudently put the question of China in brackets,
there was undoubtedly a convergence between their politics and
his own, precisely to the extent that the GP were abandoning the
classic Marxist strategies in favour of forms of anti-authoritarian
struggle not directly related to the traditional field of action of
the organised working class. A discussion from 1972 between
Foucault and Deleuze draws the balance-sheet of the work done
together with the Maoists, in which the traditional role of the
intellectual as universalising spokesman is decisively rejected.
The task of the intellectual is now to lift the barriers which prevent
the masses themselves from speaking. Theory is no longer a
commanding focus, but a 'box of tools', a 'relay' between local
struggles. The very process of theoretical totalisation is perceived
as entailing a certain danger of repression.[9]

It is perhaps this common political history, although the fact
of personal friendship cannot be left out of account, which best
explains the favourable reception which Foucault has given to
Glucksmann's books. He has suggested, for example, that
Glucksmann's analysis of the Gulag succeeds in avoiding the
major theoretical evasions which characterise discussion of
Soviet Russia: reducing the Gulag to an 'error' or 'deviation'
from the doctrines of Marx and Lenin: explaining the Gulag away
in an historicist manner, rather than considering it as a functioning
reality; continuing to view the Soviet Union through the
spectacles of Marxism, rather than exposing our Marxism to
the uncomfortable realities of dissidence; and erasing the
specificity of the Gulag in a condemnation of confinement in
general. This estimation of the merits of *La Cuisinière,* as will
already be clear, is questionable. But Foucault's sympathy for
Glucksmann's position goes further. In his review of *Les Maîtres
Penseurs* he endorses Glucksmann's blanket condemnation of the
hyphenated monster 'State-Revolution', portrayed as inevitably
devouring its own children (Foucault, 1977b). This is surprising,
given that Glucksmann's vision of the state (the vehicle of a
project of domination inscribed in the logic of Western meta-

physics) appears to run directly counter to Foucault's recent analyses of power in terms of micro-structures which cannot be resolved back into a single dominating instance. Indeed one reviewer of Glucksmann's book has used Foucault's theses on the 'materiality' of power — power as essentially invested in control of the body — as a foil to Glucksmann's metaphysical deductions (Donzelot, 1978).

It is Jacques Rancière who has suggested the solution to this puzzle — that Foucault's and Glucksmann's conceptions of power are in fact mirror-images of each other. Foucault's elusive power, which is 'everywhere' (Foucault, 1976, 122) and yet 'does not exist' (Foucault 1977c, 66), is ultimately no different from Glucksmann's power, which radiates from the Panopticon-state into every interstice of a civil society which is simultaneously a network of resistances. For the *post-gauchiste* intellectual 'power' has replaced 'value' as the ubiquitous yet ungraspable force which turns the wheels of society.[10] The plausibility of this reading is reinforced by Foucault's recent adoption of the concept of the *plebs* first popularised by Glucksmann. This borrowing not only makes clear that the traffic between Foucault and one wing of the *Nouvelle Philosophie* is not all one-way, it underlines the remarkable way in which Foucault's development, without losing its inner consistency, has continued to ensure him a place in the 'theoretical vanguard'. In the mid-sixties there was a convergence with structuralist themes (erosion of the subject, suspicion of meaning, anti-teleological view of history). Ten years later Foucault's Nietzsche-based analytic of power and resistance is equally of the moment, sharing with the *Nouvelle Philosophie* the *post-gauchiste* theoretical space. This alone would make the relation between the two worth untangling.

The *Nouvelle Philosophie's* reference to Foucault is not restricted to his more recent work, in which the relation of knowledge and power is explicitly thematised. In many respects Foucault's early book *Madness and Civilisation* is privileged above its successors, since it is here that the *Nouveaux Philosophes* find inspiration for their belief in the inherent oppressiveness of reason. In Glucksmann's *La Cuisinière*, for example, an extended comparison is drawn between the springing up of the workhouses, the 'Great Confinement' of the seventeenth century described by Foucault, and the camps and system of terror of Soviet Russia. The suggestion is that Marxism merely imitates and surpasses the oppression of classical rationalism, and this is an idea which can be found throughout the *Nouvelle Philosophie*.[11] It is persistently returned to by Maurice Clavel, the 'dissident' Christian and ex-Maoist sympathiser who now interprets May '68 as a 'cultural fracture', a re-emergence of 'human auto-transcendence', and who has acted as the self-appointed godfather of the *Nouvelle Philosophie* since its inception.[12] Clavel perceives an important cultural inflection in the contrasting receptions given to Sartre's *Critique* and Foucault's *Madness and Civilisation* at the time of their publication in the early sixties. According to Clavel, Sartre's book, in which the totalising effort of reason is seen as part of the project of liberation, was overshadowed by the 'history of madness' of a young and little-known author, in which reason, far from serving the interests of liberation, was shown to function as an instrument of oppression. Clearly, once this implication has been accepted, the next stage is to label the Enlightenment as the source of all our evils, and the way is open for the whole gamut of contemporary Parisian irrationalisms.

But the reading of Foucault offered by Clavel or Glucksmann — 'Crown of the new Reason, the General Hospital prefigures the concentration camp' (Glucksmann, 1975, 109) — seriously distorts the analyses of *Madness and Civilisation.* Where the *Nouveaux Philosophes* imagine an obscure relation of cause and effect, in which a fixed conception of reason in some way begins to function as an instrument of oppression, Foucault's concern is with the elusive moment of partition. It is not that a certain conception of reason *entails* the exclusion and confinement of those labelled insane; what is primary is the gesture of division which constitutes reason on one side and madness on the other. Nor can this gesture be reduced to a movement of thought, as the persistent idealism of the *Nouvelle Philosophie* implies. The Great Confinement of the seventeenth century took place in a Europe hit by a severe economic crisis — sinking wages, unemployment, debasement of the currency — which Foucault describes; its immediate causes were undoubtedly economic. Thus *Madness and Civilisation*, like Foucault's later works, examines a series of cultural shifts which take place at the point of articulation of discursive and non-discursive practices. The forms of theoretical reflection which accompanied the Great Confinement, as Foucault emphasizes, are neither cause nor effect — all that can be said is that they are 'in correspondence' (Foucault, 1961, 211). Institutions can form the 'concrete a priori' of discourses, but discourse nevertheless retains its own autonomy. Nor can there be any question of 'deriving' the non-discursive from the discursive. The possibility of the one is never transparently contained within the other.

Yet even if *Madness and Civilisation* cannot be read as 'proving with documents', as Clavel naïvely puts it, the oppressive nature of reason, Foucault himself has maintained that: 'It is evident today that the way in which the insane have been treated forms part of the history of Reason' (Foucault, 1977d, 14. Translation altered). Foucault, however, opposes this kind of history, whose original model is to be found in Nietzsche, from the traditional history of reason which moves from Plato to Descartes to Kant. The theoretical sleight-of-hand effected by the *Nouveaux Philosophes* here consists in drawing profit from Foucault's genealogies while retaining a *philosophical* conception of reason, of the kind which Nietzsche was among the first to attempt to demolish. Even in *Madness and Civilisation* Foucault is careful to distinguish the 'rationalism' of the classical age from a *ratio* of the West which will continue to harbour the possibility of unreason (*déraison*). His later rejection of this residual teleology only reinforces the point — for Foucault there is no 'rationality' which hovers above and determines the forms of discourse in which it is embodied. The level of 'archeology' cannot be collapsed back into either the empirical or the transcendental. Thus *The Order of Things* effects an elegant reversal in which the Age of Reason, with its aspiration to universality, is revealed as a particular cultural configuration, while its system of Representation, within which all things were to appear in their 'truth', becomes an unstable historical construct. Foucault's continual disturbance of the reassuring continuities of reflection is incompatible with the *Nouvelle Philosophie*'s fantasy of an all-dominating Reason, whose underlying model is clearly Hegelian. As in so many cases, the *Nouvelle Philosophie* simply reverses positive into negative. The principle of a movement of reason towards total self-transparency is not challenged, but this goal is now evaluated as the ultimate nightmare, against which the only possible defence is obscurity, flight, or blind rebellion. For Foucault, however, no discourse can effect such a total closure. There is no form of discourse which cannot itself become an object of discourse, as the result of an 'archeological' shift which opens a new perspective. In his more recent work this shift is seen as the result of a 'political' choice, while in his 'middle- period' books *The Order of Things*, *The Archaeology of Knowledge*) it appears as the last remaining privilege of history itself.

Yet if Foucault cannot be recruited for a global attack on 'Reason', as opposed to the dismantling of particular historical conceptions of reason, it is nevertheless in his work, since *L'Ordre du Discours* (1971a), that a critical reformulation of the relation between knowledge and power has become a central concern. Foucault has claimed in retrospect that this problem has always been central to his work, even if an explicit vocabulary of power was lacking. His researches began in the early fifties, amid the repercussions of the Lysenko scandal, and it was partly this affair, he now suggests, which first lead him to pose the problem of the political effects of scientific discourses. At the level of the natural sciences the problem becomes almost too difficult to pose; but in the case of an already 'dubious' science like psychiatry, with its far lower 'epistemological profile', it becomes possible to trace the relations between a scientific discourse and a system of institutions and socio-political controls. 'When I think back now', states Foucault in relation to his earlier work, 'I wonder what I could have been talking about if not of power' (Foucault, 1978b, 19). This interpretation is clearly plausible for *Madness and Civilisation* and *The Birth of the Clinic*, in which a particular institution — the asylum, the hospital — occupies the centre of the stage. But Foucault claims that in the books of his 'middle period', the archeologies, he was equally concerned, though in a different and perhaps obliquer way, with the question of power. His concern in these works with the 'rules of formation' of discourses can now be interpreted as a concern with the 'politics of the scientific statement', with the way in which a system of controls is established between statements within a given domain so as to produce an ensemble of scientifically acceptable propositions. What is in question here is not a power which weighs down on science 'from the outside', but the effects of power which circulate within a science in accordance with a particular discursive regime. Foucault admits however, that, at the time, he tended to confuse this idea of a 'discursive regime' with the idea of 'systematicity, theoretical form, or something like a paradigm' (ibid, 18).

The bridge between Foucault's archeology and this retrospective reinterpretation is formed by *L'Ordre du Discours*. Here Foucault has not yet developed the vocabulary of power, but discusses the constitution of what he calls 'disciplines' as one of a number of 'principles of rarefaction of discourse'. A discipline is not simply an aggregate of true statements about a given object, but is formed by a complex system of rules which determine its objects, its mode of description, the possible positions of the speaking subject. Thus a statement, in order to be 'scientific', must satisfy more than purely formal conditions for truth. Foucault cites the example of Mendel's work in heredity to illustrate the fact that a discourse can be 'true', while not being 'in the truth' (scientifically acceptable). Mendel's discoveries could not be accommodated within the system which governed the biological discourse of his day. Thus within each discipline a distinction can be made between true and false propositions, but each discipline is also bordered by a swarm of 'teratological' knowledges which do not obey what Foucault risks calling the 'rules of a discursive police' (Foucault, 1971a, 37), rules which must be reactivated by every new discourse belonging to a discipline. From here, however, it seems to be only a short step to Lévy's exegesis of Foucault, in which the 'very rigour of the rules of the *episteme*' is seen to function as a 'police of the statement' (Lévy 1975, 8). In general the idea of disciplines as constituting 'principles of rarefaction of discourse' has proved extremely useful for the *Nouvelle Philosophie*. Particularly detested forms of 'science' (such as Marxism) can be presented as repressing the burgeoning plurality of the languages of rebellion — of the feminists, the dissidents, the poets, the dreamers . . . Once the notion of scientific discourse as restrictive has been accepted, the way is open for absurd equations between 'the terrorism of science imposing its exclusive order on the real' (Dollé) and political totalitarianism. It must be asked whether Foucault's present interpretations of his earlier work have not helped to foster these conclusions.

A first error, which Foucault encourages, is involved in assuming that the rarity of statements is established by a system of exclusion. Foucault himself emphasizes in *The Archaeology of Knowledge* that rarity is not a contingent but a defining attribute of the statement. It is precisely this which distinguishes the Foucaldian concept of the statement from that of the sentence or proposition. Whereas linguistics seeks to establish a system of rules, in accordance with which an infinite number of sentences can be generated, the fundamental problem for Foucault is posed by the gulf between the totality of possible statements and the finitude of what is actually written or spoken. The question posed by the analysis of discourse is: why did this particular statement appear and no other? This question can be answered in terms of an 'exclusion' of certain statements by others, but Foucault makes clear that this exclusion does not imply a 'repression': 'we do not suppose that beneath manifest statements something remains hidden and subjacent . . . There is no sub-text. And therefore no plethora' (Foucault, 1974a, 119). This bracketing of the question of repression lead certain critics to pose to Foucault the question of his relation to Freud. In *The Archaeology of Knowledge* Foucault replied by relegating the question of repression to the level of 'formation' of discourse (the empirical conditions of its production), to be distinguished from that of archeology. But as Foucault's most recent writings make clear, his work has always implied a critique of the concept of repression as such. Power, when the concept eventually appears, is no longer primarily repressive, but positive and productive.

A similar misreading takes place in the case of Foucault's concept of the 'rules' of a discursive formation. Foucault repeatedly emphasizes that he is not searching for a set of axioms which will define a system of possible statements. In opposition to the structuralists, he is not aiming to establish a 'combinatory' or a definitive formalisation. Indeed he excludes the idea of a

discursive formation being governed by a *definable* body of rules,
'since rules are never given in formulation, they 'traverse'
formulations, and set up for them a space of coexistence' (ibid,
147). Gilles Deleuze, in his review of *The Archaeology of Knowledge*,
has stated the position well: 'The question of knowing whether
it is the space which defines the group or . . . the group which defines
the space is of little interest. There is neither a homogeneous
space indifferent to statements, nor statements without localisation
(Deleuze, 1970, 198). It makes no sense, therefore, to speak of
the 'rules of a discursive police', as if these rules were exterior
to and determined the system of statements in which they are
'embodied'. Any effective 'power' which 'circulated' between
the statements of a discipline could only operate at the empirical
level of 'formation', which is not the level at which Foucault is
aiming in his archeology, not 'interior' to the discourse. Nor is
this lack of leverage for the question of power the result of a
neglect of the non-discursive. Foucault is fully aware in *The
Archaeology of Knowledge*, no less than in *L'Ordre du Discours*,
that discourses are embedded in an 'institutional field'; and
this field is already considered to be constitutive.

The misleading nature of the image of a 'discursive police'
can perhaps be highlighted by comparison with the concept of
'tradition', as elaborated in recent hermeneutic theories.[13] The
continuity of a tradition is not assured by rigid adherence to a
pre-established rule or pattern, but by a continual process of
reinterpretation of its own precedents. This produces the paradox
of innovative conformity with which Foucault also grapples in
The Archeology of Knowledge: 'Every statement involves a field
of antecedent elements in relation to which it is situated, but
which it is able to reorganise and redistribute according to new
relations' (Foucault, 1974a, 124). In fact both Foucault's conception of a rule of discourse and his conception of rarity are
constructed on the banality that: 'There is not a single culture in
the world where everything is permitted' (Foucault, cited in
Kremer-Marietti, 1974, 99). The difficulty arises from an attempt
to interpret this fact as the result of an exercise of power. That
Foucault is aware of this can be seen from the way in which the
theses of *L'Ordre du Discours* appear to be constantly undermining
each other. The concept of the author, the commentary, the
discipline are so many 'infinite resources for the creation of
discourse', but at the same time they are 'restrictive and constraining' (Foucault, 1971a, 38). They are 'principles of the rarefaction
of discourse', but at the same time 'one must not imagine,
traversing the world and intertwined with all its forms and events,
a non-said or non-thought which it would be our task to articulate
or to think at last' (ibid, 54). How can there be rarefaction of a

commodity (discourse) which is essentially defined by its rarity? This difficulty arises from Foucault's attempt to discuss power in terms of the mere existence of institutions, rather than in terms of their specific nature. He perceives clearly that institutions are not merely imposed constructs, yet has no apparatus for dealing with this fact, which entails that following a convention is not always equivalent to submitting to a power. Admittedly the question of where these two forms are distinguishable and where they overlap cannot be definitively decided, and is necessarily subject to political debate. But without this distinction every delimitation becomes an exclusion, and every exclusion is equated with an exercise of power. This is an error which Foucault had formerly attempted to avoid. In *The Archaeology of Knowledge* it is the rarity of discourse which makes it an object of political struggle, and not political struggle which supposedly establishes the rarity of discourse.

The difficulties entailed by Foucault's overextension of the concept of the political emerge clearly in the course of his attempt in *L'Ordre du Discours* to adapt the Nietzschean notion of a 'will to truth' to his own ends. Foucault's method had always consisted in a sidestepping of the 'epistemological' problem of the criteria of truth or falsity of scientific discourse in favour of an historical analysis of the ruptures and transformations through which such discourse is constituted. But he now not only 'suspends' the concept of truth, but brings it under suspicion. Rather than posing the (metaphysical) problem of the 'surest path to truth', it is now a question of tracing historically the 'aleatory path of truth', determined by an interplay of power and desire which masquerades as an impartial search for knowledge. In its modern form the 'will to truth' is invested in a complex system of techniques, instruments, objects of knowledge which constitutes what we refer to as 'science'. For Foucault this ensemble represents a 'prodigious machinery of exclusion', since like all embodiments of the will to truth it rests on 'a primary and continually repeated falsification which poses the distinction between the true and the false' (Foucault, 1977e, 203).

The suggestion seems to be that since the truth/falsehood distinction has no absolute foundation, it must ultimately be established by a certain relation of forces. The designation of a certain form of discourse as the pre-eminent vehicle of truth will tend to prevent other forms of discourse from emerging or making themselves heard. But again the problem of the meaning of 'exclusion' in this context arises, given Foucault's conviction that there is no plenitude of 'silent discourse' waiting to be discovered and spoken. In a certain sense the instruments, techniques and discourses of contemporary physics 'exclude' those of its Newtonian counterpart, but this exclusion clearly does not imply a 'repression'. To argue that it does is to blur a vital distinction between a *politically enforced* silence, and a silence or absence which is merely the reverse side of the positivity of a given cultural formation. The neglect of this distinction allows the *Nouveaux Philosophes* to imply a fundamentally misleading parallelism, for example, between the forceful suppression of the discourse of dissidence in the Soviet Union, and the marginalisation of non-Marxist discourse by the hegemony of Marxist ideas among French intellectuals (until their own timely arrival). Thus Jean-Marie Benoist, who expresses distrust of 'big confining structures, including political ideologies' (although this does not seem to include the ideology of Giscardian capitalism), depicts Marxism as a kind of straitjacket which has long inhibited intellectual work in France, and which the empiricists across the Channel have wisely avoided. That Foucault encourages this confusion can be seen from his examples of the 'constraint and pressure' exercised by the will to truth: the fact that western literature has for centuries been obliged to seek support in the natural and the true-seeming (*le vraisemblable*), or that economic and juridical practices are increasingly obliged to seek justification in a discourse of science. These examples merely describe a given cultural configuration, and do not imply constraint in any meaningful sense.

Foucault appears to be on safer ground when he refers to the institutional field in which the 'will to truth' is embedded — the practices of pedagogy, the library, the laboratory and, more profoundly, the manner in which knowledge is divided and distributed within a society. Again however the important point is not the *fact* of these institutions, but whether they function oppressively. If they do so function it is still another step to show that this flows inevitably from the will to truth — that scientific research and teaching, for example, could not be organised in a less hierarchical manner. Such organisational changes could also alter the 'content' of science, but this would not constitute a subversion of the will to truth as such. In advocating such a subversion Foucault seems uncomfortably close to the supposition of Benoist that structures are inevitably 'confining', as if there could be any thought or action independent of structures and institutions. Even a commentator sympathetic to Foucault is unable to extract more from the conception of the will to truth as a 'machinery of exclusion' than the unexciting observation that: 'Theory is the exclusive domain of a particular group and constitutes the active principle through which others, of a different persuasion are excluded from the "fellowship"' (Bouchard, 1977, 24). Even this exposition is misleading, since the talk of 'exclusion' implies that those 'of a different persuasion' have an *interest*, which is being denied, in being part of the fellowship. In general this is not the case (why should a Lacanian consider her/himself *excluded* from being an orthodox Freudian?). And when it is the case an element of coercion is entailed which has been elided here.

Foucault's discussion of the will to truth concludes with a consideration of its relation to the two other 'systems of exclusion', which he outlines in *L'Ordre du Discours'* — the *prohibition,* manifested as taboo on the object, ritual of circumstance, or privileged or exclusive right to speak, and the *separation* between sanity and madness. Foucault suggests that these latter two systems are becoming increasingly fragile, and are being absorbed into a will to truth which both modifies and attempts to 'found' them. The denial of the right to speak and the confinement of the insane now requires a 'scientific' justification. Here we encounter one of the fundamental themes of Foucault's recent work. Prohibition and separation, he emphasizes, cannot function without the possibility of violence and coercion. But in the case of the will to truth, into which these two forms are being increase-ingly integrated, the play of power and desire is masked by the unfolding of a field of 'objective' knowledge. We are dazzled by the truth. Thus Foucault arrives at the idea, not that knowledge is connected with power, but that knowledge is a *form* of power. In *L'Ordre du Discours* this identity is only conceptualised in a tentative and inadequate way, perhaps because the notion of a 'will to truth' represents too direct a borrowing from Nietzsche to be appropriate to Foucault's needs. It is not until *Discipline and Punish* that Foucault finds the vocabulary he requires for the questions he wishes to pose, questions concerning the 'genealogy' of the human sciences.

A concern with the emergence of the human sciences is not, of course, new in Foucault. Nearly a decade before the appearance of *Discipline and Punish* Foucault published an 'Archeology of the Human Sciences', *The Order of Things*, in which he attempted to delineate the epistemological matrix within which the human sciences were born. At that time Foucault's concern was with the tensions which defined the space of possibility of these disciplines. The human sciences are not defined 'in advance' by their object — as if 'man' were an immediate pre-given which became, through an incidental shift of attention, available to science at the beginning of the nineteenth century — but by a transformation of the *episteme* which forms the conditions of possibility of both the object of science and the science in which it is 'known'. Foucault sees this object, 'man', as characterised by a fundamental instability, since at the same time that man becomes an *object* of knowledge he also becomes the *foundation* of all knowledge. An oscillation between the empirical and the transcendental is triggered off which determines the vague and uneasy status of the human sciences. Foucault suggests — and the powerful latent historicism of the work emerges here — that the epoch of 'man' is drawing to a close, that eventually we will be released from this oscillation, although it is impossible to predict the form of the new *episteme* which is beginning to dawn.

Foucault denies in *The Order of Things* that he is reducing the human sciences to the status of 'pseudo-scientific fantasies motivated at the level of opinions, interests, or beliefs' (Foucault, 1974b, 365). His intention is not to 'attack' the human sciences, but to analyse their inherently unstable structure, and to indicate the signposts — Nietzsche, Mallarmé, Artaud: inaugurators of a new conception and practice of language — which point towards an as yet unimaginable disappearance of 'man' from our horizon. Nevertheless the book can be seen as a kind of oblique preface to current orations on the 'failure of the human sciences' and the return to the primacy of artistic and literary 'truth' — the retreat from cognition to insight, and from the political to the ethical. Clavel who, with characteristic excess, considers Foucault to be 'the greatest philosopher since Kant', gleefully celebrates *The Order of Things* as having demolished the possibility of the human sciences. He recounts that, in a letter written after its publication, Foucalt expressed regret at not having gone on to undermine the 'anti-humanist' human sciences (e.g. 'structuralist' psychoanalysis and anthropology) at the same time. The disappearance of the figure of man constructed by 'anthropologising' scientific discourse is no longer the preliminary to rigorous human sciences based on the model of linguistics, as the sixties dreamed it would be, but to a 'liberation' from scientific discourse as such.

Foucault's recent work reformulates these ideas within a framework which has been given a new dimension by the introduction of the concept of power. He now admits that his concept of an *episteme,* which applied purely to the field of discourse, was in effect a dead-end. His more recent notion of a *dispositif* (the word translates as both 'apparatus' and 'system') constituted far more loosely by an ensemble of discourses, practices and institutions, represents an attempt to break with this limitation. This break coincides with the shift from his earlier 'archeology' to a Nietzschean method of genealogy whose principles are most clearly presented in an essay on Nietzsche written shortly after *L'Ordre du Discours* (Foucault, 1971b). Here Foucault emphasizes Nietzsche's conception of the role of force, error and accident in history as disruptive of the continuities of origin and meaning. What we take to be the 'essences' of things or 'natural' forms of behaviour are merely the result of linguistic and social conventions imposed in the course of a struggle for power. Thus in contrast to *The Archaeology of Knowledge*, where the emergence of scientific discourse is thought in terms of the successive crossing of a series of thresholds of formalisation, Foucault now sees such discourse as constituted and caught up within relations of domination. Following Nietzsche's conception of the body as the 'surface of inscription of events', he now gives an account of the 'origins' of the human sciences which is far more vividly 'political': 'It is in the mechanisms of power which have invested the body, gestures, forms of behaviour, that we must construct the archeology of the human sciences' (Foucault, 1977f).

Discipline and Punish represents a first realisation of this programme. It is organised around what Foucault terms 'a reversal of the political axis of individualisation' which roughly coincides with the emergence of bourgeois industrial society. Foucault perceives a privileged illustration of this reversal in the transformation of penal practice in France between the end of the eighteenth and the beginning of the nineteenth century. Under a feudal and monarchical system individualisation is greatest at the summit of society. Power is visibly embodied in the person of the king, while its 'objects' and modes of operation tend to be relatively haphazard and imprecise. An extreme example of this polarity can be seen in the practice of punishment by torture and execution, which ensures no systematic social control, but which makes manifest in a spectacular way the 'excess power' (*surpouvoir*) of the king, the person against whom all crimes are ultimately an offence, over a more or less anonymous social body. Foucault's concern is with the change to the kind of regime which is still ours today in which, as power itself becomes more indifferent and functional, its objects become increasingly defined and individualised. This transformation is symbolised by Bentham's invention of the Panopticon, already discussed in relation to Glucksmann, a device permitting unrestricted surveillance of workers, inmates, or prisoners by a guardian who cannot her/himself he perceived by those she/he watches. The development of such forms of observation allows a new detail in the regulation of physical gesture and activity which can be employed to increase productivity. For Foucault the emergence of the carceral system is merely one aspect of the spread throughout the institutions of society of what he terms a 'political technology of the body'.

The most significant aspect of Foucault's argument in the present context is his suggestion that the deployment of these techniques of surveillance produces at the same time a field of objectification which permits the constitution of scientific knowledges. The prison provides the clearest illustration of this process — in the hothouse conditions of permanent observation and control it provides, the discourses of penology and criminology, of the 'maladjusted individual' and the 'deviant personality' can flourish. Indeed the supposed expressive unity of the individual and her/his 'personality' — the human 'soul' — is itself constituted by relations of power in which the formation of knowledge plays a central role. It is through the internalisation of such knowledge that the individual is first produced as a 'subject' on which the strategies of power can operate. Subjectification, in this sense, is the necessary preliminary to subjection. Furthermore, once it has been set in motion, the relation of power and knowledge produces a cycle of constant self-reinforcement. The development of knowledge increases control, and hence power, which leads to the laying bare of further fields of objectification. Foucault is prepared to advance the general conclusion that 'there is no relation of power without the correlative constitution of a field of knowledge, nor knowledge which does not suppose and constitute at the same time relations of power (Foucault, 1975, 32). Thus it can no longer be a question of liberating science from ideological distortion, or uncovering a truth obscured by the effects of power. Against those philosophers who suppose that knowledge is the reward of a disinterested pursuit of truth, Foucault suggests that knowledge and power form an articulated unity (he refers to a *pouvoir-savoir*), and that truth itself, as *L'Ordre du Discours* had already hinted, is always dependent on a particular regime of discourse.[14]

In the hands of the new 'post-Foucaldians' these theses have been put to devastating use. It becomes all too easy to suggest that 'science equals oppression', that particularly the human sciences oppress, and particularly among the human sciences — of course — Marxism. Thus François Ewald, in his review of *Discipline and Punish*, suggests a *rapprochement* between Foucault's theses and the ideas of Glucksmann's *La Cuisinière*. Just as Foucault has demonstrated that, in general, power produces knowledge, and knowledge in its turn reinforces power, so Glucksmann reveals Marxism to be: 'an extraordinary instrument of power, unbelievable principle of production, production of concentration-camps, and production of camps as an apparatus of production, formidable principle of blindness, obliteration, prohibition, exclusion and death' (Ewald, 1975, 1232). The lurid rhetoric of this passage is characteristic, but is not our main concern here. Nor is the remarkable fact that this kind of writing is now widely accepted in France as coming 'from the left'. More important is the question of how these opinions find their justification in Foucault.

In *Discipline and Punish* certain sciences of the individual such as criminology are seen as born out of a tightly-woven system of procedures of observation and control. These sciences then function within this system to increase the leverage of power on the body, which in turn advances the field of objectification. One of Foucault's arguments for this way of conceiving the operation of power is that it seems to provide a far more 'materialist' account than those which rely on the concept of ideology, which implies the — presumably 'idealist' — concepts of 'consciousness' and 'representation'. It can be argued, however, that Foucault again overextends his position here. The functioning of criminology and penology within the 'carceral archipelago' is effectively established, but Foucault then goes on to speak in the following general terms of the human sciences: 'It seems probable that (their origin) is to be found in these inglorious archives where the modern play of coercions on the body, gestures, forms of behaviour, was elaborated' (Foucault, 1975, 193). At least two factors make this generalisation untenable. The first is Foucault's own reluctance to grant a 'science' such as criminology any more than bastard status. He points out that the discourse of criminology is of such banal utility that it does not even bother to provide itself with a coherent system of concepts. This is clearly not Foucault's view of the human sciences in general. The second is the fact that the intimacy of the relation between knowledge and control of the body is absent in the case of disciplines such as sociology or economics. Such sciences are evidently employed within strategies of power. But it is also possible for them to prove an embarrassment and a danger to power (in the Soviet Union, for example, sociology is deliberately restricted to a survey-gathering empiricism), and this is an aspect of their functioning which Foucault has failed to emphasize. The *Nouveaux Philosophes*, of course, ignore it.

Foucault's view of the human sciences can be seen as giving comfort to the *Nouvelle Philosophie*. His method of arriving at this view cannot. In his haste to cement the Foucault-Glucksmann alliance Ewald fails to perceive that, like all current deductions of the Gulag from Marxism, Glucksmann's position offends against the most elementary principles of genealogy as Foucault understands it. Glucksmann's work must be seen as 'metaphysical' in a pejorative sense, since 'Placing the present at the origin, (it) makes us believe in the obscure labour of a destination which would seek to appear from the very first moment' (Foucault, 1971b, 155). For Nietzsche, on the contrary, the cause of the emergence of a thing and its ultimate use are inevitably disparate. The history of the development of an object, a custom, an organ, is the history of the struggles and seizures which have taken place around it. Every overpowering and mastering is a reinterpretation.[15] Foucault's fidelity to Nietzsche on this point is strikingly revealed by the disjunctions and non-coincidences he describes between the reality of penal institutions and the discourse of the criminologists and reformers. The projects and plans of the 'ideologues' of the eighteenth century, who envisage a finely controlled balance, a psychological calculus of crime and public punishment, are followed by the abrupt emergence of the very different institution of the prison. At first attacked as a moral abomination, the prison finds apologists who suggest that its role is the rehabilitation of the criminal. But since it has never played this role (Foucault shows that its real function was to produce and maintain a utilisable form of delinquence) it can be shown that prisons and projects of prison reform were born in the same moment. There is nothing here of that transparent relay between theory and practice which, assumed by the *Nouveaux Philosophes*, leads them to search for the seeds of 'totalitarianism' in the *1844 Manuscripts* or Hegel's *Logic*. Such a search perceives the 'anticipatory power of meaning' where there is only a 'hazardous play of dominations' (ibid, 155).

Foucault's use of Nietzsche clearly reveals the idealism of the *Nouvelle Philosophie's* attempt to derive real effects of oppression from the conceptual structure of Marxist discourse. At the same time, however, it implies a critique of the totalising theory of Marxism as having a braking effect on forms of struggle in their inevitable locality and specificity. For Foucault, prior to any attempt to evaluate the epistemological claims of Marxism, the question to be posed to any supposed demonstration of the 'scientificity' of Marxism (the primary target here is clearly Althusser) is: 'What subjects of speech and discourse, what subjects of experience and knowledge do you therefore wish to "minoritise" when you say: "I who hold this discourse am holding a scientific discourse . . ."?' (Foucault, 1977h, 170). Thus what is significant is not the content of discourse but the institutional field — traditionally for Marxism the political party — within which its effects of power are deployed. (It must be emphasized that the two aspects of this critique by no means hang together in the way both Foucault and the *Nouveaux Philosophes* seem to assume they do. 'Totalising' theories do not inevitably crown institutions, even less *oppressive* institutions; and non-theoretical — irrational — discourses can exercise formidable effects of power.) In bracketing the epistemological question and judging in terms of effects of power Foucault is following a principle he enunciated long ago: 'It is not in the name of a political practice that one can judge the scientific quality of a science . . . But in the name of political practice one can question the mode of existence and functioning of a science' (Foucault, 1978a, 23). The question of the 'truth' of a system of scientific statements is thus deprived of a priority which Nietzsche would claim to be dependent on certain 'moral' assumptions. Foucault criticizes the position taken up by certain Maoists, which entails the introduction of political criteria into the epistemological domain (defence of bourgeois/proletarian science division, qualified rehabilitation of Lysenko), but only to reach an even more radical position, since epistemology seems to give way entirely to politics. Thus the novelty of the critique of Marxism formulated by Foucault and the *Nouveaux Philosophes* consists in its taking the diametrically opposite line to traditional critiques such as that of Popper. It is an irrationalist and not a rationalist critique. 'If we have an objection to make to Marxism', says Foucault, 'it is that it could effectively *be* a science (Foucault, 1977h, 169).

For the *Nouvelle Philosophie* this is the end of the story. In a bizarre sense, as we shall see in the case of *L'Ange*, Marxism is oppressive because it is 'true', or at least represents the, 'untranscendable philosophy of our time'.[16] But this is not so in the case of Foucault. He may claim at some points to avoid epistemological judgements, but at the same time his work, ever since the beginning, has contained an implicit and explicit critique of Marxist concepts. Of the concept of ideology as a relation of correspondence or representation, for example, or more recently of the juridical elements in the Marxist conception of the state. Furthermore Foucault does not erect an opposition between a monolithic science and dispersed capacities for resistance which inevitably take the form of non-thought ('always a don't-think throws down its challenge to the 'supreme' I-think' — Glucksmann). He considers one of the major events since May '68 to be what he terms 'the insurrection of subjected knowledges' — the knowledge of the prisoners, of the psychiatrised and hospitalised, whose communication and circulation is blocked by the codified discourses of criminology, psychiatry or medicine. For Foucault the force of the critical discourses of the post-'68 period is drawn from the fusion of historical studies of the emergence of institutions, produced within the traditional academic context, with these localised and subordinated knowledges. The term 'genealogy' refers to precisely this fusion, genealogy being understood not as a more attentive ōr exact science, but rather as an 'anti-science'. Anti-science, however, does not mean ignorance. Foucault's elaboration of this point could have been written in explicit polemic against the *Nouvelle Philosophie*: 'Genealogy does not claim the lyrical right to ignorance or to non-knowledge; it is not a question of refuting knowledge (*savoir*) or of putting into play and into practice the prestige of an aquaintance (*connaissance*) or experience not yet captured by knowledge' (ibid, 169). A corollary of this position is that for Foucault it makes no sense, even if it were possible, to reject Marxism *en bloc*. Marxism continues, as does psychoanalysis, to provide indispensable theoretical tools, indeed it provides the general horizon within which historical questions are now inevitably posed. But the creative use of Marxism involves its being shattered as an (imaginary) theoretical unity in order that the critical dimension of its analyses can be released. Thus Foucault declares his admiration not for Marx's economic theory, which he claims to be derivative of Ricardo, but for the political analyses of the *Eighteenth Brumaire* or Marx's remarks on the role of the army in the development of political power. This attitude is linked with Foucault conception of the 'tactical polyvalency of discourses'.[17] There is no single unitary divide between accepted and excluded, dominating and dominated discourses, but a multiplicity of strategies in which fractions of discourse can play alternating roles. Thus Foucault suggests that although in the West psychoanalysis functions as a means of normalisation, there are other sociopolitical contexts (he is thinking of South America) where it is still a subversive force. But the rule of tactical polyvalency clearly also applies, despite the efforts of the *Nouveaux Philosophes*, to Marxism. Foucault's recent position, in the end, seems close to that of Rancière, at the moment of a break with Maoism which did not result in a surrender to fashionable simplifications: 'The appeals of certain people to forget Marxism will not prevent the class struggle from existing or Marxism from retaining the ambiguous function which it exercises today: as a system of multiple identifications, a place where discourses of revolt intersect, and where the language of subversion is ceaselessly being exchanged for the language of order' (Rancière, 1974, 224).

The desire of the *Nouvelle Philosophie* to replace the necessary ambiguities of political action with the vision of a world riven by abrupt dichotomies — reason and madness, state and civil society, Marxism and dissidence — undoubtedly finds its most fanatical embodiment in Lardreau and Jambet's *L'Ange* (1976). Under the patronage of Maurice Clavel the book aroused much discussion of a supposed new ideological phenomenon termed *'christiano-gauchisme'*. The label may appear bizarre, but becomes less so if one recalls the quasi-religious fervour of the militants of the *Gauche Prolétarienne*. Indeed even enemies of the book, with its extravagant patristic metaphors, have been obliged to admit its fidelity to certain aspects of the experience and vision of the GP. But whereas, for most people, the comparison between the Maoist

militant and the gnostic heretic would provide the definitive condemnation of the politics of the GP, for Lardreau and Jambet it is
a source of glory. Their aim is not to abandon what they imagine
to be 'Maoism', but to drive the implications of the doctrine
through to their conclusions: 'we had not to become apostates,
but to go even further in our imperfect conversion' (Lardreau and
Jambet, 1976, 10). Rejecting the recuperative continuity implied
by the Marxist idea of the new society being born from the womb
of the old in favour of Mao's injunction to 'break the history of
the world in two', Lardreau and Jambet are nevertheless haunted
by the possibility of a recuperation of revolt. Hence *L'Ange*
announces itself as an 'Ontology of Revolution', an attempt to
establish on what 'metaphysical' preconditions rebellion is not
only justified, but possible.

The conceptual scaffolding of the world in which Lardreau and
Jambet seek to establish the possibility of rebellion is lifted
from Lacan. The Lacanian thesis of the primacy of the Symbolic,
of language as determinant in a constitution of sociality thought
in terms of a mythical enunciation of the Law, is turned by
Lardreau and Jambet against any form of naturalism, or any
theory of the 'liberation of desire'. For the Lacanian desire does
not express the spontaneity of a nature which pre-exists and
must be bridled by the Law. Rather desire and the Law are
coterminous, since desire is nothing other than the traversal of
the signifying chain by the metonymy of a 'want-to-be', of an
absence installed by the capture of the subject in the network
of the Symbolic (traditionally theorised by psychoanalysis as
castration). This absence, the alienation of the subject in the
Other which is the place of language, cannot be articulated as
such. This is because desire, which impells the subject to speak,
is always supported by what Lacan terms the *objet petit a*, the
metonymic replacement of the Other, which generates a
momentary appearance of being *(un semblant d'être)*, but which
fades in the moment of desire's realisation. Thus however urgent
the attempt at rebellion (however radical the desire of the Other
— the desire to speak the whole truth), this rebellion can only
result in deepened submission, since the Other is in fact the
'place of the signifier' which determines the law of the desirer's
subjection. In Lardreau and Jambet's terms, the desire of the
Rebel, lured by the *semblant*, results in a discourse identical with
the discourse of the Master. *L'Ange* draws the conclusion that,
on strictly Lacanian premisses, 'the real is pure oppression',
governed by the ineluctable law of castration.

But Lardreau and Jambet are not strict Lacanians. They are
what their friend Clavel terms 'Lacanian protestants', convinced
that Lacan offers the only credible ontology (he is the third of

the three ontologists that count, with Leibniz and Hegel), but convinced at the same time that the rebellion which this ontology renders 'impossible' has taken and will continue to take place. Thus against Lacan's pessimism Lardreau and Jambet assert the necessity of a pseudo-Pascalian wager — we must gamble on the denial of the universality of the *objet petit a*, on the possibility of a world which is not the world of desire. If our subjection results from the permanent disharmony between sex and language, then radical freedom depends on the order of sexuality not being coextensive with the order of the body, on the discourse of the Master not being coextensive with discourse as such. Lardreau and Jambet 'break the history of the world in two' to reveal two histories, each of which is entirely foreclosed from the other. Their resolute dualism supposes that the history of the Master, in which the *objet petit a* reigns supreme, can know nothing of the history of the Rebel, in which desire is no longer the desire of one's own subjection. Thus from the point of view of the Master his[18] domination is coextensive with the real. But this domination is revealed as illusory by the irruption of a transcendent other history symbolised by the book's title. The Angel, to whom sex is 'impertinent', escapes the slavery of desire. Since the Angel *is* the masses in their unconscious spontaneity, its function is to symbolise salvation for the intellectuals.

This metaphysics of rebellion is concretised in the central section of the book, which consists of a long comparison between the theologies and heresies of the early christian church and the doctrines of the Great Proletarian Cultural Revolution. The comparison is organised around the distinction between the concepts of 'ideological revolution' and 'cultural revolution'. The first of these conforms almost exactly to the Marxist conception of a transformation of superstructures accompanying, and ultimately determined by, the change from one mode of production to another. Indeed Lardreau and Jambet go as far as to state that the Marxist account of revolution can be accepted as 'true' — but only from a point of view which affirms the unity of history in order to foreclose the Rebel. The ideological revolution expresses the desire to do away with the Master, but only in the interests of installing a new Master. Cultural revolution, by contrast, strives to change the world systematically through a transformation of 'hearts and minds'; its aim is the abolition of the Master as such. If these two forms tend to appear at the same time, this is not because the cultural revolution, like the ideological, can be explained in terms of a transition from one mode of production to another. The coming of the Rebel is strictly without cause. It is rather because the ideological revolution attempts to exploit and 'domesticate' the themes of the cultural revolution, to transform the discourse of the Rebel with the lure of a *semblant* of rebellion.

The spread of early Christianity coincided with the crisis of the ancient world, and the agonised centuries-long transition to feudalism. At this period, claim Lardreau and Jambet, the themes of the cultural revolution emerged with force, themes which undermined the very foundations of the domination of the Master: 'radical rejection of labour, hatred of the body, refusal of sexual difference' (Lardreau and Jambet, 1976, 100). A profusion of dualist and manichean doctrines challenged every established authority, urging women to leave their husbands, children their parents, and slaves their masters. *L'Ange* paints the fanciful picture of a 'mass movement' of heretics and ascetics thronging the highways and sweeping across the deserts of the ancient world. Men and women chastely intermingled sustained themselves solely by begging, and even banditry. This movement, which threatened the fabric of ordered society, was the cultural revolution against which the Church Fathers were obliged to do battle. Despite the profound dualism of their own temperament they found themselves forced, in order to defend the Church as an institution, to turn theology against sensibility. By means of subtle distinctions between the 'body' and the 'flesh', the institution of marriage could be defended against 'anarchic practices of virginity'. The dignity of labour was reaffirmed within the tightly controlled forms of monasticism. And the practice of self-flagellation had now to be interpreted as an *imitatio Christi*, and not as a mortification of the body as such. By means of the concept of 'vocation' the practices of the cultural revolution could be limited to a small minority, and even turned to the profit of the new order established by the ideological revolution. By a subtle process of transformation the hatred of abstract learning, of the wisdom of this world, became an abject submission to the wisdom of authority. The energy of the cultural revolution, after a long and intense struggle, was diverted and channelled into the hierarchical world of feudal Christianity.

Lardreau and Jambet have no difficulty in demonstrating the affinities between the ethos of early Christianity and the Cultural Revolution in China. The religious dimension is clear in the intense emphasis on 'inner transformation' ('everyone needs re-education'), the cultivation of a spirit of humility and self-sacrifice ('the man who is too concerned with his food and clothing grows distant from the masses'), or the stultifying repetition of readings from a sacred text ('he could go without food or sleep, but not without studying the works of Chairman Mao').[19] It is even possible, as Lardreau and Jambet show, to find identical *topoi* in early Christian hagiography and the edifying parables of Maoist China. For them the grandeur of the Cultural Revolution consisted in its spirit of revolt against all established order, which passed via the desire to 'transform what is most profound in man'. Yet even here doubts begin to arise. The fundamental principle of both Christian and Maoist ascesis, the forsaking and forgetting of father and mother, seems to lead only to subjection to a new and 'higher' authority, 'as if one forgets one's parents only in the name of the Father'. The Lacanian resonance of this last phrase introduces a disturbing possibility. Perhaps the Lacanian analysis of psychosis, as the result of a failure of the paternal metaphor to be installed as support of the Law, can be applied to the discourse of the Rebel. It would then be rebellion which was merely illusion, the return in delirious guise in the Real of a castration foreclosed from the Symbolic. Against this possibility, that rebellion is merely the 'paranoia of humanity', Lardreau and Jambet can only fall back on their tacit Kantianism. It is *necessary* to believe that the world of the Rebel is the true world, the history which makes history possible. This belief is justified by the action it sponsors. Its truth is undemonstrable.

At first sight Foucault's recent work, firmly rooted in historical investigation, seems as far removed as possible from the sub-Lacanian *Schwärmerei* of *L'Ange*. While Lardreau and Jambet, for example, affirm that 'desire is nothing but the specular image of the Law', one of Foucault's persistent themes has been the critique of what he terms the 'juridico-discursive' conception of power, according to which power essentially resides in the capacity to enunciate the law. At the socio-political level this conception leads to an overemphasis on 'sovereignty' and the role of the state, and a corresponding blindness to procedures of 'normalisation' — the production of 'useful' and conforming individuals within the systems of power which form the fine mesh of social institutions. But this model also has serious effects at the level of a discipline such as psychoanalysis. Whether, as in classical Freudianism, desire is perceived as a kind of rebellious energy which must be contained, or whether, in the wake of Lacan, desire is seen as dependent on the Law with which it ruses, Foucault claims that it is the same negative and prohibitory conception of power which dominates. For a number of convergent reasons Foucault began to find this conception unsatisfactory, not the least of these being the difficulties involved in explaining how such power 'holds'. If power is indeed merely negative and repressive, argues Foucault, it is hard to see why power relations are not far more unstable and fragile than they appear to be. In *Discipline and Punish* Foucault begins to suggest that the way out of this problem is to stop considering power as simply negative. Power can also be, and perhaps is predominantly, positive and productive.

In Foucault's latest book, *La Volonté de Savoir*, this suggestion is illustrated and deepened in the course of what turns out to be an overthrow of one of the commonplaces of cultural debate — the assumption of an historical repression of sexuality which reached its apogee during the nineteenth century and from which we are still struggling to emerge. Far from finding evidence for such a repression, Foucault is struck by the extent to which Western societies, from the confessional box to the psychoanalyst's couch, have established elaborate systems for the 'putting into discourse' *(mise en discours)* of sex. What characterised the event we perceive as an intensification of repression was not the fact that what was once openly discussed was driven back into silence, a silence from which it is only now beginning to emerge, but rather a transformation of the regime of discourse concerning sexuality. Thus the purification of vocabulary, the new restrictions on when and between whom it was possible to speak of sex, associated with the Victorian era, were accompanied by the flourishing of medical, paramedical and psychiatric discourses which described sexual behaviour and its 'aberrations' with meticulous devotion to detail. It was more a question of a change in the 'economy' of sexual behaviour than of its restriction. These developments can only be comprehended, Foucault suggests, if we cease to think of power and pleasure as standing in a relation of exteriority. The very rigour with which the space of the family comes to be ordered and controlled — polarity between parents' and children's bedrooms, segregation of male and female, obsessive attention paid to infantile masturbation — and invested by the discourses of education, medicine, religion, constitutes a *dispositif* whose effect is not to repress, but to prolong, intensify and refine the possibilities of pleasure: 'Pleasure and power do not cancel each other; they do not turn against each other; they pursue, overlap, and release each other (Foucault, 1976, 66—7).

In this way *La Volonté de Savoir* confirms the 'analytic' of power which Foucault began to outline in *Discipline and Punish*. Foucault employs the term 'analytic' to distinguish the premises of his historical investigations of particular 'power technologies' from the construction of a general theory of power. Such a theory, he suggests, will inevitably take the form of a search for origins, whether these are found in a Rousseau-esque 'social contract' (Foucault denies the usefulness of the concept of 'consensus'), or in a Marxian original division of society into classes (for Foucault power cannot be reduced to a 'function', such as that of securing the reproduction of relations of production). Foucault's analytic therefore implies an attempt to avoid from the outset the

traditional dichotomy between 'integrative' and 'coercive' theories
of power. Nevertheless it does depend on certain general 'propositions', which Foucault formulates systematically in one chapter
of *La Volonté de Savoir*. Power, within his analytic, is always
already present. Indeed it is 'omnipresent'. Produced at every
point in the social structure, or rather in every 'relation of force'
between points, it constitutes and traverses individuals, invades
and informs the gestures of the body, circulates within regimes
of discourse, and produces effects of knowledge and pleasure.
At the same time every advance of power produces 'resistances'
as an inevitable counter-effect, although these resistances are as
minute and dispersed as the relations of power themselves.

This pursuit of power into the finest channels of the social
body leads to a reversal of the traditional conception of power
as invested in a central organising instance (i.e. the state) from
which it filters down to successive levels. It is now the 'micro-
relations' which are primary, but which may be co-ordinated
or 'crystallised' so as to produce certain global effects of
domination (eg. that of a class).[20] An important aspect of this
conception is that there is no immediate parallelism between
the micro-powers which form the tissue of social relations and
the global 'strategies' which are supported by them. The father
in his role within the family, for example, is not the 'representative' of the state. While the specific relations of power within
the family can be used within a broader strategy, the form of this
exploitation cannot be predicted (otherwise power would be
reduced to a kind of structural determination). Function cannot
be deduced from form.

One of the major contentions of *La Volonté de Savoir* is that
the *dispositif* constituted by the ensemble of discourses, practices,
and institutions which have developed around the 'problem' of
sexuality, is central to strategies of power in 'societies of
normalisation'. Since sex is at the same time central to the life
of the individual and to the life of the species, sexuality forms
the hinge between the 'disciplines' which Foucault studied in
Discipline and Punish, and which are concerned with the maximi-
sation of the docility and utility of the body, and the regulations
and controls concerned with population: its rate of growth, its
distribution, its health, its mortality. Foucault points out that
the emergence of the idea of a 'population' (rather than a nation
or a people) marks a new event in human history — the entry,
roughly contemporaneous with the rise of capitalism, of the
life of the species into the arena of political debate and decision.
Thus the nineteenth-century concern with sexuality was expressed not simply in a tracking-down of desire into the nuances of
behaviour and the recesses of dreams, but in an obsession with

the themes of racial 'purity' and 'degeneration', and in campaigns of popular moralisation. The *dispositif* of sexuality linked these two forms of the exercise of power. It provided the common point of leverage for an 'anatomo-politics of the body' and a 'bio-politics of population'.

Foucault admits that at the beginning of his investigations he had assumed a primary reality of 'sex' beneath the distortions and displacements of a manufactured 'sexuality'. The new genealogy was to proceed on the lines laid down in Foucault's earlier books, with their implied dialectic of nature and culture, of 'madness' and 'civilisation'. Yet the conclusion of *La Volonté de Savoir* operates a striking reversal of these assumptions, entailing what Foucault considers to be the definitive break with a naturalism which pervaded his earlier books. 'Sex' is no longer the pregiven which *dispositifs* of power occlude; it ceases to be, as the prophets of the century (Freud, D. H. Lawrence) would have us believe, the most secret and authentic reality of our being. It becomes simply the projected point of convergence of certain strategies of knowledge and power, the imaginary unification of a plurality of relations, functions, and pleasures. Foucault goes on to draw the conclusion that the struggle for 'sexual liberation' can only serve to perpetuate our subjection to the *dispositif* of sexuality, and that a real counter-attack must reject our enslavement to this particular form of the 'will to knowledge'. Our reply must take the form, not of a demand for more and better 'sex', but a rediscovery of the 'body', of the diversity of its pleasures and its capacities for resistance.

While an assimilation of Foucault's conclusions to the theses of *L'Ange* would clearly be abusive, it is impossible to ignore the echoes between the two books: their common suspicion of 'sexual liberation', the discovery that sex-desire is in fact an apparatus of subjection, the vision of history as what *L'Ange* terms 'the principle of dispersion of tiny unities of power and rebellion' (Lardreau and Jambet, 1976, 47). In Foucault, of course, the position is far more nuanced. He admits that the liberationist demand, with its naturalist underpinning, may form a necessary moment of certain struggles (eg. Women's and Gay Movements), but maintains that their impetus must ultimately carry them beyond the problematic of 'repression'. But here we encounter a difficulty. For the notion of the 'body and its pleasures' can only become, on strict Foucaldian premisses, a component in another strategy of power, if the present *dispositif* were to break up. The alternative to this would be to see the idea of the 'body and its pleasures' in a naturalist perspective, which would coincide with Baudrillard's suggestion that the disappearance of repression from Foucault's

analyses is an illusion. All that has happened is that Foucault has
pushed the process one stage back: it is no longer a question of
a repression *of*, but of an equally grinding repression *by* sex
(Baudrillard, 1977, 26). But Foucault valiantly strives to avoid
the naturalist reading. He affirms that 'resistance' is always
resistance to a power — which entails that once the power
'retreats' the resistance must either disappear or itself be transformed into a new power. The dilemma of all social revolutions,
seen from the *gauchiste* viewpoint, is thus transferred to the
'micro-level'. Liberation is not only not where we thought, it no
longer seems to be anywhere at all.[21]

These difficulties are inevitable, given Foucault's general
conception of power as a kind of *a priori*, producing discourses,
knowledges, pleasures, but not itself reducible to any other kind
of relation. His assertion that we are never 'outside' power, that
points of resistance are internally related to the operation of
power, begins to look remarkably like the Lacanian notion, which
he opposes, of a Law which desire may ruse with, but which it
can never transgress. This impression is reinforced by a significant
tendency — despite Foucault's emphasis on the multiplicity of
micro-relations — to speak of power in an anonymous third person
singular, as if it were a kind of homogeneous current circulating
through the social body; it is never a question of whose power and
for what purpose, since the 'purpose' of any power can now only
be its own expansion. This accounts for the noticeable convergence
between the idea of the Rebel promoted in *L'Ange* and Foucault's
conception of resistances. For in both cases power is seen as
coextensive with the real (or at least with social reality), so that
any 'counter-attack' can only take the tautological form of a
desire to be no longer oppressed by power.[22] Thus Foucault
describes resistances as 'coextensive and contemporary with
power' — not as a nature opposed to culture, but as the ever-
present counter-effect of its action. At the level at which Foucault
is operating, however, the attempt to separate power and resistance
becomes less and less feasible. The rule of tactical polyvalency
takes its revenge. As Baudrillard has pointed out: 'on this
microscopic scale, the atoms of power and the atoms of resistance
get confused — the same fragment of gesture, of body, of gaze,
of discourse, encloses the positive electricity of power and the
negative electricity of resistance' (Baudrillard, 1977, 51). The
inevitable terminus of this pulverisation of relations of power
is reached by Foucault himself. Pressed on the question of political
alliances he states: 'There are not, immediately given, subjects
of whom one would be the proletariat and the other the bourgeoisie.
Who struggles against whom? We all struggle against each other.
And there is always something in us which struggles against

something else in us' (Foucault, 1977c, 75). What these two 'somethings' might be is perhaps more clearly formulated by the authors of *L'Ange*, in a humanist rhetoric which Foucault would no doubt find uncomfortable, as the 'desire for submission' and the 'love of freedom'.

A number of commentators have observed a convergence between Foucault's analytic of power, with its abandonment of class analysis in favour of the vision of a complex of forces which continually dissaggregate and coalesce, and the characteristic positions of American-style functionalism.[23] The comparison does not seem entirely unjustified, given Foucault's tendency to slide from the use of the term 'power' to designate one pole of the relation power-resistance, to its use to designate the relation as a whole. (Foucault wants to say both that power constitutes the social as such, and that its 'antagonist', the resistances, is equally mobile, ingenious and extensive). What is implied is that resistances cannot be 'constitutive'. The dice are always loaded, since it is only power which is positive and productive, while resistance is simply a reaction to its productions. But this entails that power is always 'on the same side'. There can be no such thing as a 'subversive institution', for example, since any institution is already a crystallisation of relations of power. Following this logic the *Nouvelle Philosophie* arrives at the conclusion that the left-wing parties, the trade unions, even the proletariat, are pillars of the established order. In a parody of ultra-leftism, Lévy suggests that elections are irrelevant since the Eurocommunist parties 'already have power' (Lévy, 1978, 27). Indeed, given the functionalist premiss, any social transformation can be interpreted as the ruse of an anonymous and all-pervasive rationality. One disciple of Foucault sees the spread of the private car, for example, as the consolidation of a formidable 'disciplinary instrument' (Ewald, 1975, 1255).

A further difficulty with Foucault's analytic is its tendency to elide the necessary dimension of coercion in the exercise of power. As early as *L'Ordre du Discours* Foucault had seen the at least minimally coercive forms of prohibition and the sanity/madness partition as being absorbed in a 'will to truth' invested in the more dispassionate procedures of science. This theme is taken up in *Discipline and Punish*, where the Panopticon becomes the central symbol of this 'dematerialisation' of power. In his extended description of the Panopticon Foucault seems to revel in the paradoxes of a device which makes possible the exercise of power by means of continuous, minute and unrestricted surveillance. It is as though one of the most cherished assumptions of 'metaphysics' had thus been overthrown — the contemplative attitude, the attitude of *theoria*, with its implication of freedom from practical or political constraint, now becomes the embodiment of the dream of absolute domination. Not the darkness of the cavern, as in Plato, but 'visibility is a trap' (Foucault, 1975, 202). What Foucault appears to forget, however, is that the internalisation of controls on behaviour by an inmate held in a field of visibility is effective only because of the possibility of sanctions in the case of disobedience. The production of a field of visibility cannot in itself constrain. Knowledge does not, as Foucault often suggests, *equal* power.

One of the more recent developments in Foucault's analysis of power, as has already been mentioned, has been his discovery of the usefulness of Glucksmann's notion of the *'plebs'*. This he interprets not as a 'sociological reality', but as an 'inverse energy', a 'centrifugal movement', which 'replies to each advance of power by a movement of disengagement' — *The* pleb does not exist, but 'there is "*plebs*" (il y a "de la" plebe . . .). There is always something in the social body, in classes, in groups, in individuals themselves, which in a certain way escapes relations of power' (Foucault, 1977i, 92). What is remarkable about these descriptions is not only their implicit restoration of the dominant centre/rebellious margin imagery ('centrifugal movement'), inevitable given Foucault's tendency — despite his own cautions - to speak of power as if it were a single unified instance. They also reveal the incoherence of the idea of the *plebs*. For at the same time that Foucault describes the *plebs* as the *irreducible* limit, the reverse side of power, he also suggests that the *plebs* can be 'reduced' by its 'effective subjection', or by its utilisation as *plebs*, as in the case of the controlled exploitation of delinquency described in *Discipline and Punish*. A third kind of reduction takes place when the *plebs* 'fixes itself according to a strategy of resistance'. Thus Foucault's wish to avoid any kind of naturalism (there is no beach under the paving-stones any more), combined with the contradictory desire to deny that power is coextensive with the real, leads inevitably towards the *Nouvelle Philosophie* conception of a pure essence of rebellion, which is neutralised as soon as it sets itself any positive goal.

The lesson to be learned here concerns the need for discrimination — politics always consists in a choice *between* powers, and not in a stand *against* power as such. The apparently radical shift entailed by the discovery that, since relations of power are everywhere, 'everything is political', was swiftly followed by the discovery that the revolution may no longer be desirable, and that we are consequently 'living the end of politics' (Foucault, 1977j, 160). The affirmation that 'a revolutionary undertaking is directed not only against the present, but against the rule of "until now" ' (Foucault, 1977k, 233), becomes the conclusion that 'the only socialism which deserves the inverted commas of derision is the one which leads the dream-life of ideality in our heads' (Foucault, 1977i, 92). The extension of the concept of power to all social relations empties it of any political content. In one sense everything becomes contestable, since power is everywhere; but at the same time power itself is no longer worth contesting, is no longer unconditionally sterile and malign, the enemy of the richness and spontaneity of nature. This situation is perfectly illustrated by the spurious politics of the *Nouveaux Philosophes*, which combines verbal support for 'marginals', ecologists, the Italian 'metropolitan indians', with a fundamental commitment to the values of bourgeois-liberal democracy. An over-reaction to the dangers inherent in the exercise of political power leads to a denegation of the importance of the state, in itself or as an arena of struggle, either by means of the suggestion that the state is merely one apparatus among many (Foucault), or by depicting the state as so uniformly monstrous that it is not worth having anything to do with (Glucksmann). The conviction seems to be that we can in some way significantly transform society while leaving the question of power to the 'paranoiacs' (Lévy). This dominant mood, which the *Nouvelle Philosophie* refracts, can be illustrated by a quotation chosen almost at random: 'What has really begun to change in these last ten years is most notably the fact that a number of us, following Michel Foucault, have renounced the idea of revealing THE TRUTH, while showing that in the hollows of our illusions there were *spaces of truth*. In the end this is the whole distance and difference which separates those who proclaim "LIFE must be changed" from those who more modestly, but this time accomplishing an authentic social and cultural *rupture*, can say: "We have begun the work of changing *our* lives" ' (Laplantine, 1978, 61).

It is clearly both a risk and a temptation to try to draw general conclusions from the emergence and rapid consolidation of this 'Liberalo-libertarianism'. In many respects the *Nouvelle Philosophie* is such a characteristically French — and even Parisian — phenomenon, that there seems little point in seeking for parallels elsewhere. There has never been in Britain, for example, the kind of generalised currency of Marxist ideas to which the *Nouvelle Philosophie* is undoubtedly in part a reaction. A generation of intellectuals who were formed by Althusserian Marxism-Leninism have ended by asserting with virulence the subjectivity and immediacy which that philosophy sought so radically to eclipse. The close interweaving of the origins of the *Nouvelle Philosophie* with the story of May '68 and its aftermath adds a further element of particularity. Ten years after the events, which many saw at the time as heralding a new era of intensified class conflict, the French intelligentsia is predominantly composed of anti-Marxists (Lévy and associates), non-Marxists (Foucault, Deleuze), and ex-Marxists (including Sartre, who announced in an interview given to *Lotta Continua* in autumn 1977 that he had stopped being a Marxist three or four years ago). The decade which began with hopes of radical social change has seen a reflux of energies after 1974 from far-left militancy towards the major parties which ended only in the bitterness of electoral defeat. In these circumstances it was inevitable that a large section of a 'generation of '68', with the revolution rapidly fading from a collective experience to a personal mirage, would try to salvage those aspects of that experience which could be prolonged within the interstices of capitalism. In contrast to the Anglo-Saxon countries, where the 'counter-culture' underwent a certain politicisation, in France the development of a counter-culture marked the ebbing of political militancy. The *Nouvelle Philosophie* has taken this movement to its logical terminus, with its replacement of politics with poetry, and its urging of an escape from the 'political view of the world'.[24]

Yet despite the particularities of the French situation, the *Nouvelle Philosophie* must be seen in the context of an ideological resurgence of the Right, and a dissolution of Marxist certitudes on the Left, which is taking place across the advanced capitalist world. In Britain too the ideas of strident reaction have gained a new respectability, while the modish Left is beginning to assert the plurality and specificity of social practices against class analysis (termed 'class essentialism'), to suggest the priority of political over epistemological criteria in the assessment of theories, and to suspect Marxism of being a dangerously totalising discourse. In many cases the inspiration for these positions is drawn from the same sources as that of the *Nouveaux Philosophes*: the writings of Lacan and Foucault. Already the first skirmishes have been fought between this new 'post-Marxism' and the defenders of an orthodoxy which only a few years ago represented the advance guard of radical theory.[25] In the United States the left-wing intellectuals grouped around the journal *Telos* are also 'moving on' — this time not from Althusser .to Foucault, but from an Hegelian and phenomenological Marxism to 'alternative traditions' of socialist and libertarian thought. It seems unlikely however that the *Nouvelle Philosophie* itself, which in many ways represents the 'unacceptable face' of the French approach to theory, will find any echo in these very different political and cultural climates. A wider knowledge of the *Nouvelle Philosophie*, and of its roots in the Lacanian and Foucaldian vulgate, may even have a positive effect in encouraging a review of the widespread assumption of a spontaneous affinity between theoretical 'radicalism' and socialist politics.

Notes

1. See *Les Nouvelles Littéraires*, 10 June 1976. The *Nouveaux Philosophes* presented in the dossier were: Jean-Marie Benoist, Jean-Paul Dollé, Michel Guèrin, Christian Jambet, Guy Lardreau.

2. See *Time*, 5 September 1977. The article, with its crude conflation of the *Nouvelle Philosophie* with the human rights ideology of Jimmy Carter, is typical of the exploitation of the *Nouvelle Philosophie* by the Right. A brief but informative account from the Left can be found in Jenkins (1977). There is a collection of short articles by *Nouveaux Philosophes* and opponents, mostly taken from a series run by the *Nouvel Observateur*, in *Telos* 32 (Summer 1977).

3. This is the fundamental thesis of Lecourt (1978). Although much of what Lecourt says is correct, the idea of 'objective guilt' only plays into the hands of the *Nouveaux Philosophes*.

4. Given the purely cosmetic nature of *Tel Quel*'s politics, this evolution was not only unsurprising but predictable. Even before May '68 a sceptical commentator had forseen that *Tel Quel* would probably continue 'the escalation which, in order to save their sacrosanct *écriture*, will end by denouncing revolutionary ideology itself.' (Pingaud, 1968.)

5. The exception to this rule is Jean-Marie Benoist, who has always been an old-fashioned political liberal. Having written a book called *Marx est Mort* in 1970, Benoist justifiably felt entitled to some of the limelight. More recently he has alienated some of his colleagues by standing for the Giscardians in the legislative elections.

6. For exemplification of these attitudes see the special issue of *Les Temps Modernes*, No. 310bis (1972): 'Nouveau Fascisme, Nouvelle Democratie'. This issue was produced entirely by the Maoists grouped around *La Cause du Peuple*, i.e. the Gauche Prolétarienne after its banning in 1970.

7. The theory of the 'new fascism' is expounded in Glucksmann (1972).

8. See Glucksmann (1972).

9. See Foucault (1977a).

10. Some followers of Foucault have raised this substitution to the level of unconscious parody in speaking of the extraction of a 'surplus value' or 'profit' of power. See Ewald (1975).

11. The feeling that oppressions which justify themselves with a global theory or philosophy of history are somehow more monstrous than those which don't is a common feature of philosophies of rebellion, and clearly favours the Right. In Camus' case a profound hostility to Communism was combined with support for France's war in Algeria. In the *Nouvelle Philosophie* Marxism becomes the paradigm of all oppression.

12. For a brief sketch of Clavel's ideas and of his relation to Glucksmann see the review of his *Deux Siècles Chez Lucifer*, *T.L.S.*, 27 October 1978.

13. See Gadamer (1975).

14. See Foucault (1977g), p. 14.

15. See Friedrich Nietzsche, *On the Genealogy of Morals*, II, 12.

16. Cf. Bernard-Henri Levy: 'we are condemned for a long time yet to the language of *Capital*, in so far as we resign ourselves to playing the game of politics'. Lévy (1977), p. 127–8.

17. See *La Volonté de Savoir*, IV, 2, 4.

18. The Master is always masculine, since reason is always masculine. For a critique of the anti-feminism of *L'Ange* see Le Doeff (1977), p. 7.

19. These slogans are cited from texts of the Cultural Revolution in Lardreau and Jambet (1976), p. 137.

20. In fact this conception is not as original as it seems. Nor is it alien to Marxism. '(Power) is not an object at all: it is the totality of differential relationships which make up a society . . . They include a myriad microsocial formations: families, schools, universities, factories, offices . . . These formations in turn make up larger agglomerations.' (Anderson, 1966, 235–6.)

21. There are fundamental weaknesses in Foucault's critique of the concept of repression, which entails the vanishing of 'liberation'. (These weaknesses account for the vague impression of sleight-of-hand which the book generates.) Foucault falls into the trap of his self-proclaimed nominalism. He mobilises a tacit assumption – aided by the illusory polarity of the French terms *dit* (spoken) and *interdit* (forbidden) – that what is verbally formulated cannot be prohibited, so that the burgeoning of discourse *about* sexuality is equated with sexual activity itself. Yet what is spoken of can at the same time be fiercely repressed, as the Freudian notion of 'working-through' makes clear. A direct revelation to the analysand of the 'contents' of his or her unconscious not only does not lift repression, but can have a seriously regressive effect. Lacan's notion of *la parole vide*, an ineffectual veracity opposed to 'truth', represents an elaboration of this idea.

22. As so often, Lévy provides a clear and crude formulation of what is only implicit in other texts. He refers to: 'what I call *Resistance*, which has nothing to do with the paranoia of power, nothing to do with the fantasm of revolution, which aims at nothing except the pure contingency of its own coming, and desires nothing but the force which bears it onward and the rage which moves it.' (Lévy, 1978, 33.)

23. See Lefort (1978) and Poulantzas (1978).

24. See, for example, Kristéva (1978).

25. See, for example, Rosalind Coward's Lacanian critique of the Birmingham Centre for Cultural Studies in *Screen* vol. 18, no. 1 (1977), and the reply from the Centre in vol. 18, no. 4. Or the exchange between Stuart Hall and the Editorial Collective in *Ideology and Consciousness* no. 3 (Spring 1978).

References

Anderson P. (1966) 'Problems of Socialist Strategy', in *Towards Socialism*, Fontana.

Baudrillard J. (1977) *Oublier Foucault*, Editions Galilée.

Bouchard D. (1977) 'Introduction' to *Language Counter-Memory, Practice*, Blackwell.

Deleuze G. (1970) 'Un Nouvel Archiviste', *Critique* no. 274.

Dolle J.-P. (1975) *Désir de Revolution*, 10/18. Original edition *Grasset* 1972.

Donzelot J. (1978) 'Misère de la Culture Politique', *Critique* no. 373–4.

Ewald F. (1975) 'Anatomie et Corps Politiques', *Critique* no. 343.

Foucault M. (1961) *Histoire de la Folie*, Plon.

Foucault M. (1971a) *L'Ordre du Discours*, Gallimard.

Foucault M. (1971b) 'Nietzsche, la Généalogie l'Histoire', in Bachelard *et al.*, *Hommage à Jean Hyppolite*, P.U.F.

Foucault M. (1974a) *The Archeology of Knowledge*, Tavistock.

Foucault M. (1974b) *The Order of Things*, Tavistock.

Foucault M. (1975) *Surveiller et Punir*, Gallimard.

Foucault M. (1976) *La Volonté de Savoir*, Gallimard.

Foucault M. (1977a) 'Intellectuals and Power', Donald Bouchard (ed.), *Language, Counter-Memory, Practice*, Blackwell.

Foucault M. (1977b) 'La Grande Colère des Faits', *Le Nouvel Observateur*, 9 May 1977.

Foucault M. (1977c) 'Entrevue: le Jeu de Michel Foucault', *Ornicar?* no. 10.

Foucault M. (1977d) 'Prison Talk', *Radical Philosophy* no. 16.

Foucault M. (1977e) 'History of Systems of Thought', *Language, Counter-Memory, Practice*, Blackwell.

Foucault M. (1977f) 'Potere-Corpo', *Microfisica del Potere*, Einaudi.

Foucault M. (1977g) 'The Political Function of the Intellectual', *Radical Philosophy* no. 17.

Foucault M. (1977h) 'Corso del 7 Gennaio 1976', *Microfisica del Potere*, Einaudi.

Foucault M. (1977i) 'Pouvoirs et Strategies', *Les Révoltes Logiques* no. 4.

Foucault M. (1977j) 'Power and Sex: an Interview with Michel Foucault', *Telos* 32.

Foucault M. (1977k) 'Revolutionary Action: "Until Now"', *Language, Counter-Memory, Practice*, Blackwell.

Foucault M. (1978a) 'Politics and the Study of Discourse', *Ideology and Consciousness* no. 3.

Foucault M. (1978b) 'Verité et Pouvoir', *L'Arc* no. 70.

Gadamer H.-G. (1975) *Truth and Method*, Seabury Press.

Gavi P., Sartre J.-P., Victor P. (1974) *On a Raison de Se Révolter*, Gallimard.

Glucksmann A. (1972) 'Fascismes: L'Ancien et le Nouveau', *Les Temps Modernes* no. 310bis.

Glucksmann A. (1975) *La Cuisinière et le Mangeur d'Hommes*, Seuil.

Glucksmann A. (1977a) 'A Ventriloquist Structuralism', in *Western Marxism: A Critical Reader*, N.L.B.

Glucksmann A. (1977b) *Les Maîtres Penseurs*, Grasset.

Jenkins T. (1977) 'The New Philosophers', *International* vol. 2, no. 4.

Krémer-Marietti A. (1974) *Michel Foucault*, Seghers.

Kristéva J. (1978) 'La Littérature Dissidente Comme Refutation du Discours de Gauche', *Tel Quel* no. 76.

Laplantine F. (1978) 'Du Romantisme, au Nihilisme, au Pragmatisme', *Autrement* no. 12.

Lardreau G. and Jambet C. (1976) *L'Ange*, Grasset.

Le Doeff M. (1977) 'Women and Philosophy', *Radical Philosophy* no. 17.

Lecourt D. (1978) *Dissidence ou Revolution?* Maspero.

Lefort C. (1978) 'Then and Now', *Telos* no. 36.

Lévy B.-H. (1975) 'Le Système Foucault', *Magazine Littéraire* no. 101.

Lévy B.-H. (1977) *La Barbarie à Visage Humain*, Grasset.

Lévy B.-H. (1978) 'La Preuve du Pudding', *Tel Quel* no. 77.

Pingaud B. (1968) 'Où Va Tel Quel?' *La Quinzaine Littéraire* 1–15 Jan. 1968.

Poulantzas N. (1978) *L'Etat, le Pouvoir, le Socialism*, P.U.F.

Rancière J. (1974) *La Leçon d'Althusser*, Gallimard.

Rancière J. (1975) 'La Bergère au Goulag', *Les Révoltes Logiques* no. 1.

CHAPTER 5

Strategies for socialists?
Foucault's conception of power

Jeff Minson

Abstract

This chapter draws out the relevance of Michel Foucault's work
on forms of 'social' regulation and training to a socialist audi-
ence. In an introduction to his conception of power, Marxist
theory is implicated in Foucault's criticisms of classical conceptions of power-as-sovereignty. Some untenable 'Nietzschean'
ingredients of his position, particularly his preoccupation with
'power' and 'subjectification' are distinguished from a more
rewarding emphasis on the construction of specific categories
of social agent and their attributes; and on the formation of the
politically ambiguous domain of 'social' policies and programmes. These emphases render problematic current socialist
conceptions of 'socialization' and 'social' revolution.

This piece concerns Michel Foucault's project of a genealogy of
the forms of domination — the 'morals' — characteristic of modern
societies. Respecting the political motivations of Foucault's work,
emphasis is placed on the implications of his approach for the
analysis of conditions of current political struggle. To this end,
reference to Foucault's published work is mainly confined to
Surveiller et Punir (1975, now translated as *Discipline and Punish*,
1978) and *La Volonté de Savoir* (1976).[1] If the first book offers
a synoptic historical view of the general domain of investigation of
the genealogy of morals, the second contains a more developed
account of the concept of power on which the project turns. They
will be henceforth referred to as DP and HS respectively. What
follows is not a full-scale review but a reconstruction, criticism
and tentative extension of one particular theoretical position
which finds its most elaborate but not necessarily its best expression in these texts. That is why reference is made to Jacques
Donzelot's book *La Police des Familles* (1977); this genealogy of
the construction of the modern family in 'social' policy and
administration and related forms of expertise and moral instruction represents a rigorous implementation of Foucault's project.

The main aim of this paper is to show that for all its flaws certain aspects of Foucault's position presents (Marxist dominated) socialist theories and politics with some inescapable challenges. On the constructive side, it enlarges the scope for rethinking many of the parameters of socialist struggles and their objectives — the 'ends' of socialism — and this in a non-utopian way. The parameters in question concern the domain of 'the social' itself, as presently constituted; that is the assorted forms and contents of what is variously called 'social' policy, the 'social' wage, etc, and not forgetting the correlative functioning demarcations of the individual, of the personal or private realm which are constructed within this domain. However, socialist thinking may only profit from Foucault if these 'positive' aspects of his work can be detached from the untenable central concern of the position as a whole, which reduces politics to domination. It is argued that a consistent bifurcation in Foucault's approach licences this detachment.[2]

I Introduction to genealogy

Let us run through the main arguments of one of Foucault's genealogies of morals, to see the concept of power at work. Apart from their theoretical reflections on power both DP and HS take a particular field of investigation which is then located in a broader domain common to them both. The fulcrum of each book is an historical question, and we can see how this 'historical question' becomes integrated into a general investigation of *pouvoir/savoir* through an examination of HS.

The historical problem for HS concerns the conditions for the emergence and success of an organized *mis-en-discours* of sexuality in 'Western' societies, and in particular, of its most developed expression, psychoanalysis (HS: 10, 130). The specific domain of investigation to which the latter belongs is termed the 'apparatus of sexuality'. Before describing it, it might be helpful to rename this domain the 'family-sexuality complex'. For the 'effects of domination' of this apparatus always pertain to family relations, branching on to them and transforming certain traditional familial characteristics just as, according to DP social work, legal psychiatry, forensic science and prison itself batten on to traditional juridical forms to form a 'scientifico-legal' complex (HS: 106–112; DP: 16–24).

This proposal helps to make some sense of HS's specific historical focus. Psychoanalysis is deemed the most achieved exemplification of *scientia sexualis*, of the peculiarly 'Western' propensity to construe sexuality as a vital subject of self-knowledge and scientific expertise (as opposed to an 'Eastern' hedonistic art of loving). Given the symbiotic relations of the 'techniques' of the apparatus of sexuality and the 'discipline' and morality of family life, psychoanalysis, with its technique for inducing unconscious sexuality to 'speak itself', cannot on this argument be judged an unambiguously liberating discourse, but is instead implicated in a nexus of 'familialist' power relations.

What is this 'sexuality', if it is possible to conceive of its having a history, and if this is to be written primarily as a history of discourses (HS: 68–9)? As distinct from the traditional 'repressive hypothesis' concerning social attitudes to sex since the seventeenth century, where *what* is repressed is a universal datum, Foucault proposes a genealogy of the construction of sexuality in and across practices ranging from Catholic confession to legal psychiatry to 'consciousness-raising' groups as everybody's 'Secret Life' which *must* (though it will not) be spoken of. Repression and censorship there undoubtedly were, but these were part of that wider 'economy' of power relations which Foucault terms the 'apparatus of sexuality': 'an ensemble of effects produced on the body, on modes of behaviour and so social relations by definite apparatuses based on a complex technology of power' (HS: 127). Side-by-side with censorship a history may be traced, of a 'regular and polymorphous incitement to discourse' (beginning with changes in Christian confessional forms); a proliferation in the volume and diversity of learned discourse of sex, eg, those involved in the two-century-long war on masturbation; and lastly a proliferation in the very forms of sexuality themselves in the course of a medically-dominated 'psychiatrization of perverse pleasures'. This latter involves an 'implantation' of categories of perversion into their subjects, a real work of sexual identification. In this perspective, sexuality as a universal human attribute does not exactly vanish, but becomes a feature of those definite discourses and social (power) relations in which sexual relations become, as in no other culture, central objects of scientific and self-knowledge, of regulation and desire.[3]

The 'apparatus of sexuality' forms a hinge connecting the two axes of the general political technology of modern power. This domain comprises both the 'disciplinary techniques' discussed in DP and the 'regulatory procedures' characteristic of *biopolitics*. The latter bears not directly on 'individuals' but on the fecundity, hygiene and moral health of national populations (ibid: 25–6 139 ff). It implicates individuals and 'private family' by imposing disciplinary norms in pursuit of biopolitical objectives (e.g. 'national efficiency' in the U.K.), making the latter matters of e.g. parental or pedagogical responsibility. How are these modern powers to be understood? The exegesis of *pouvoir/savoir* which follows begins with the 'traditional' problematic of power which he constructs as a foil to his own.

I Power, sovereignty and legalism

This problematic, which his earlier programmatic (1971) text partly retains (Gordon, 1977: 15), Foucault christens the 'juridico-discursive' conception of power (HS: 82). What this term is generally intended to convey is the common tendency to construe political forms in terms which are dominated by the language and imagery of law. Crucially, he vacillates throughout between seeing this tendency as mistaken *per se*, and as more or less adequate to the political forms of a bygone age (Feudalism, Absolutism), hence merely 'superannuated'. We may go along with this indeterminacy for the present, leaving the demonstration of its determinants and effects for later.

The 'superannuated' juridico-discursive conception is ruled by two basic assumptions which emerge in its treatment of illegality and the powers arraigned against it. Firstly, illegality is defined as offence against the sovereignty of the established order, and this, even where as today crime is characterized not as an affront to the Sovereign's person but as 'anti-social'. Secondly, the sovereign legal-political order is an essentially *negative* one, but also dual. The paradigmatic mode of expression of sovereign *authority* is discursive, a rule or principle legislating what is forbidden. Moreover, turning from the form of Sovereign law and order to its sanctions, the paradigmatic mode of expression of sovereign *power* is repression. The law of the land impinges on political subjects who defy it in the form of a *levy*. This concept of power as levied (prélèvement) is central to Foucault's differentiation of 'sovereign' and 'disciplinary' punitive regimes in DP. The point of punishment-as-levy is to restore and symbolically to make manifest the supreme authority (*surpouvoir*) of the sovereign, by physically impressing it on the offender's body. If offences are not paid for with the offender's life or limbs, the punishment takes the form of confiscation of goods. In either event sovereign power entails a 'deduction' from the 'forces' available to those subject to it (HS. 89, 135—6). By contrast, and contrary to the adage, 'you can't keep a good man down', the 'productive', disciplinary, form of power is so exercised as to positively *augment* the forces of those subject to *its* 'government', in direct proportion to the degree of their subjection. Its aim is manipulability for productive purposes (DP: 208).[4]

What are the consequences for the political analysis of modern social forms of its continuing to be dominated by legalism in the above 'juridico-discursive' sense? Two sets of implications may be noted.

1. Power is construed in a global and subjectivist manner. Power flows from its *possession* by unitary, 'sovereign' political forces. This proposition entails then

2. that the key problems for political analysis concern (i) the identity of the dominating forces and (ii) the legitimacy or legitimations of their rule. To show how these consequences flow, I shall consider firstly the perhaps unexpectedly far-reaching functions of the concept of possession in current forms of political differentiation and secondly the reasons for the political significance accorded to ideology, particularly in historical materialism.

Why, we may ask, are 'People's Democracies' so-called?. What are the implications of this category? These questions are raised here to illustrate with respect to the first set of consequences noted above why Foucault wants to line up Marxism with other currents of political thought in his pungent charge that the task of decapitating the King in political *thought* has still to be accomplished (HS: 89). 'People's democracy' occupies the same classificatory space vis-à-vis forms of state as 'bourgeois democracy' by virtue of their common theoretical provenance in the Marxist concept of political dictatorship. This classification basically differs from classical political theory over the locus of political power. Forms of state differ, ultimately, according to prevailing economic class relations and these, crucially, are predicated upon the form of 'economic' *possession* (relations of production). A people's democracy is realized to the extent that means and conditions of production are 'collectively' possessed. Political power passes to the possessors to the extent that socialization effects a passage from 'formal' to 'real' appropriation.

Following a remark in Balibar's (1974: 162–3, Note 65) we may wonder how the term 'real appropriation' can designate *extra*-legal 'objective' economic relations or how capitalist legal property rights can express these relations when Marx's distinction itself replicates a *legal* distinction between kinds of possession (possession-as-right). Given this problem, which ironically points to the presence of a 'juridico-discursive' tendency within Marxist economic theory itself, and thence, in its political thinking, the congruence of Marxism and bourgeois or classical political philosophy over the question of power becomes a more plausible idea than Foucault's explicit observations to this effect would suggest.

Classical political theory (i) generally assumes the existence of some distinctive given area of social life which is political; (ii) identifies that domain with whatever 'officially' falls within the preview of the State administrative apparatuses; (iii) conceives of the State as a homogeneous entity; (iv) whose characteristic mode of action is the dominion exercised through its administrative *instruments* (civil service, police, treasury, etc.) as by a sovereign subject, over other subjects. The form of dominion (political practice as domination) is classically construed as the realization of the will of a sovereign body/subject, the content of this will according with the legitimizing principle on which this sovereignty is based. Thus the UK is classified politically as a Parliamentary 'democracy' without reference, for instance, to whether the democratically *un*accountable powers enjoyed by various State apparatuses (its so-called instruments) are greater or less than in the case of their equivalents in 'totalitarian' states.

Of the above four properties of classical political philosophy, classical Marxism arguably disagrees only in respect of (i) and (ii). By contrast with mainstream political thought Marxism makes the *location* of the political domain a problem requiring analysis in that it refuses to restrict it to the standard institutional locations. But as others have argued (Cutler, *et al.* 1977) it cannot, except at the cost of theoretical indeterminacy, refuse the assumption of the homogeneity of political power. When all the recent complications of Marxist political theory are taken into account, the figure of the ruling class can still be discerned insistently playing the same unifying function with respect to what counts as political in those Marxist discourses that specifically depend upon Marxist theory as the various incarnations of political forms, Princes, Sovereigns, Legislators, etc., play in classicial political theory.

Regarding the second set of consequences of this theoretical legalism, if power has an ultimately unitary and subjective locus, then one can see immediately why a key question for political theory is the identification of the locii of power — of the forces that possess or that contend for power. Since power on any understanding of the term entails a capacity to dominate another, and given the premise of a unitary subjective locus, it follows that the necessary and sufficient conditions for the effective exercise of power is its possession by a subject. Let us now set down why the problem of justification arises so insistently. In the first place it is necessary to locate in an elementary and crude fashion the problematic of ideology in relation to the juridico-discursive presuppositions of political philosophy.

Put simply, power is in these terms a relation between those who have it and those who do not. If as in the bulk of social theory agents are construed as human subjects, then by virtue of their natural possession of will and consciousness, political agents subject to a form of rule are in this scheme of things bound to submit to their subordination in one of two ways: either willingly or unwillingly. This then in turn generates a finite set of possibilities. If willingly then the mechanism of domination is the consent of the governed. Consent in turn may be obtained by fair or rational (legitimate) means or foul. If the former, we are in the traditional territory of moral and political philosophy, e.g. the problem of the grounds of political obligation, the general conditions under which claims to legitimacy by rulers succeed or fail, and so on. If foul, then we are in the encyclopaedic, residual domain of ideology: the management of consent, legitimation as 'make-believe' albeit not outright duplicity, etc. If not by consent, then by force. The political pertinence of 'ideology', or within political philosophy, of 'opinion' or rational consent is standardly registered in terms of either a contrast or complementarity with coercive powers.[5]

We are now in a position to see two grounds on which Foucault takes issue with this aspect of Marxist political analysis. The concept of *pouvoir-savoir* runs counter to the concept of ideology as defined (a) in opposition to science, to some discourse which knows ideology to be ideology and (b) as opposed to violence or force. Although discussion is here restricted to (b), Foucault's concept cross-cuts the poles of both these oppositions. For instance, military drill and penitentiaries built along the lines of Bentham's Panopticon proposal were calculated to produce definite mental effects whilst remaining of a physical order. The Panopticon prisoners' own minds and knowledge form a crucial component of their subjection to this power of surveillance (DP: 202–3) without any element of 'make-believe' being involved. This brings us to the nub of Foucault's strictures against juridico-discursive conceptions of power.

This is — and the problem of the management of consent in any theory of ideology exemplifies this most clearly — that it takes the subjectivity of the individuals that are subject to its power as a mere datum in respect of the problems of analysing forms of power. Indeed both superordinate and subordinate subjects are assumed to exist, even if not unconditionally per se, then independently of the powers they assume or those which are exercised over them. Having reviewed the critique Foucault makes of classical conceptions of power, we have now only to turn it round to arrive at Foucault's own view of the fundamental prerequisite of an adequate understanding of power.

Relations of power, subjectivity and the notion of strategy

Power in its actual exercise must be ever constitutive of the subjectivity of the agents of power relations. It therefore may only issue in subjection, in the conventional sense of domination if it also undertakes this work of 'subjectification'. Foucault's term *assujetissement* carries this two-fold significance. (HS: 60)

The notion of *pouvoir-savoir* satisfies this prerequisite in the following way. Subjectivities are constituted by and rendered instrumental to a particular form of power through the medium of the orders of discourse 'immanent' to that form of power. *Autre pouvoir, autre savoir* (DP: 226). Thus, the commemorative discourses of Sovereign power (genealogies, ballads, heraldry) and its ceremonial rituals institute a 'memorable man': to be individualized is to be famous (or infamous). It is a privilege enjoyed by and large only 'where sovereignty is exercised and in the higher echelons of power'. In a 'reversal of the political axis of individualization', discipline in effect 'lowered the threshold of describable individuality and made of this description a means of control . . . .' (DP: 191–2) it makes *calculable* individuals of us all.

The human individual constructed in such discourses is calculable to the extent of being subject to comparative, scalar measures and related forms of training and correction. The objective of disciplinary techniques is normalization. They homogenize individuals whilst simultaneously individualizing their objects insofar as individuals deviate from the norms of such populations. That is, the child is more individualized than the adult, the insane and delinquent more than the normal, and normal, healthy law-abiding adults are individualized not, as in times past, by illustrious deeds but by their secret singularities, fantasies, failures. The modern individual is the product of a power which individualizes those on whom it is exercised in proportion as it becomes itself anonymous, eschewing the symbolic trappings and spectacles of Sovereign power (ibid: 192–194).

What distinguishes Foucault's treatment of these frequently rehearsed motifs of anonymity, objectification and so forth is that no appeal is made (at least *prima facie*) to a prior human ethical subjectivity whose *in*calculable essence discipline threatens to envelope in a straitjacket of conformity. That which *resists* normalization far from simple representing an obstacle is the *sine qua non* of discipline's operation, discipline does not merely repress individual differences, and offend against humanist virtues, but rather produces them as its supports.

Subjectivism in political theory is not restricted to the treatment of human beings; all political forces may be treated like subjects in political discourse. In Foucault, however, power is not the stake of independently constituted political forces. Nor are they simply made dependent on forms of power, rather Foucault in a sense brackets them off. For instance, his account of Sovereign power in Absolutist France pays no regard to major political forces of the day, the Court at Versailles, the Church, Parlements, seigneural courts and so on, even where they bear directly on his main theme — the form of Absolutist punishment and its popular supports.[6] Rather the concept of *pouvoir-savoir* bids him lead off with the question of the form in which power is exercised. From this theoretical choice (conceived as being between the problematics of the exercise and possession of power) flows its relational, symbiotic character.

A form of exercise of power may be defined by the nature of the resistances it produces, confronts, fixes in place and manages. The multiple points of resistance established by an ensemble of power relations thus play the role of *support* as well as that of adversary or target. Resistances are always already implicated in power relations as their 'irreducible vis-à-vis' (HS: 96).

They derive their means of struggle, their very social location from the prevailing form of power. We have then a distribution of heterogenous interdependent possibilities and forms of exercising power within a 'strategic field' of relations (HS: 95—6), an ensemble of powers that cross-cuts the distinction between the haves and the have nots. It follows that main force or repression *may* be marginal to, at all events not essential to the successful exercise of power. That may depend as much on the promotion of some kinds of resistance as on the effectiveness of the means mobilized against them. This means — particularly since if resistances or forms of individuality are promoted by power this is to the detriment or exclusion of more unstabling forms — that *un*successes in the exercise of power cannot be simply registered as such. Tactical failure may be accounted in more than one sense, a strategic advantage.

In what senses and with what theoretical implications we shall see shortly. Here I want to sketch out Foucault's points about the economy of power and the non-essential role of repression. Foucault's perspective on the repression and emancipation of sexualities may be read as raising, and providing one answer to the difficulties (on which see Coward 1978: 9—11) of evaluating movements of sexual liberation, and of formulating political objectives in the whole area of sexual relations using categories drawn from the register of oppression or repression (repressive tolerance, desublimation, etc). His focus on the development within and between the very institutions associated with sexual oppression of organised rituals of obligatory sexual confession might well make possible a less celebratory assessment of, say, certain rituals of 'coming out'. How adequate is the view of this as the freeing of a hitherto undisclosed experience, the assertion of a true sexual identity? 'Coming out' as *a* bisexual, a lesbian or whatever, implies speaking out. One is then caught up in a quite specific range of discourse and patterns of behaviour which are no less obligatory and determinate, for their 'informal' nature, in the absence, that is, of any 'institutional' locations or sanctions. Voluntary organizations such as consciousness-raising groups may well share a number of characteristics with psychiatry and related disciplines of 'the apparatus of sexuality'.

Attention is here being drawn not to some necessary unavailability of 'official' discourses to progressive causes, to the political invalidity of *sans culottisme* as such, but to the possibility that posing progress in the sexual domain in terms of liberation may be tactically naive. The language of homosexuals' medical disqualification may be effectively adopted by its intended targets to constitute a 'counter-discourse' employed on the rebound (*discours en retour*) to effect their 'social' requalification (HS: 101–2). This might affect the strategic place of homosexuality in the current configuration of sexual relations, partially removing it from the category of socially dangerous deviant sexualities. But *that* place was never simply *'anti*-social'. Or rather, as such it was located within the particular domain of 'the social' constituted, by among others, the administrative-legal-psychiatric-pedagogical 'apparatus of sexuality'. Homosexuality does not cease to be a deviation suitable for treatment (isolation, control including a good measure of repression) if under certain conditions self-management is the order of the day. Perhaps the dilemmas of 'political' as opposed to 'closet' gay teachers or public figures exemplify the way making one's sexuality public may be instrumental to the very power it seeks to defy. At least the possibility must be faced that coming out is not invariably an effective recipe for changing the current order of sexual relations.

It is respecting just such possibilities that Foucault describes the discourse of *pouvoir-savoir* as, 'tactical blocks in a field of force relations' (ibid). Conflicting moves could be strategically complementary. Or the same discourse may circulate unaltered in opposed strategies. In any event Foucault's approach clarifies and renders problematic the unwitting, atactical character of current emancipatory 'social' requalifications of deviant sexualities.

This illustration of the dispersed economy of power and the limited role of repression will doubtless raise doubts in many people's minds, especially as concerns the strategic-cum-tactical aspect of *pouvoir-savoir*. In Foucault's book ensembles of power relations are identified and unified in terms of the 'strategy' in accordance with which they operate. What is identified here, re-

member, is a type of *exercise* of power. If these ensembles are nominated 'strategies'; then Foucault's use of this term is evidently not going to coincide with the usual range of political-cum-military connotations, which refer primarily to a *plan* of action. Foucault's notion of a strategy denotes a regularly reproduced *pattern of effects, including the (re-)drawing up of e.g. reformative plans.* Yet in some respects there is an overlap. For example there is a superficial, yet more than terminological affinity with Walker's (1972) 'strategic' approach to penal sentencing policy. The concept of strategy is ambiguous again in that it does not stand or fall with the adequacy of 'power relations'. In view of the centrality of 'strategy' to both of the positions which I argue can be constructed from Foucault's writings, a thumbnail exegesis of the term would be misleading at this stage. Pending detailed consideration of its theoretical and political implications in Parts III and IV below, it is more appropriate here to play the part of 'Doubting Thomas':
(i) How can a strategy be simultaneously intentional and yet non-subjective? (HS: 94—5).
(ii) If ensembles of power relations are identified as such by common strategy that informs them, what differentiates this term from a *principle* of identity and unity, a principle of intelligibility? Relatedly, what is its relation to discourse, notably to attempt to articulate strategies? If a strategy can be identified with particular proposals, how is it different from the juridico-discursive problematic's accordance of a controlling role to the discursive instance of the rule (HS: 83)?
(iii) How then can *strategy* and *tactics* be subject to a (methodological) rule of reciprocal or 'double' determination as Foucault claims (ibid: 100)? What does it mean to make *strategy* dependent for its very form on 'the specificity of possible tactics', such that these 'micro-powers' are not *derivable* from 'the logic of a global strategy' (ibid: 97), even if the local focii (*foyers locals*) of power depend on such an overarching 'strategic envelope' in order to function? Can the two forms of determination really be at par and do they not contradict each other?
(iv) For if strategy is conditioned by tactics this implies that the global character of a strategy belongs to the order of effects. It is contingent on the success of a variety of tactical interventions. Is the contingency of tactics compatible with the fact that if power is defined by the forms of 'resistance' it institutes, then 'power' must designate both the relation in question and one of its terms (Poulantzas, 1978: 150). The question is of course whether and how a form of power so defined can ever lose, whether opposition is not necessarily confined to resistance immanent to *a* strategy? Is not failure here always necessarily strategic? In which case the

polymorphous character imputed to tactics is gestural. Tactics would be variant expressions of a controlling strategy, and power would have exactly the unitary character Foucault began by attacking. If power forms subjects, the question arises, *what* is enveloped and thereby 'subjectified' through power relations? Social agents cannot after all be identified with their 'subjective' attributes or 'soul', which Foucault characterizes as a 'real albeit incorporal element in which the effects of a certain type of power are articulated, and the reference of a body of knowledge' (DP: 29). His answer to the above question is: power operates on the body, attempting to master its forces. We thus arrive at the reason for Foucault's alternately terming strategies 'techniques' or technologies and his own project, a political 'anatomy', and through that, at his project for a genealogy of morals. For Foucault's proposal is that the genealogy of 'the individual' celebrated in modern social thought be written as a 'political history of the body', i.e. a genealogy of the investment of human bodies by a variety of 'political technologies'. In this perspective the individual, person human subject or whatever — as distinct (ethically and epistemologically) — from an order of physical entities — is identified as the product of discipline and its willing 'self-disciplined' instrument. This 'soul' is specified through an analysis of the discourses immanent to these technologies of power, and this means in particular the 'social' sciences and their 'disciplinary' precursors.

To implicate the human sciences in procedures of social control is scarcely original and Foucault's endeavour in this direction is not unproblematic. One thing that sets it apart is his emphasis, derived from Nietzsche's concept of genealogy, on the diversity of the 'roots' whose confluence produces the disciplinary mode of exercise of power. Demonstrating as it does how elements of this form of power arise and combine in a variety of originally marginal institutions such as monastries, maritime hospitals, Jesuit and military colleges and in isolated cases, in nascent capitalist enterprises, *Discipline and Punish* refuses the idea that the 'disciplinary' institutions are essentially capitalist in origin and nature. Rather capitalist economy and pro-capitalist politics are related to disciplinary forms by a variety of mutual dependencies (DP: 220—221).

To appreciate the intricacies of Foucault's project, some further discussion is necessary. Firstly in order to elucidate and build on the 'strategic' analysis of social relations it is necessary to locate the extent to which Foucault's approach is tied to his retention of power as a theoretical category and relatedly, whether and if so why, a genealogical approach is necessary to make those social (power) relations intelligible. For this it is necessary to refer to

Nietzsche's writings. Secondly, to understand the discursive mechanism of *pouvoir-savoir* we must refer to some of the concepts for
the description of discourse and positions for agents of discourse
elaborated in the *Archaeology of Knowledge* (1972).

II Foucault, Nietzsche and the genealogy of morals

It would be misleading to place the entire responsibility for the
limitations of Foucault's 'genealogies of morals' on to their
Nietzschean dimension. One can in fact make some telling points
from at least one (anarchic) Nietzschean standpoint *against*
Foucault's treatment of modern power relations, as Rajchmann
(1978) has shown, and this precisely on account of what Foucault
does *not* take from Nietzsche. Nevertheless there are at least four
major and interconnected theoretical problems associated with the
concept of *pouvoir-savoir* and the form of historical discourse
(genealogy) to which it gives rise, which a consideration of their
'Nietzschean' filiations may illuminate.

Firstly, social (power) relations in being construed as forms of
pouvoir-savoir are necessarily periodized in an historicist manner.
Historicism in Foucault is bound up with his preoccupation with a
problem of modernity, in the result that only two fundamentally
different forms of power are conceivable and these can only *be*
conceived in a 'before-and-after' retrospectivist manner.

Secondly, the problem with the concept of a will-to-knowledge
is that it retains a 'representational' conception of discourse. Both
forms of *pouvoir-savoir* presuppose representing subjects constituted independently of the discursive orders of which their subjectivity was theoretically to have been the effect.

Thirdly, *pouvoir-savoir* is a problematic notion to the extent that
it entails a relational totality, the relations in question being essentially relations of domination. This means (i) confining political
analysis to the identifying of means of subjection and (ii) exclud-
ing the possibility of forms of individuality or positions for and
attributes of social agents which are not the exclusive 'property' of
the dominant ensemble of power relations. The 'power' of Foucauldian power relations to constitute subjects is as unconditional
as that of the subjects of mainstream political thought to constitute
power relations.

The fourth problem is the obverse of the third. Having bracketed
off political forces in the course of framing the problem of *assujetissement* Foucault provides no new way of reconceiving them save
for a nebulous concept of the forces of a political subjectivity
based on properties of the body. We thus return to the first point,
the problem of historicism. Disciplinary technique answers to the

question of the intelligibility of 'modern' societal action as a whole
on an originary (political, hedonistic) body-individual. We have returned therefore through a series of deviations to the antinomies
and themes of the old philosophical problem of order. To back up
the first point about the connection between genealogical enquiry
and *pouvoir-savoir* (and its historicist consequences) let us try as a
preliminary to reconstruct Nietzsche's approach to the domain of
morals and to place Foucault's project in relation to it. For the
purposes of my argument, these tasks may be combined by outlining just three ways in which Nietzsche and Foucault differ over
the periodization of the history of morals.

In Nietzsche[7] the essential division is between a 'natural' prehistory, that of the morality of mores and its product, the 'sovereign' conscience of the human individual, and an *un*natural history
of cultural 'decadence' which Nietzsche identifies with the domination of the will to power of the Judaeo-Christian religious tradition. These 'slave' moralities are unnatural in the sense of being a
will to power which denies its true nature as such. Christianity in
particular turns naturally self-overcoming human instincts back on
to their possessors; it forces men to lacerate the animal side of their
nature; thus it moralizes the sovereign conscience, transforming
the hard-won privilege of 'the right to make promises' and a
certain 'memory of the will' (the products of prehistory)[8] into the
'gnawing worm' of the *bad* conscience. Master moralities build on
the instinctual prehistoric labour of the morality of mores. Slave
moralities 'help' the weak, the underprivileged (and incidentally
help to keep them that way).

Nietzsche establishes these differences by a combination of
philosophical argument and philology. Whereas the difference between sovereign and disciplinary power is at least partly established
by an historical argument, they partly conform to recognizable
historiographical landmarks (the politics of French Absolutism,
the 'social' consolidation of capitalism, etc). The Judaeo-Christian
tradition may mark an historical era in some discourses, but not in
Nietzsche's. Foucault transposes Nietzsche's concepts and problems,
which are got up to deal with philosophical representations of
morality, into a form amenable to particular historical enquiries.
'Archaeology' indeed requires such an historical (-geographical)
anchorage (1972: 117).

This difference is related to a second, which concerns their
respective treatment of humanism. Nietzsche's various polemical
targets share an attachment to the 'ascetic' ideals of Christianity.
Humanist philosophies and values are treated either as poor sur-
rogates for it or else as wily subterfuges, testifying to its tenacity.
In Foucault 'the modern soul' is sharply distinguished from the

Christian one. Considering its indifference to the well-being of the body and its concern with spiritual salvation, the Christian soul is situated in a pre-disciplinary era, prior to that of *biopouvoir*, a 'relative mastery over life' (HS: 142). The social disciplines transform both the traditional soul and the traditional religious deprecation of the body. No longer the latter's prisoner, the soul-unity is made an instrument for rendering the body docile, reducing it as a political force, the better to maximize it as a useful force (DP: 221). The critical force of Foucault's genealogies is thus specifically anti-humanist. The timeless subject of humanist ethics, social science, etc, in Foucault's book is an instrument and effect of discipline, the barely two hundred years old 'prison of the body' (ibid: 30).

Lastly, in Nietzsche the human subject is the product of a power (the will to power of the morality of mores) which is invariably at once repressive *and* 'productive' (Nietzsche, 1969: 58—9). In Foucault these two aspects of will to power are split up and distributed to sovereign and disciplinary power respectively. (Rajchman, op. cit.)

We may now begin to see why Foucault's concept of power, insofar as it derives from *will to power*, necessarily leads in the direction of genealogy. Judaeo-Christian morals do not merely represent one possible form of will to power but an *un*natural form which negates its essential nature. Two points may be made regarding the 'nature' to which Nietzsche appeals when he identifies the will to power with it (all, not only human, life as a perpetual movement of self-overcoming). First, it has a simultaneously *a*historical and pre-historical status. At least one attribute of human subjectivity, the 'memory of the will', (and hence the right to make promises; the key to the powers of reason and purposiveness) is an evolutionary product of the morality of mores. The bloody and cruel social practices associated with the latter are accounted to instinct; to a natural pre-history. Moreover the latter continues into civilized, decadent times (1969: 71). Nietzsche's attempt to have it both ways, to pose the form of morals (master morality) most in keeping with 'true' will to power as both the product of a history and as a natural origin, must be set besides a second feature of Nietzsche's 'naturalism'. Nietzchean nature is a *'de-deified'* nature (1974: 169), which is to say it is constructed by stripping the standard philosophical concept of nature of all its Judaeo-Christian accretions, as once and for all Divine creation, in some sense a complete, law-like order; and then inverting these characteristics to produce a concept of nature (equals will to power), which is as unChristian as Christianity is unnatural.

This circularity is crucial to at least one way Nietzsche's discourse on power works. It is equally clear from the 'Second Essay' that the way the impression of the natural superiority of one form of power over the other is created and validated is *via* the genealogy of morals which discovers them and provides them with a supposed historical, concrete anchorage. The necessity of the genealogical approach to Nietzsche's concept of will to power is bound up with this 'diacritical' definition of the forms of power, and with the implication of that circularity, which restricts the forms of power to two. In fact if genealogy and will to power dovetail, this is because they compensate for each others's deficiencies. One deficiency of Nietzschean genealogy in particular may be brought out. This will bring us back to Foucault's genealogies.

A genealogical dilemma

The dilemma is how genealogy should proceed, in view of a discrepancy between its methodological point of departure and its critical-cum-moral goal, a 'revaluation of all values' in Nietzsche's case. Genealogy treats moralities as so many masks, 'sign-systems', which are by no means directly revelatory of the practices associated with them but conceal their nature, i.e. their will to power, or at most betray or manifest it, e.g. where Nietzsche discerns the 'cruelty' in the 'bloodless' rationalism of Kantian ethics (1969: 65). The object is to unmask such moral interpretations of phenomena and this, by enquiring into their conditions of emergence of these moralities. Genealogy discloses the immoral bases of morals (Nietzsche, 1973: 15). This is not a 'scientific' discovery; there are no moral phenomena, only moral interpretations (1972: 55); interpretations are signs of a will to power. Genealogical 'interpretation' in Nietzsche's sense then involves a revaluation of all values which dichotomize good and bad into two essentially distinct orders whereby evil, sin, and transgression, have a purely negative significance.

What sort of historical discourse could have this critical force? Nietzsche distinguishes his historical method from that of teleological histories of morals which write history backwards, under the assumption that the emergence of e.g. a punitive practice can be explained by reference to some unitary current utility or moral justification. In contrast to this identification of origins and outcome Nietzsche's starting point is that 'the cause of the origin of a thing and its eventual unity, its actual employment and place in a system of purposes, lie worlds apart'. (1969: 77).

Genealogy discovers not one unitary ultimate justification but a variety of either amoral or immoral origins. These are subject to contingent mutations and displacements and hence are irreducible to a single trajectory of development. Their confluence produces the practice in question. Needless to say these origins are as unedifying as they are unsuspected.

Yet genealogy of morals must also posit an essential connection between origins and outcome or else where could be the critical point of the enterprise? Reconstructing the prehistory of a practice may only serve as a vehicle of critical-moral instruction if that prehistory discloses its real nature. So which way is genealogy to go, since its critical objective seems to necessitate the very identification of origins and outcome that genealogical method begins by refusing? Here then is the dilemma. It can remain faithful to its methodological starting point and maintain the dissociation of origins and outcome, in which case its moral-critical presumption falls down since origins are no longer constitutive of their product. The alternative is to insist on the constitutivity of origins, but then the original grounds for distinguishing genealogy from teleological history collapse. Either genealogy remains a variant on teleological history or it is irrelevant by its own standard of relevance.

Both the validity and the force of this argument may be doubted. Why do these alternatives exhaust the possibilities? Surely there is a place for genealogical investigation which does not assume conditions of emergence to be necessarily constitutive of a practice, determining all its parameters, its possible mutations, etc., in short its identity, from the outset. There is no need to assume *a priori* that the genesis of a practice has any bearing whatsoever on its current operation. Rather it suffices for genealogy if, in some instances, some of the constituents of a current practice may be illuminated by genealogical enquiry. Genealogy comes into its own if currently operative 'disciplinary' strategies, sinister interests, or whatever, were originally proposed or put into effect with a frankness that is no longer manifest, in their current expression. For instance an 'ideological' analysis of crucial parts of Frederick Taylor's classic *Scientific Management* would be virtually superfluous, since the intentions of Taylorist managerial techniques, the status of these techniques as means of struggle relating to augmenting the 'effective possession' of capitalist means and conditions of production is quite explicit. Traces of Taylorist techniques of control may well be discerned in modern production engineering manuals and production processes notwithstanding their merely technical appearance, without its being the case either that such industrial techniques are intrinsic to capitalist relations and forces of production alone or that such modern production engineering is reducible to these techniques.

Clearly then there is genealogy and genealogy. Once remove certain *a priori* totalizing assumptions and the foregoing 'dilemma' may at most apply to Nietzschean genealogy. What then is the point of setting up the dilemma, or rather of reconstructing the logical discrepancy between method and objective *as* a dilemma? Well, framing it thus would help to account for the bi-polar retrospective structure of genealogy of morals, if this structure may be viewed as an attempt to resolve the said dilemma. The theoretical problem is how to realize the moral critical purpose of genealogy by genealogical methods. The problem is resolved if the differences genealogy constructs are themselves morally and critically significant. The condition of possibility of this compromise is that these differences should have the form of 'diacritical', binary antitheses. In other words these differences will be morally instructive if and only if, in Foucault's terms, ensembles of power relations are so interdefined that one form of power is specified through a contrast with, and by registering the absence of, the characteristics of its antithesis. In fact, the work of inter-definition involved here is not quite so straightforwardly circular. To say that this conceptual structure limits forms of power to two, is to say that any account at all governed by this structure is bound to subsume a variety of, say, forms of law and punishment under the one *negative* rubric. (What unites these forms of power is solely their not possessing the characteristics of the 'modern' form, e.g. their not representing forms of 'bio-power'.)

To cap the argument, we have only to point out how snugly the circularity of the Nietzschean concept of power fits the dilemma of genealogy, since as we saw the concept of will to power is so constructed as to admit of only two diametrically opposed exemplifications, the one that affirms its essential nature, and the one that 'denegates' it. Here are a set of differences with which genealogy can work. Concommittantly the Nietzschean concept of power can only be used in a more or less speculative, 'historical' discourse on social life. Historical, in that such discourses (whether or not they recount a story, a transformation or whatever) can only specify social forms as either 'modern' or 'traditional'. Speculative in that it involves charting the 'outcome' of analysis in advance. For a Nietzschean grid-reading, genesis is of necessity constitution.

Foucault's genealogy: either/or

Does Foucault's project partake of this bi-polar structure? To decide this issue, consider firstly the ambiguous status of the juridico-discursive conception of power. In places, Foucault definitely

identifies the actual mode of operation of sovereign power with
its 'ideological' expressions in Absolutist legal principles and penal
symbolism. Power in the jurisprudence of natural law (e.g. Pufen-
dorf) emanates from the Sovereign who disposes over the life
and death of all his subjects. Its vehicle is a 'symbolics of blood'
(HS: final chapter). Yet in DP the discussion of the Absolutist
power to punish is conducted in a relational mode. The royal
power depends for its functioning on a set of popular 'infra-
powers', for instance the great punitive spectacles require elaborate 'scaffold services' (DP: 59) which the populace might demand
as of right or refuse to perform in the event of an unpopular
conviction; to say nothing of the extensive 'margin of tolerated
illegality' from which all social strata derived benefit (ibid: 82).

The identification of Absolutist power and the juridico-discursive conception is not an isolated slip. A 'relational' treatment of
Absolution cannot be sustained, as will be clear when we consider
the diametrically opposite sort of ambiguity which prevails in respect of disciplinary power.

This in places is so specified as to accord with the general conception of power relations, as in Foucault's characterization of
hierarchized surveillance (DP: 176–177), where

> power . . . is not possessed . . . or transferred as a property . . .
> (cf Absolutist power) . . . although . . . its pyramidal organi-
> zation gives it a 'head' it is the apparatus as a whole that pro-
> duces 'power' and distributes individuals in this permanent
> and continuous field. . . . Discipline makes possible the opera-
> tion of a relational power. . . .

What follows from these two identifications is a tendency to conceptualize law (and also symbolic forms) in modern societies as
residual domains. Law as such is an essence, the 'highest instance'
of the Absolutist regime. Today law is pertinent just insofar as it
is enveloped and its essential, traditional modes of operation
recast by the 'infra-legal' disciplines 'which should be regarded as a
sort of counter-law (DP: 222–3; cf. also DP: 16–22, 227 and
HS: 144).[9] Power is no longer, except residually, expressed through
a 'symbolics of blood' (HS: 147) but through an asymbolic 'analytic of sexuality' (on which see Rajchman, op. cit.).

Returning to Foucault's treatment of the relations of Absolutism the difficulty is that a thoroughly relational account of pre-
disciplinary power requires the specification of certain forms of
assujetissement which the necessarily genealogical form of development of this concept of subjection does not permit. The reason
is that if a consistently relational account of Absolutist power
were sustained, then the subsequent account of the emergence
and 'swarming' (DP: 211) of disciplines could not get going.

On Foucault's own account of Absolutist power, the King's subjects must somehow be 'interpellated' . . . as *spectators*, if the 'political operation' of ceremonial punishment is to function. Is popular 'interest' in the condemneds' last words, in the fate of their souls hereafter, and so on, to be attributed to some unconditional Renaissance experience? If not, there must be forms of discourse, art and ritual available to constitute 'ignoble', undistinguished, forms of individuality.

The general reason for Foucault's silence on this matter bears on his committment to the problem of the constitution of the human subject, which I have argued elsewhere (Adams and Minson, 1978: 46–50), cannot be coherently posed. Foucault's genealogical 'approach' to modern morals represents an ingenious attempt to evade the circularity in which this problem is inevitably caught. How may the subject-as-effect not be resolved into an originary unity and presupposed in its own explanation?

No doubt in Foucault's book 'the subject' is the progeny of the very techniques of normalization which according to pessimistic humanist cultural critics and social scientists threaten to envelop it totally. However, the price of this achievement is the collapsing of all forms of individuality and all questions of the formation of particular subjective attributes or of the agents of specific social relations into the problem of the formation-cum-regulation of *the* subject, and the subsequent identification of subjectivity-in-general with the object, target, instrument and effect of disciplinary *pouvoir-savoir*.

This conflation is apparent in the characterization of disciplinary *assujetissement* as involving a 'reversal in the political axis of individualization'. Yet surely *that* contrast — between memorable and calculable individuality — need not coincide with Absolutist and disciplinary *assujetissement*. As subjection, power individuates the (ig)noble or (in)famous few under Absolutism and, latterly, the previously anonymous compact popular masses, now a known quantity of 'separated individualities' (DP: 201). Subjectivity under Absolutism is an ascribed status, under discipline it is incorporated into its human supports as an essential identity. Nevertheless, by definition *assujetissement* forms human identities. However, pre-humanist commemorative discourses, rituals, etc., did not only individualize human beings but *inter alia* families, clans, gods, angels, guilds, cats and horses. Following these conflations, the formation of particular categories of social agent and associated sensibilities can only be framed as a problem for analysis if they are the focus of some dominant formative 'power-knowledge'. For instance there could be no specifically 'Renaissance' forms of sexuality unless they pertain to the genealogy of the panopoly of sexologies, the transformations in domestic architecture, and (primarily) the discourses which construct sexuality as the privileged object of *scientiae sexualis*.[10]

Whence the explanation of Foucault's silences. For the account of disciplinary *assujetissement* to get going, *some prior non-subjective material is required for it to work on*. This precondition is satisfied by a naturalistic (e.g. sexually undifferentiated) adamic 'body' whose unruly pre-discursive pleasures and powers are an irrepressible fount of 'political' force even for discipline, as the recent prison unrest testifies: 'revolts at the level of the body, against the very body of the prison' (DP : 30).[11]

In fact pre-disciplinary body individuals are pre-social in a more fruitful sense too. In the Foucauldian account, various forms of what would otherwise naturally be termed social relations are conceptualized as pre-social: this is the theoretical status of the popular masses (DP: 201), and of 'the apparatus of alliances' (HS: 106) together with the 'blocs of dependence' and 'networks of solidarity' which in Donzelot (1977: 49) characterise pre-disciplinary family relations in terms of their relations to various economic, political and local community practices. These categories are pre-social in that they predate the particular domain of 'the social' which is constituted in biopolitical 'social' politics and programmes from the eighteenth century onwards. Foucauldian genealogies inevitably concern the birth of 'the social' correlative with that of 'the individual', its orderly milieu, and the province of those familial, assistantial, insurantial, and carceral practices which recast the old private-public divisions as they 'police' the health and security of individuals. (On the 'old-fashioned' meaning of 'police' see Pasquino (1978).)

The strength of Foucault's claim rests on its promising identification of the 'social' domain in this restricted sense, a sense which does not depend on the bipolar retrospective structure of *pouvoir-savoir*. In my forthcoming study of Foucault's genealogies detailed demonstrations of the grid-readings which flow from this structure will be provided (Minson, 1980). For the time being, we consider for the purposes of illustration an aspect of Foucault's essentialist treatment of judicial torture, while noting that analogous points could be made against his treatment of 'punishment for suspicion'.

Foucault's reconstruction of the Absolutist penal system in DP revolves around the eighteenth century reformer's humanist misconceptions on the one hand and various contemporary legal texts on the other. The latter are read, for the most part, merely as inversions of humanist valuations. As a corrective to the received view of Absolutist law as barbaric, irrational, arbitrary and so on, DP is invaluable. Nevertheless the non-'humanist' elements of the 1670 French Ordinance, on which Foucault draws heavily, are not all of a piece. For instance its inclusion of judicial (investigative) torture among the punishments was an innovation in Absolutist legal discourse, which according to the legal historian Langbein, testifies to the silent emergence of a subsidiary system of proof, the *poena extraordinaria*, alongside the late medieval Roman-canon system. Whereas the latter necessitated investigative torture the former, by and by, made it redundant. When torture *began* to be legally classified as also one punishment among others (as in the 1670 Ordinance), this was the signature of its fate, a tacit invitation to the courts not to use it.

One condition of possibility of this 'revolution in the law of proof' (Langbein, 1977) was the emergence of new, if scarcely humanitarian or 'corrective' (ibid: 31–2) forms of punishment for serious crime such as galley service in the Royal fleet. 'Perpetual' or 'determinate' galley service, ran the message of the 1670 Ordinance, could be imposed '. . . on the same quantum of circumstantial evidence for which medieval law permitted only investigation under torture to obtain full proof' (ibid: 59). Judicial torture (and the 'patient's' confession) became redundant when compelling circumstantial evidence could be deemed sufficient to convict for serious crime, and the 'free judicial evaluation of the evidence' which this presupposed (and which the Roman-cannon law system ruled out or at least attempted to minimize), could be deemed permissible. The crucial point to note is that these conditions of possibility for the abolition of torture simply do not figure in the reformers' calculations, which simply rehash inconsequential, centuries old reservations and offer no realistic alternatives (even those which already existed!). Foucault misses this transformation in the law of evidence too and consequently only reinforces the customary historical overestimation of the reformers' role in securing the abolition of torture (and also the 'blood sanctions'). Instead we get a critical gloss, in terms of power, on their humanist motivations and objectives.

The point of the form of criticism mounted here is to draw attention to certain classes of phenomena which Foucaldian genealogy appears to exclude in principle. Langbein's arguments concerning the law of proof and the 'fairy-tale' concerning its abolition might be disproved, but it would remain that to construe law in terms of *pouvoir-savoir* is to render such changes in legal discourse and their consequences invisible. Law is the symbolic expression of Sovereign will or it is residual, its non-symbolic effectivity depending on its investment by 'infra-legal' techniques. Drawing this part of the analysis to a close, I now propose to consider a more general problem of the category power in which Foucault is caught and indicate means by which it can be avoided.

Is power a theoretical problem?

Reference has been made to Foucault's silence respecting a variety of specific Absolutist discourses. The problem does not only arise vis-à-vis the populace but, also in connection with the conflicting political forces in the Absolutist legal-political-religious arena which, as we noted, (p. 9 and n.6 above), he brackets off. Why should all the discourses (and the social practices of which they are a part) which were available at that time to constitute and support various categories of agent, their attributes and objectives; religious believers, witches, lawyers, landowners, etc., be immanent to *a* dominant form of power?

This problem is a general one, which relates to the construction of political forces as well as individual human agents. Power, contrary to Nietzsche's dictum, be it taken as empirical generalization on life in general, true of amoebas and men alike, or a statement on the logic of the concept power, does not necessarily thrive on resistance. Therefore, all means, objectives and points or resistance cannot be construed as necessarily invested in the dominant form of power, Foucault himself understands the global character of power, as we saw, as an effect (cf. also HS: 99—100). If the limits to its successful diffusion were determined immanently, there could only ever be one form of power.

This problem pertains to any concept of power employed in an explanatory capacity, whether or not it be construed as a possession. Not all the elements of a political conflict are attributable to some particular political force. Rather the latter may derive strength from strategies of 'government' which are not the property of any 'side'. However why must we choose between conceiving power as a function of either its possession *or* its exercise? We might refuse to treat possession as a unitary function, and construe, say, the differential effectivity of legislation or democratic constraints in terms of forms of possession. But if a legally invested right is effective, its effectiveness cannot be *explained* by reference to the particular form of either possession *or* exercise of some power. Whether an Act has 'teeth', whether, for instance, legislation to reorganize the NHS could be so framed as to ensure the provision of abortion at least within the terms of the 1967 Abortion Act, depends on its capacity to overcome resistance from various quarters ranging from feeling within sections of the medical and nursing professions, NHS organizational considerations, to pressure on MP's via Party constituency organization by antiabortionists. Recognizing that not all these sources of opposition are locatable in terms of means and conditions of struggle peculiar to *specific* political forces, but may be attributable to 'technical' practices and relations in the social services and elsewhere with equally formidable political consequences, is important and central to the contribution Foucault's ideas can make to any socialist political analysis. But in accounting for, or calculating on, the outcome of such an NHS Reorganization Act, *what* is exercised or possessed more or less effectively in the course of the construction, passage and implementation of the legislation is not power as such. *That* can only be the conditional *product* of the clash of the forces, policies and means of action involved.

I submit that the concept of power lacks any explanatory force or theoretical significance. Nothing can be explained in terms of power because on any understanding, one thing (be it political subject, economic structure or whatever) must be attributed the unconditional capacity to dominate another. Rendering power as an attribute with a causal efficacy means that the outcomes of (power) struggles must be either deducible in advance from the power attributes of the forces or relations involved, or else beyond calculation altogether, inexplicable. For power-as-attribute is un-limited. To set conditions on a capacity to dominate is to deny that a thing *has* that capacity. We may use the military-political thought of Mao in illustration of this implication.

Mao's notorious dismissal in 1946 of atomic weapons as 'paper tigers' was based on the view that Clausewitzian military principles are not obsolete in the age of nuclear power. In particular, war remains an instrument of political policy and defence retains its advantages over attack. It is not to deny the proven efficacity, under *some* modern conditions of anti-imperialist people's wars, if we reject the move from considering the political constraints on the use of nuclear weapons to dismissing them as a mere scare-tactic, and locating the real power equally unconditionally elsewhere: 'The outcome of a war is decided by the people, not by one or two types of weapons' (cited in Glucksmann, 1968: 37).

What we may distill out of the foregoing arguments is that both the bifurcated order of freedom and its antithetical correlate, determinism as an objective realm of necessary effects, must be cast aside. Instead, 'powers' might be conceived as *differential advantages* (or disadvantages) regarding the possibility of social agents being successful in realizing certain objectives, particularly, wherever the compliance and support of other agents is a prerequisite. It is not necessary to construe those differential advantages and disadvantages such as popular aspirations, morale, responsibilities, principles, rights or virtues as essential human or subjective factors belonging to a moral domain. Rather it is possible to treat these phenomena of the moral or personal life as always determined by the specific discourses and social relations in which they are formed and where they exercise definite, albeit limited effects.

They are no less 'objective' or more conditional than a police-man's power of arrest or the power of a gun to penetrate a body or of a manager to sack an employee. Statutes, gun manufacturers' instructions, manuals of military drill stipulate or calculate powers. A clenched fist or a muscular physique may symbolize powers. But these signified powers, *pace* Foucault, are not of themselves productive of anything. Moreover their possession and exercise from some standpoints may represent positive disadvantages with respect to the attainment of certain objectives. Whilst signi-fied powers are not automatically effective, as Foucault himself emphasizes, they implicate agents as supports. They may be effec-tive in ways which their agent supports, by virtue of their partaking of other discourses and practices, may not want. The discussion of the familial powers of women below will illustrate this point.

The point of the displacement of power by differential advant-ages (and of human or moral subjects by categories of social agent) may be seen to good effect when we consider some of the 'archaeo-logical' aspects of *pouvoir-savoir*, some of which are locked into the problemàtic of power I want to set aside, some of which are not.

III Archaeology and problems of social agency

'The human soul is made of paper'. In Tournier's fable (1974: 35) the consequence of a benevolent person's destroying all official written files on individuals is their gradual adoption of brutish ways. Like Tournier's papier-maché man, the human soul which on Foucault's account is constructed by the social disciplines as their common 'reality-reference' (DP: 29) is a biographical entity; the product of a panopoly of petty techniques invented in the eighteenth century and which Foucault groups under the general heading of examination: a combination of hierarchical surveil-lance and normalizing judgement. These techniques, employed in hospitals, barracks, schools and private homes constitute indi-viduals as 'cases', each with their own 'history'. A crucial condi-tion of possibility for the emergence of philosophical conceptions of both human beings and societies as essentially historical indi-viduals, and hence of social science, was the humble *exercise,* involving in all its forms a gradual inflection of deportment or of inculcated knowledge towards an ideal state (DP: 160–161). Exercise permits the genesis of its subjects to be traced and their future development organized and shaped in a continuous practice of writing and interrogation.

On all fours with 'examination' are the forms of individualiza-tion dependent on self-examination. Rituals of confession produce *assujetissement* by virtue of the presumptions of (i) coincidence of speaking subject and subject of the statement, hence (ii) another to whom one confesses, who interrogates, passes judgement, consoles, etc. (iii) resistances and their overcoming as testimony to the truth of confession and (iv) effects on the confessor produced by the act itself (blushing, emotional relief, spiritual joy) (HS: 61—2).

Examination and avowal: here we have two general discursive mechanisms for the formation of human subjectivity in its modern form. We have already noted some of the theoretical costs of this advance over other accounts, and the precariousness of the advance itself. If power evaporates as a theoretical problem so must *assujetissement*. The question then arises, how intrinsically are 'discursive practices' such as these forms of confession and examination and the very project of archaeology implicated in power-relations and Nietzschean genealogy? And following this, what remains of the project of a genealogy of morals, once the two totalities, power and the subject, are peeled off?

Genealogy traces the double genesis of the subject and disciplinary society in terms of a political history of the body, of its investment by power knowledges. Two ingredients of the project of archaeology are *prima facie* particularly discrepant with this project. Firstly, Foucault forever insists on the *limited* character of his archaeologies, which reconstruct specific configurations of statements, 'regions of interpositivity', and attempt to describe the historical conditions which made it possible for a statement in such a region to be uttered and there and then, in conjunction with certain statements and not others; to find the same 'rules of formation' operating uniformly in other contemporary 'regions' would signify a *failure* of archaeological descriptions, the recovery of a *Weltanschauung,* or some other brand of totality (Foucault, 1972: 158—9). Disciplinary society and the subject are surely just that.

But secondly, 'statements' are not given essentially as representations. Theoretically speaking, what Foucault tries to do in this (1972) book, by various means and with varying success, is to conceptualize discourse in a non-representational mode, to displace the oppositions of thought and being, word and object. Genealogy does no such thing. It appeals to an undifferentiated body as the point of application of domination and the forms of the latter (modalities of 'the power to punish') are analysed primarily as forms of representation (DP: 131). Thus we have in archaeology a project to describe the complex relations of coexistence and dispersion of limited groups of statements, and to trace their conditions of emergence, transformation and mutation.

Statements are treated as 'traces' (1972: 109), whose inter-relations and dependencies are to be described without reference to another order of being 'outside', either in (un)consciousness (as the source of their 'meaning') or in a domain of objects (ibid: 120–1). Statements and the discursive formations to which they belong are understood to have a material existence and effectivity. This materiality is both peculiar to discourse and yet in other respects at par with the materiality of the social relations and entities to which it refers and on which it depends in various ways. The ambiguity in the form of materiality that is claimed for discourse is reflected in the concept of discursive practice, a category which leads Foucault into difficulties, some of which are common to the genealogical problematic of power.

Discursive practice occupies a mysterious place, 'at the limit of discourse' (ibid: 46). Ultimately it is accorded the transcendent status which is traditionally accorded to subjectivity or the objective world. It is doubly reductive. Firstly it tends to subsume elements of social relations which are irreducible to discourse. For instance the subject fabricated in confession does *not* 'emerge only in discourse' (ibid: 47), but in certain confessional *rituals*, in one form of which specially constructed church furniture is a crucial ingredient. We say nothing of other social practice in which forms of discourse do not, as in confession, occupy a 'primary' place. On the other hand archaeology can be charged with reductivism in an opposite direction, namely that it reduces discourse *to* social relations. This occurs in a number of ways but most relevant to archaeology's genealogical affinities is its treatment of statements as *events*. Foucault presents the reader with the alternative of treating discourse as 'an ideal timeless form that also possesses a history' and as systematically dispersed events, historical 'from beginning to end' (ibid: 117). Needless to say, these alternatives do not exhaust the options. Canguilhem's work on the emergence of scientific concepts, e.g. his *Formation du concept de réflexe* (1955) testifies to that. In Foucault the 'discursive formations' to which statements are assigned comprise their *a posteriori* reconstructed conditions of possibility or historical *a prioris'*. If discourse is reduced to history, and its statement-events are, as noted above, reducible to social practice, then it is possible to see how Foucault, for all his hostility to construing discourse as essentially representative, reinstates the opposition of discursive and non-discursive in a genealogical reduction of discourse to a supposed non-discursive order of 'primary relations' (1972: 45).

Discursive formations and statements are subject to four different forms or levels of description, which one takes depends on which seems least straightforward (ibid: 65). None of Foucault's studies claim to be exhaustive of their chosen object. For instance, in his sketch of the rituals of confession in HS, the interest lies less in the formation of religious and therapeutic concepts than in the formation of the 'enunciative modalities' and 'objects' of sexual avowal. What does this mean?

Confessional rituals bring into relation at least two ensembles of discourses and a set of behavioral regulations. In each case what is prerequisite for the enunciation, efficacy and value of a confessional statement is the assignment of categories of social agent to definite positions. These 'enunciative' positions include the *sites* from which certain statements derive their source, point of application and authority and the *perceptual situations* it is possible to occupy in relations to domains of objects. Sites and perceptual situations are also allied to the *statuses* with which a discursive agent must be equipped to be entitled to make statements in a particular discourse. These determinants of subject positions Foucault terms the 'enunciative modalities' of statements. Not just anyone can receive or make a confession and the latter varies considerably, from the Catholic confessional (with its distinctive authoritarian 'perceptual situation' governing the form and order of interrogation and the 'patient's' verbal and facial responses) to the perpetual autobiography of Puritanism; from the exorcism of 'possessed' women to psychiatric therapy. The problem with these enunciative modalities is that as stated by Foucault they carry a subjective load which, however, they can arguably well do without.

Foucault insists (1972: 95) that *subject of a statement* is not to be identified with the authorial subject of a formulation. Yet he often writes as if such human persons are the bearers of these statuses, or the occupants or supports of perceptual positions (ibid: 50–55), as if there were but a series of sociological modifications of or external constraints on human perception. This line of thought is reinforced by the above-noted conception of a level of 'primary' relations between social forms which are 'independent of all discourse' (ibid: 45) and an eclectic specification of the conditions of emergence of discursive objects (vague talk of social processes, behavioural patterns, etc., on which see Williams (1974)). Yet in spite of this sociological overlay, Foucault does not return us to the old theoretical battlefield of social institutions and human subjects or persons.

For that to be the case a sixty-four thousand dollar question must be satisfactorily answered. This concerns *what* occupies this or that position in particular discourses, what is positioned and thus enabled or disabled as an agent of that or related discourses and the social relations of which they are a part. Moreover such 'positions for agents' are themselves constituted partly through discursive forms, instructions to priests, statutes, etc., and may not work out as they are supposed to. Agents themselves, of course, may, under certain conditions, transform or at least disconcert those positions. To illustrate the possibility of slipping the control of the ill-starred philosophical oppositions of freedom and determinism in accounting for these possibilities, we shall reconsider the avowal.

What are the effects of the above-mentioned *variations* in the confessional form on the 'enunciative modalities' proper to the making of statements on the side of *the one who comes to confess*? The form of the confessional intercourse will be radically affected by whether one comes *as a sinner* or under some general psychiatric designation. To put this point in Foucault's terms, 'the speaking subject', who in the general description of confession above is identified with 'the subject of the statement', must itself always be the bearer of specific 'statuses' if it is to figure in the confessional discourses on concupiscence or sins of the flesh, as opposed to those concerned with 'nervous' convulsions. So what comes to be positioned as a confessing agent is always one or more specific category of agent, albeit of a sufficiently general character to qualify the agent to figure in other social relations too. Here is a task for a genealogy of current morals which would investigate the construction not of subjectivity as such, but rather that of 'personal' categories, the human person, the child, mother, father, sexual identities, etc. as variously represented in ethical and 'social' discourses. To illustrate the non-given, and limited character of these general categories, let us see what this project implies in repsect of the child and the personal space of the family, drawing briefly on Donzelot's account.

The child, *qua* product of 'social' policies, is a category defined in terms of a variety of moral and physical dangers or insecurities from the standpoint of 'biopolitics' and ethico-religious discourses, which various extra-familial authorities are qualified to detect and treat, if the child's parents fail to secure his or her welfare unaided. This child 'in danger' (from servants, incestuous or violent parents, itself) is, as never before (Aries, 1973) 'socially' recognized as a moral individual, a legal person, a psychological being, in a variety of knowledges, and concommittantly as a corporal and/or mental resource which must be conserved and harnessed. The imputation of 'personality' a normal trajectory of 'development', etc., to the child was crucial to the 'involution' of the relational, geneaological form of family organization which began (in 'bourgeois' families) in the mid-eighteenth century and was extended (by different means) to the proletariat and the poor in the nineteenth (Donzelot 1977). The persecution of masturbation for instance is one of a series of 'child-oriented' campaigns which strategically were in fact directed equally at the conduct of better-off parents, and which imposed units of domestic 'personal' existence, that are simultaneously *cellular* and 'internally' differentiated according to 'external' norms. These 'norms' define frequently conflicting or unfulfillable responsibilities, competences and incompetences, sentimental and sexual orientations which are distributed to individual family members. It is these categories of individual, child, sister, mother, etc., with their conflicts, failures and the dangers they represent which provide the point of entry of 'outside' agencies and discourses. Whether through their complaints against particular family members, intervention, arbitration, regulation by specific 'social' agencies (divorce proceedings, family violence, ungovernable children) or through disputes in which appeal is made to more general familial 'normative' criteria, and which do not involve institutional interventions, it is these categories of individual familial agent who conduct disciplinary norms within the domestic setting. Unless their 'personality' is construed as a status, the sociality of the familial space itself is unintelligible. The 'social' instrumentality (limited but indispensable) of humanist ethical/legal categories such as person, consist in their role in constituting that strategic common ground on which familial problems, conflicts and failures can be staged. Consider 'women's place' as housewife and mother. Donzelot is not alone (see Cott, 1977) in documenting how a 'humanistically' justified promotion of the status of women, and the work to which they were said to be fitted was crucial to the emergence of the 'cellular' family and to the construction and positioning of women as housewives and mothers.

If the paring away of some paternal powers and the provisioning of women (and children) with definite rights and responsibilities and competences can be termed an equalization (Donzelot 1977; Trumbach, 1978), this term pertains strictly to their status as persons. The heterogenous 'social' practices which bestowed and recognized these 'powers' *privilege* familial agents over against each other: father, where e.g. housing and labour markets are concerned; mother, in respect of e.g. education, apparatuses of juvenile justice, the training of children and domestication of husbands.[12] Appeals to the realms of the personal in struggles to liberate women from these typecast domestic positions must be assessed in the light of the 'familialist' conditions of emergence of these categories. The 'powers' which attach to such positions may well be 'disadvantageous' from the standpoint of some

socialist and feminist objectives, but as has been argued elsewhere (Adams and Minson, 1978), with all their miserable consequences, these liabilities are not illusions foisted on 'brute'
persons.

One feature of Foucault's and Donzelot's approach worth
remarking in conclusion is its treatment of the social theories
and philosophical assumptions against which it is constructed.
Global conceptions of social relations and the concept of human
subject are not simply criticized but displaced on to the terrain
of social practices under investigation. Thus society as a totality
'governed' by some unifying principle in this perspective becomes
a defining mark and an asymptotic objective end, hence a functioning ingredient of certain disciplinary, biopolitical 'social' strategies
and the domain of 'the social' set up thereby. It does not subsume
all social relations even if a 'social' theory-cum-programme of
human improvement such as Bentham's might aspire to just that.
Similarly the essential 'humanity' and 'subjectivity' of human
social agents are a functioning discursive component of technologies
of the individual such as psychopathology.

(i) 'Strategies', their limits and effects

The task is now to salvage Foucault's concept of strategy from
the notion of *pouvoir-savoir*. For this purpose Foucault's meta-
phorical use of Jeremy Bentham's Panopticon proposal as paradigmatic of discipline, together with his thesis concerning the
failure of imprisonment will be considered.

The Panopticon, recalling our point about Foucault's treatment
of global social theory, could be regarded as a vulgar empiricist's
dream . . . a privileged place for experiments on men, for analysing
with complete certainty the transformations that may be obtained
from them . . . a kind of laboratory of power (DP: 204); a power
of control which proceeds at minimal expense through the sub-
jectificatory effects of a perpetual visibility. This economy makes
it an administrator's dream also: an architectural inversion of the
costly spectacle (DP: 216). However Foucault insists that the
Panopticon is no utopian 'dream building' but 'a diagram of a
mechanism of power reduced to its ideal form . . . a figure of political technology . . . detached from any specific use' (ibid: 205).
Moreover panopticism is not tied to 'institutional' forms: everything from tachographs in heavy goods vehicles to electronic
'in vivo' monitoring and treatment/punishment of drug addicts,
sex offenders, untrustworthy categories of parolees, etc. (Schwitz-
gebel, Ingraham and Smith, in Dinitz, Dynes and Clarke, 1975:
487—510) would fall in some respects under the panopticist

rubric. Both 'total' institutional and semi-institutional disciplinary forms (halfway houses, out-patient drug addiction centres, etc.) intersect to form a 'carceral archipelago'. However, if Panopticism is no dream does this not imply that disciplinary institutions work as they should? Is this not contrary to fact?

Of course, taken either separately or in aggregate, 'disciplinary' institutions do fail to work to almost anyone's satisfaction. Time and again, disciplinary institutional historiography runs up against the 'problem' of their perpetuation in the light of their perpetual failure; their degeneration into a custodial function, attraction and inmixing of inappropriate clientele, and so forth. (Rothman, 1971; Ignatieff, 1978). But in Foucault's symbiotic perspective the failure of the penitentiary is a functioning component of the Panopticist strategic field. Partly this is a question of focussing on the actual discursive forms in which failure is registered and their dependencies and effectivities. No need for a theory of power here. If prison disappoints all hopes, it does so for different, opposed, reasons. Certainly, though Foucault does not do so, it is possible to show (Minson, forthcoming) how these oppositions are symbiotically related at a purely discursive level, e.g. how retributivists and utilitarians elaborate in opposite directions the same hierarchized sets of conceptual oppositions, how, in terms of archaeology these registrations of failure are articulated in a definite 'space of dissension'. (1972: 152). In DP, Foucault is more immediately concerned with the political effectivities of such oppositions, treating them as 'tactical blocks in a field of force relations'.

The function he actually accords to penitentiary failure and its registration is more controversial. It is the consequence of a successful joint-strategy of depoliticizing illegalities and (re)producing a delinquent population. The latter lacks popular support for their activities, constitute no political threat yet provide the occasion for multiplying and intensifying disciplinary measures directed at the population at large. This may smack of a latent functionalism. Perhaps Foucault's thesis may indeed be read as a functionalist one, but not simply on the grounds that the notion of strategy makes 'failure' under some conditions functional. It can happen. Failure may be 'specific, differentiated . . . and opportunity to refine techniques, re-define targets, extend the field of operation, include more factors and make tactical adjustments' (Burchell, 1979: 133–134). As we saw, the modern familial 'mechanism' is sustained by discrepancies between 'social' familial norms and actual functioning, which provide the occasion for 'social' agencies to intervene if familial agents cannot or will not carry out their 'socially' defined familial responsibilities.

(Hodges and Hussain, 1979: 90, 93). Again, given the existence
of competing versions of strategies and hence the possibilities of
conflict between 'social' agencies, it is not hard to see why failures,
if they can be localised, seldom need to be seen as warranting the
abandoning of a strategy. Either the competing strategy was
adopted or the true first principles were never properly applied.
Thus the monotonous century-and-a-half-long critique of the
prison — insufficiently punitive, insufficiently corrective — 'prison
"reform" is virtually contemporary with prison itself' (DP: 234).

We may therefore acknowledge that 'failure' may operate to
the advantage of a strategy under definite conditions. But the
objection might be pressed further.

If failure is only conditionally functional, then strategies cannot be *designed* to fail. An unintended consequence, then? But if
so, how is it so systematically reproduced? So by a familiar structural functionalist route, an intentionality and unconditional
constitutivity must then be accorded to the global ensemble of
disciplines. This objection is serious but misses the point. Failure
may be functional to a strategy, but what fails is not the strategy
itself but always some particular social policy or programme of
correction, which cannot be *identified* with a strategy even if it
attempts to state and apply it. Strategies are irreducible to theories
or principles, they have no unitary locus, and above all their
global character belongs to the order of *effects.*

Perhaps Foucault himself puts one off the track by employing
as a metaphor of discipline Bentham's Panopticon scheme (Panopticism). To see why, let us first consider the implications of the
fact that the concept of intentionality which is causing problems
here does not presuppose the category of conscious or even
unconscious subject. An intention signifies the point, rationale,
objective of an action. It is derived by inference from a set of
effects. This action need have found no prior discursive expression
of intention which the action then realizes, and of course statements of intention may mislead concerning the action to which
they ostensibly point. It is thus not so mysterious of Foucault
to insist that strategies may not originate either in a human individual or an institution. Rather strategies traverse quite heterogenous practices and objectives, creating strategic similarities in
the mode of implementation of radically different 'social' and
political policies and objectives: e.g. in the mode of 'government'
of individuals in late eighteenth-century English prisons, irrespec-
tive of who builds and administrates them, 'Whitehall' or county/
urban borough authorities (Ignatieff 1978: 96).

Strategies are constructed, by derivation, from the effects or
outcomes of the branching one on to the other of a set of prac-

tices, in the result that a relatively stable system of mutual support is formed. Social work in all varieties, the psychiatric complex, national insurance, education, family life, family law, legal psychiatry and so on are not realizations of some one deliberate project of 'social order', yet they form a strategic 'social' configuration, an ensemble of 'government' which without radical alteration could be incorporated in left and right political programmes.

Why is it misleading to identify disciplinary strategy with the Panopticon? Retracing our steps, we answer, precisely because it leads to a juridico-discursive mode of describing and assessing strategies. Discipline becomes identified with a particular principle or 'idea': in this case the inspective principle, as Bentham states it and as embodied in the architecture and geometry of certain buildings, which is then *applied,* as Bentham said, to grind rogues honest, and so on. Strategy is subsumed within the opposition of stated ideal and real practice. But evaluation of the Panopticon in such terms is absurd. The most cursory inspection of the 1791 text reveals its epistolary form, its innumerable qualifications and revisions, which are then elaborated in successive appendices, its neurotic concern both to anticipate every possible abuse of the inspective force whilst also attempting to maximize it; even the famous diagram of the Penitentiary, Panopticon is represented as being in an 'improved but as yet . . . unfinished state' (Bentham, 1843, Vol. iv). The whole text has this character: you could say, with apologies to Lichtheim, that Panopticism is at least as difficult to preach as it is to practice. The Panopticist ideal may be unattainable in principle and in the light of a comparison of the idea and its realizations. But strategic principles have neither a unitary locus, a stable form of existence nor, above all, a fundamental constitutive role. They may be variously stated in various locations. They may be the subject of controversy, or fail to find any adequate expression. And the construction of controversy over the practicality of particular strategic ideals i.e. in *that* set of terms, rather than in other, 'political' terms is part and parcel of an effective working strategy.

Returning to the objection of functionalism, that discipline is an unconditional relational totality, a brief response is required to bring out in general what hangs on this problem of the globality of discipline, where the relevance of the latter to socialist theory and politics is concerned. There is no reason to infer from the notion as I have tried to sketch it out (independently of a notion of power relations) that discipline (including biopolitics in this) renders every conceivable social practice and agent immanent to itself. Nevertheless a conditional, relatively global influence of disciplines might, I say might, obtain in this restricted

domain of 'the social'. In which case, the implication that social-
ist demands and involvements in this arena would then be
implicated in disciplinary strategy might be no objection to
Foucault's position. For existing socialist 'social' programmes
are arguably all too often committed to a disciplinary, biopolitical sanitization of 'irrationalities' and excrescences attributed to
capitalism. Yet *when the form, the means of its implementation
are taken into consideration,* this sanitization is frequently hard
to distinguish from that ensemble of 'socializations' introduced
with the precise intention of taking the wind out of the revolutionary socialist movement's sails (Donzelot, 1979), not only in
capitalist countries but in those of Eastern Europe as well.[13]

This consideration of socialist politics and existing 'social'
strategies, I want to argue, far from implying that a 'socialist'
future must necessarily involve the further extension of the
social disciplines and in particular of their depoliticizing effects,
rather necessitates a progressive political reclamation of a number
of 'social' arenas and could be useful in developing *socialist* political work in these arenas.

IV Social strategies and Socialist politics

Foucault, in an interview published under the title 'Revolutionary
Action: Until Now', contends that:

> . . . to imagine another system is to extend our participation
> in the present system . . . this particular idea of 'the whole of
> society' . . . arose . . . within this highly individualized histori-
> cal development that culminates in capitalism. We readily be-
> lieve that the least we can expect of experiences, actions and
> strategies is that they take into account 'the whole of society'
> . . . But I believe that this . . . means imposing impossible con-
> ditions on our actions because this notion functions in a manner
> that prohibits the actualization, success and perpetuation of
> these projects. 'The whole of society' is precisely that which
> should not be considered except as something to be destroyed.
> (1977b: 230, 232–3)

The question is, could anyone conceivably call themselves socialist
and say that? In the anarchist tradition the state must be brought
down, that society may flourish. Whatever Foucault's practical
politics may be, the political implications of his written work on
this showing are not straightforwardly anarchist. What are they,
then? What follows is an extremely tentative and provisional
answer.

The utility of Foucauldian analysis of 'the social' to socialist thought and politics is unthinkable insofar as the latter is over-arched by Marxist theory. By that I mean that certain aspects of Marxist-socialist politics, such as the revolutionization of capitalist economic and 'social' relations into non-commodity, democratically collectivized forms and the 'withering away' of State administration are warranted by a global historical and social theory. Suppose, however, socialization or withering were conceived not as theoretical derivatives, as defining marks of individual forms of society which constitute general political ends of successive stages of the historical process, but as possible political objectives here and now, or at one remove from currently attainable objectives. And suppose that the practices which are both the products and instruments of their realization did not cease to be political insofar as they succeeded in these objectives, but that on the contrary, retaining their political character was part of their continuing struggle to flourish *as* socialist practices. No doubt these practices would need to take other practices 'into account', but 'the whole of society'? Might not that be part of what one was up against? In that case, the question must be faced, must a socialist politics that is not committed to perpetuating the present 'social order' be committed to constructing a new one? Are radical changes in social relations, including insurrection and wars of liberation, unthinkable except in terms of some change from one *type of society* to another, whether this change be conceived in revolutionary *or* evolutionary (reformist) terms? To suggest this may be to go against the grain of almost any political theory on which a socialist is likely to draw. But it may be more practically consonant with some existing socialist forms of struggle than one might imagine, as well as with some barely existent but readily desirable ones.

One step at a time. At least three elements of Foucault's contestation of Marxism are significant for this purpose: his attack on global conceptions of social relations; his relocation of such categories of social totality as a functioning component in the limited field of 'social' strategies; and lastly his attack on 'possessive' conceptions of power and concommittantly his emphasis on the determinants and effects of the 'technical' forms of implemenation of policies, 'strategic' programmes, etc., in this 'social' domain.

The first of these simply poses an obvious problem for socialist thought. If in characterizing social forms no appeal is made to a structure or foundation which in the last analysis determines the overall cohesion and identity of social forms, what becomes of the very idea of socialism? In short what could be meant by socialist society or social formation? What basis of coherence and of the affixing of political priorities would be available for socialist struggle or reconstruction?

In classical Marxism (witness its refusal of utopian blueprints) collective appropriation of surplus labour only provides a foundation on which a variety of non-commodity, non-authoritarian relations might be constructed; their form cannot be foreseen or deduced in a general theory. It follows that if a 'whole society' bears the stamp of socialism this identity amid diversity must be in part an ideological-political construction. If notions of fundamental structure or foundation are dropped, and Foucault is not alone in suggesting this, the unease of socialists is readily comprehensible. When it is proposed that the proper form of socialist economy is itself not given by any theory but is a political matter, then in Marxist terms is the ideological constituent of socialist construction not being asked to bear an impossible load? Without an 'objective' foundation the basis for the coherence of socialist policies and practices could only be a kind of negotiated ideological common denominator, which would express the current aspirations of a multiplicity of political forces, such as party and trade union organizations, social movements, issue campaigns and significant sections of the electorate. Even if a satisfactory common socialist-progressive formulae could be found such political ideological constructions at most are a means of *aligning* political forces under a common banner, they do not address the problems of effectively *allying* socialist forces and the fields of practical activity in which they are engaged. An ideological common denominator is of necessity indifferent to the specific interests of not only individual practices but of particular *configurations of practices.* Strategic alliances, say, within the complex of legal, psychiatric and social work practices cannot be forged on the basis of common socialist ideological attitudes alone.

Neither is it a question of bringing together socialist ideals with an appropriate set of existing political mechanisms. Turning to Foucault's relocation of social totality, the next question concerns what socialist ideals are taking on board, in the light of the pre-socialist and anti-revolutionary 'traces' of the 'social' domain which Foucault and his colleagues' genealogies have picked up.

Let us briefly consider the socialist feminist demand for the socialization of child care and domestic tasks. It has been shown how a certain socialization and various measures of 'women's liberation' provided some of the conditions of emergence of the involuted private modern family. Some of the East European countries furnish examples of the combination of ostensibly progressive measures of socialization happily co-existing with an iron committment to the nuclear family as both a relay of 'social' disciplinary norms, and as a site of private 'promotion' (Donzelot, 1977), and a condition of political quietism amongst the population.

Similarly Riley (1979) has brought out the nuclear familialist objectives of (Fabian) socialist recommendations for continuing the provision of war nurseries in the U.K. Her question — what would a feminist demand for nurseries look like? — assumes what I have been arguing, that 'progressive' forces have no monopoly on the objective of socialization and that as a general formula it has extremely limited value. In this particular domain the conspicuous absence of a socialist politics of the modern family (which is on the contrary the main if not the unique receptacle for the 'social' ameliorations demanded by the labour movement and promised in left-wing party programmes) cannot be construed as evidence of their revisionism. For as Donzelot has emphasised (1977: 11) the *attacks* on the family in the Marxist nineteenth-century classics were politically vacuous, depending as they did on the 'colander-concepts' (ibid: 13), of 'crisis' and 'contradiction' of and between 'private' and 'public' realms, and on the idea that the family served to reproduce bourgeois ideological domination. Whereas, as a 'social' hybrid of private and public, it both thrives and enables a variety of political orders to flourish *on account of* its crises and contradictions. The development of a socialist politics of the family would be a major step forward in any progressive political reclamation of 'the social' domain. The development and alliance of struggles in the NHS and the Social Services, in the domain of school 'government', in housing and planning departments and the housing market, to mention no other areas, would not be adjuncts of struggle over family and sexual relations but part of it.

Two comments might be made concerning this sort of politics. Firstly, the cardinal importance of Foucault's position on this familial domain — and this point holds equally for the 'socialization' of economic relations — consists in its demonstration of the need for socialists to cease fuelling the mindless identification of socialism with interventionism, any State control over private or personal spheres or a 'civil society' supposedly constructed independently. The notion of the withering away of the State consequent upon the achievement of a socialist 'social' order cannot easily avoid this identification. If the quotation from Foucault above is re-read in terms of Marxist theory, we could say he has good reason to want to turn the 'withering' process into an immediate political objective, and that what is to be withered away is not 'the state', but the peculiar 'private' and 'public' anti-political hybrid of the 'social' order, 'the whole of society'.

The second point to recall is that the latter is, to repeat, a functioning category in an ensemble of 'social' and 'psychological' practices which certainly do not in fact form a seamless whole subsuming all social relations, but are open to a variety of possible socialist interventions of both Parliamentary and extra-Parliamentary sorts, to the organization of both technical, professional 'specific intellectuals' (Foucault: 1977a) and the clients of the institutions they serve. Exploitation of the dependencies and intersectionings of the 'social' disciplines by socialists has scarcely begun. The strength of alliances in the 'social' domain would derive not merely from ideological solidarity and numbers, in a unity of opposition, but from the political, 'strategic' advantages implied in their joint professional positions.

We come now to the last constituent of Foucault's challenge to Marxist socialist thought: the critique of power as possession and the focus on technical and strategic forms of exercise of power. The first point to be made is that the absolute precondition for socialist programmes not becoming implicated in the construction of an anti-political 'quarantine' is that their objectives *incorporate* their means of implementation. Whether it is a question of introducing more egalitarian wage structures or taxation systems, or health, therapeutic and welfare measures, the means of calculation and 'administrative' implementation must always be seen as a decisive constraint on the range of objectives it is possible for political forces of any persuasion to even propose, let alone attain. This does not entail that technical expertise must always be subordinate to democratic decisions, the objectives of some 'watchdogs' might be to tighten up professional expertise. Nor is it anti-centralist on principle. This introduces the second point.

If we were to go by the Pantopticist grid, all forms of supervision would be at par. Centralized hierarchical authority within corporations, government departments, etc., would be indistinguishable from any move to institute centralized control *over* these leviathans. But to focus on the forms of implementation of policies and objectives does not preclude the possibility that e.g. a higher level of popular involvement in the running of the NHS might depend on a greater measure of central control. The freedom of self-perpetuating professional bodies from 'external' government interference is a contributory factor in their freedom from internal and direct control over their operations. *Mutatis mutandis*, the form of operation and 'social' strategic supports of NHS institutions limit the effectivity of central government interventions.

To conclude, on what it might mean theoretically to destroy 'society as a whole'. The network of 'social' practices to which a socialist politics might lay political claim is of a complexity that belies the assumption that any analysis which does not take account of some social totality or structure falls into a factorialism and a political naïveté about the obstacles to transforming sets of social relations. With regard to Foucault's conception of power, nothing testifies so eloquently to what his work has to offer independently of that ultimately historicist notion, than the radical anti-historicism of his challenge to the subsumptive power over political thought and action of the category of 'the whole of society'. No doubt what this challenge implies is the repudiation of the ideal of 'social' revolution, the transformation of one society into another, truly social, one. But must socialist political practices be committed to that? The question is whether socialists who are so committed, are not committed to *completing* a revolution which started without them and which from its inception has spelt death to the plural forms of popular democratic social organization which socialists want to bring about. In response to the question overarching this discussion, concerning the utility of 'strategies' for socialist politics, it may be suggested that it be confined to a (possibly) useful term for describing and analysing the current 'social' orders. An alternative socialist 'social' strategy would represent a perpetuation of the present, not 'a revolutionary undertaking directed against the rule of "until now" (1977b: 233). What is at issue in this hypothesis is the need to reconsider current relations of political parties and programmes to specific 'social' struggles; and in particular whether the movements of women, blacks, prisoners, anti-psychiatry and so on are necessarily furthered by their being as easily subsumed as they currently are within party-political programmes.

Notes

1. Recently translated from the French as *The History of Sexuality, Volume One: An Introduction* (1979). Five further volumes are promised: *La Chair et Le Corps, La Croisade des Enfants, La Femme, La Mere et L'Hysterique, Les Pervers,* and *Population et Races.* For a summary c.f. Morris (1977). Quotations are the author's own translation, reference to both editions is given where appropriate. For a summary of DP see Hussain (1978).
2. The present work elaborates on and complements some of the arguments of 'The "subject" of feminism' (Adams and Minson, 1978). Notably, the problems associated with 'the problem of the subject' and of its supposed construction which are brought out in that article are rather taken for granted in this one, for all their relevance to the problem of power. The direction of my discussion of Foucault's concept of strategy is considerably indebted to Nikolas Rose, Athar Hussain, Jill Hodges and Graham Burchell, who gave me access to drafts of the articles which appeared in *Ideology and Consciousness No. 5* (1979) under their names; and to discussions held in a seminar on Politics and the State over the last year at Birkbeck College, University of London. The treatment of the general category of power is indebted to Barry Hindess. Finally a longstanding debt to Terry Counihan must be acknowledged.

3. Crucial to the organized avowal of sexuality is the 'myth' of its 'intrinsic latency', (HS: 61, 156–7) which provides resistances with their evidential value vis-à-vis one's true sexuality.

4. Students of 'Utilitarian' thought and politics may profit from this definition of discipline, which encapsulates the historically specific significance of 'utility' as a theoretical and political concept. In this perspective Benthamite *ethics* no longer appear as the foundation of Utilitarian 'social' programmes, policies, etc. but functions within them as a kind of multi-purpose 'professional' – administrative ethic. This view builds on Lyons (1973). On this see Minson (forthcoming).

5. T. Counihan drew my attention to the agreement of Weber and Poulantzas in their definition of the (for Poulantzas, *capitalist*) State in terms of monopoly access to the legitimate use of force. (Weber, 1964: 154–156: Poulantzas, 1973: 226–227). Leaving aside considerations such as the proliferation of private security, note the politically immobilizing consequences of construing the military and the police as essentially 'special bodies of armed men'. That description at best denotes *one* set of conditions (constraints? opportunities?) constraining political activity within such institutions. Issues of working conditions, housing, health, sexism, etc., arise on e.g. military bases as anywhere else, and if they arise differently, such differences are not necessarily traceable to a military organization's strictly repressive functions; for instance the current problems in the US military medical service, which partly derive from its being organized along the lines of an NHS whilst drawing on a staff unaccustomed to 'socialized' medical practices.

6. On the conflicts between the Royal judicial power and the seigneural courts (numbering up to 80,000 during the eighteenth century), see Dawson (1960: 79). On the consequences of the Royal victory for the abolition of judicial (investigative) torture see Langbein (1977: 55–60).

7. This reconstruction is based mainly around the celebrated 'Second Essay' of *The Genealogy of Morals* (1969). The concepts of decadence and will to power, however were only explicitly stated and developed in later works.

8. Nietzsche imbues human subjects with an originary 'apparatus of repression', that is, a faculty of 'active forgetfulness' which enables them to *have done* with past experiences, to make room for new ones. This 'form of robust health', the 'condition of all cheerfulness and hope', must nevertheless suffer modification, at the hands of the 'memory of the will', which is exactly the desire *not* to rid oneself of *some* things desired once ' . . . to ordain the future in advance'.

9. In practice Foucault *et. al.* frequently treat the infra-legal constituents of legal forms non-essentialistically, opening up for analysis what is usually registered in terms of contradictory 'principles', themes of contamination of a legal essence, etc. Thus in Donzelot (1977: 91–109) and Burchell (1979: 125–135) it is made clear in respect of juvenile justice, how (far from being rendered marginal) legal jurisdiction may be extended by 'disciplinary' means.

10. Recalling the account of HS in Part I above, it is not obvious that the only alternative to (Foucault's) reduction of sexuality to (a particular set of) 'social' determinants is some kind of essentialism which allows no place for the effectivity of social relations in determining diverse forms of sexual drive. Here it is only possible to notice the failure in HS or anywhere else of Foucault to take seriously the fundamental concepts of Psychoanalysis (drive, the unconscious, repression, transference, etc.).

11. Particular statements, e.g. (DP: 25), or even entire books which testify to our author's awareness of how 'the body' is variously constructed in diverse discourses do not save the concept of *pouvoir-savoir* from these implications.

12. On the latter Donzelot (1977: 38) writes: 'In place of the contract which by virtue of the dowry gave the man the possibility of an exterior autonomy, she inserts him into the dependence of an interior . . . reserved for him as his domain, which she may give him but also take back at any time'.

13. Evidently reference to 'democratization' *per se* is insufficient to differentiate socialist socialization, when we recall the provision for the supervision of Panopticon officials by what Bentham elsewhere calls 'the watchful and tutelary eye — the antiseptic influence — of the Public Opinion Tribunal' (1843: Vol. IX, 611).

References

Adams, P. and Minson, J. (1978) 'The subject of feminism'. *m/f*, No. 2: 43—61.

Aries, P. (1973) *Centuries of Childhood*. Harmondsworth, Penguin.

Balibar, E (1974) *Cinq Etudes du Matérialisme Historique*. Paris, Maspero.

Bentham, J. (1843) *Works* ed. Bowring, J. 11 vols. Edinburgh, Tait.

Burchell, G. (1979) 'A note on juvenile justice'. *Ideology and Consciousness*, No. 5: 125—135.

Canguilhem, G. (1955) *La formation du concept de reflexe aux XVII et XVIII siècles*. Paris, Presses Universitaires de France.

Cott, N. F. (1977) *The Bonds of Womanhood: 'Women's Sphere' in New England, 1780—1835*. New Haven, Yale University Press.

Coward, R. (1978) *'Sexual liberation and the family'. m/f* No. 1: 7—24.

Cutler, A., Hirst, P., Hindess, B. and Hussain, A. *(1977) Marx's Capital and Capitalism Today, Vol I*. London, Routledge and Kegan Paul.

Dawson, J. P. (1960) *A History of Lay Judges*. Cambridge, Mass. Harvard University Press.

Dinitz, S., Dynes, R. and Clarke, A. eds. (1975) *Deviance: Studies in Definition, Management and Treatment*. London, Oxford University Press.

Donzelot, J. (1977) *La Police des Familles*. Paris, Editions de Minuit.

Donzelot, J. (1979) 'The poverty of political culture'. *Ideology and Consciousness* No. 5: 73—86.

Foucault, M. (1971) *L'Ordre du Discours*. Paris, Editions Gallimard.

Foucault, M. (1972) *The Archaeology of Knowledge*. Transl. Sheridan Smith, A., London, Tavistock. Originally published as *L'Archaeologie du Savoir* (1969).

Foucault, M. (1976) *Histoire de la Sexualité: Tome 1, La Volonté de Savoir* Paris, Editions Gallimard.

Foucault, M. (1977) *Discipline and Punish: The Birth of the Prison* Transl. Sheridan, A., London, Allen Lane. Originally published as *Surveiller et Punir: Naissance de la Prison* (1975), Paris, Editions Gallimard.

Foucault, M. (1977a) 'The political function of the intellectual'. *Radical Philosophy*, No. 17, Summer: 12—14.

Foucault, M. (1977b) *Language, Counter-memory, Practice: Selected Essays and Interviews*. Ed. Bouchard, D. F. Transl. Bouchard, D. F. and Simon, S., Oxford. Basil Blackwell.

Foucault, M. (1979) *The History of Sexuality. Volume I: An Introduction*, London, Allen Lane.

Gordon, C. (1977) 'Birth of the subject'. *Radical Philosophy*, No. 17.

Glucksmann, A. (1968) 'Politics and War in the thought of Mao Tse-Tung'. Transl. Brewster, B. With an 'Introduction to Glucksmann' *New Left Review*. No. 49: 35—57.

Hodges, J. and Hussain, A. (1979) 'Review article: Jaques Donzelot, *'La Police des Familles'.Ideology and Consciousness* No. 5: 87—123.

Hussain, A. (1978) 'The anatomy of power: a review article'. *Sociological Review.*, Vol. XXVI, No. 4

Ignatieff, M. (1978) *A Just Measure of Pain: the Penitentiary in the Industrial Revolution, 1750—1850*. London and Basingstoke, Macmillan.

Langbein, J. (1977) *Torture and the Law of Proof: Europe and England in the Ancient Regime*. Chicago and London, University of Chicago Press.

Lyons, D. (1973) *In the Interests of the Governed*. Oxford, Clarendon Press.

Minson, J. (forthcoming 1980) *Social Relations and the Sovereignty of Ethics*. London and Basingstoke, Macmillan.

Minson, J. (forthcoming) *The Utilitarian Yoke: Benthamism Reconsidered*. Hassocks, Harvester.

Morris, M. (1977) 'Review article: Michel Foucault, *La Volonté de Savoir (Histoire de la Sexualite, I)'. Working papers: Studies in the discourses of sex, subjectivity and power*, No. 3: 8—26.

Nietzsche, F. (1968) *The Will to Power* Transl. Kaufman, W. New York, Vintage Books.

Nietzsche, F. (1969) *On the Genealogy of Morals* (with *Ecce Homo*) Transl. Kaufmann, W. New York, Vintage Books.

Nietzsche, F. (1972) *Twilight of the Idols* with *The Anti-Christ*. Transl. Hollingdale, R. Harmondsworth, Penguin.

Nietzsche, F. (1973) *Beyond Good and Evil*. Transl. Hollingdale, R. Harmondsworth, Penguin.

Nietzsche, F. (1974) *The Gay Science* Transl. Kaufmann, W. New York, Vintage Books.

Pasquino, P. (1978) 'Theatrum politicum: the genealogy of capital: police and the state of prosperity'. *Ideology and Consciousness*, No. 4: 41–54.

Poulantzas, N. (1973) *Political Power and Social Classes*. London, New Left Books.

Poulantzas, N. (1978) *State, Power, Socialism* (1978) transl. Camiller, P. London, New Left Books. Originally published as *L'etat, le pouvoir, le Socialisme* (1978) Paris. Presses Univérsitaires de France.

Rajchman, J. (1978) 'Nietzsche, Foucault and the anarchism of power'. *Semiotexte* Vol. III, No. 1: 96–107.

Rothman, D. J. (1971) *The Discovery of the Asylum: Social Order and Disorder in the New Republic*. Boston, Little, Brown.

Riley, D. (1979) 'War in the Nursery'. Feminist Review 2: 82–108.

Tournier, M. (1974) *The Erl-King*. Transl. Bray, B., originally published as *Le Roi des Aunes*.

Trumbach, R. (1978) *The Rise of the Egalitarian Family*. London, Academic Press.

Walker, N. (1972) *Sentencing in a Rational Society*. Harmondsworth, Penguin.

Weber, M. (1964) *The Theory of Social and Economic Organization (Part 1 of Wirtschaft und Gesellschaft)*. Transl. T. Parsons, New York, Free Press.

Williams, K. (1974) 'Unproblematic archaeology' *Economy and Society*, Vol. 3, No. 1: 41–68.

CHAPTER 6

Power and power analysis: beyond Foucault?

Gary Wickham

Introduction

This chapter is an attempt to develop a framework for non-essentialist power analysis. By 'non-essentialist analysis' I mean analysis which does not understand its object in terms of an all-important essence (like the economy, the state or the creative individual). As Barry Hindess describes it:

> Essentialism . . . refers to a mode of analysis in which social
> phenomena are analysed not in terms of their specific
> conditions of existence and their effects with regard to other
> social relations and practices but rather as the more or
> less adequate expression of an essence (Hindess, 1977, 95).

A non-essentialist analysis treats its objects in terms of its specificity, its particular conditions of existence, without reference to an eternal, external essence. In this way a non-essentialist analysis allows a far more thorough understanding of its object as it is not restricted to considerations in terms of an essence. An essentialist analysis, on the other hand, is bound by such restrictions — it must ignore or marginalize those aspects of the object being analysed which are not seen as important in terms of the essence being maintained. But an essentialist analysis is not only analytically debilitating, it is also politically debilitating. Essentialism means that strategies and tactics developed to achieve policy objectives must be limited to considerations only in terms of the essence maintained and not in terms of the specific conditions of existence of the policy concerned.

An analysis produced through a framework built around the essence economy (an economistic analysis), for example, must consider its object, say the demolition of a group of houses to make way for an office building, only in terms of the economy — considerations such as the relationship of this object to the maintenance of a capitalist economy (the potential profits of development and finance companies, the importance for such companies of office space compared to housing space, etc.). And it must do so at the expense of considerations of this object and its specific conditions of existence in their own right, free from any essence (government policies on development and housing, housing laws, council procedures, deliberations of planning bodies, etc.). A policy of resisting the demolition of the houses based on such an essentialist analysis will be limited to strategies and tactics concerned with critiques of and attempts to change companies' concentration on profitability and companies' building priorities, at the expense of strategies and tactics concerned with the specific conditions of existence pointed to above.

Of course this does not mean that a non-essentialist analysis must ignore economic factors. In considering the above object and its specific conditions of existence a non-essentialist analysis will consider such things as the potential profits of development and finance companies, the importance for such companies of office space compared to housing space, etc. But it will consider them as specific conditions of existence of the object — alongside the other conditions of existence pointed to — not as aspects of a determining essence.

The notion of conditions of existence, it must be stressed, should not be confused with the notion of 'real causes'. As developed by Paul Hirst and Barry Hindess 'conditions of existence' is a term which refers to the means by which the connections between an object — as a specific site or specific set of relations — and other objects are theorized. It refers to the way they are theorized free from the requirement to grant one or more of these other objects a causal status, that is, free from the requirement to grant one or more of them the status of determining essence (Hindess and Hirst, 1975, ch. 6). So, to continue with the above example, to say that government policies on development and housing, housing laws, council procedures, etc., etc., are specific conditions of existence of the object of analysis -- the demolition of a group of houses — is not to grant any one or any group of these the status of 'the real cause' of this object. It is not to suggest that any one or group of these objects is or are the real and eternal determinant of this object. Rather, it is to suggest that as a specific site or specific set of relations this object is connected to these other objects in a way which effects its specific form and therefore these other objects must be considered in any analysis.

My attempt to develop a framework for non-essentialist analysis will focus on some of the work of Michel Foucault, who can reasonably be said to be a pioneer of this type of analysis.[1] Foucault says his commitment to this type of analysis stems from his determination to go beyond the two forms of analysis which 'people of my generation were brought up on' and which continue to dominate power analysis – 'one in terms of the constituent subject, the other in terms of the economic in the last instance, ideology and the play of superstructures and infrastructures' (Foucault, 1980(b), 116).

Two things must be stressed about the reading of Foucault's work which will form the basis of this chapter. Firstly, I will be concentrating solely on several interviews with and lectures by Foucault[2] rather than on his major texts. I will do so not just because the interviews and lectures have received far less attention than his books, or because they are the only place where he discusses power in a general way (of course he does so to a considerable extent in his two most recent books, *Discipline And Punish* and *The History of Sexuality Volume One*). I will do so mainly because his general treatment of power in these interviews and lectures is more extensive than in his books. It is a treatment which allows us, I suggest, a 'warts-and-all' look at Foucault's understanding of power. Secondly, I will be attempting a reading of these interviews and lectures which exposes serious weaknesses in Foucault's treatment of power. In fact, I will go so far as to suggest that in many respects Foucault has not gone far along the road towards the construction of a truly non-essentialist framework for power analysis. This may seem overly harsh on Foucault, especially as I will be using only the lectures and essays as a basis for this criticism. But it must be remembered that I will be producing a *reading* of these lectures and essays. I will not be attempting to present the 'total Foucault', the 'complete author'. Such a figure is not a 'real' entity which must be considered if a study of texts under his signature is to be worthwhile, but simply the product of one particular, institutionally-promoted, essentialist reading of texts under his signature. This is a point Foucault himself makes in his essay 'What is an Author?' (Foucault, 1979 (b)) where he argues that the notion of author should be replaced by that of 'author-function' and also in an interview where he says of Marx:

As far as I'm concerned Marx doesn't exist. I mean, the sort
of entity constructed around a proper name, signifying
at once a certain individual, the totality of his writings, and
an immense historical process deriving from him
(Foucault, 1980 (g), 76).

In attempting the construction of a non-essentialist framework for power analysis I will not be involved in the posing of a general theory of an entity which has a particular form.[3] Power will be treated as relations which have no necessary, essential form and the analytical framework is a grid which can be brought to bear on particular sites so that these relations can be understood in their specific forms. In this I agree with Foucault's point that to construct a general theory of power would be to 'be obliged to view it [power] as emerging at a given place and time and hence to deduce it, to reconstruct its genesis', whereas if we view power as relations with no necessary form 'the only problem is to provide oneself with a grid of analysis which makes possible an analytic of relations of power' (Foucault, 1980 (f), 198—199).

In working towards the development of a new framework, I will discuss Foucault's conception of the way power works, the location of power, the possibility of resistance and struggle and the nature of power. I will conclude with an outline of the new analytical framework I am arguing is necessary.

How power works

Foucault tells us that power is 'co-extensive with the social body' and that 'relations of power are interwoven with other kinds of relations' (Foucault, 1980 (c), 142). We must ask what path power takes in doing this interweaving. Foucault suggests that all power starts in the 'smallest elements' of the social body: 'the family, sexual relations, but also: residential relations, neighbourhoods, etc. As far as we go in the social network we always find power as something that runs through it, that acts, that brings about effects' (Foucault, 1979(a), 59).[4] Power works then, from the bottom up and must be studied in this way:

> One must . . . conduct an *ascending* analysis, starting that
> is from its infinitesimal mechanisms, which each have
> their own history, their own trajectory, their own
> techniques and tactics, and then see how these mechanisms
> of power have been — and continue to be — invested,
> colonised, involuted, transformed, displaced, extended etc,
> by ever more general mechanisms and by forms of
> global domination (Foucault, 1980(a), 99, his
> emphasis).[5]

In treating power in these micro terms Foucault often calls into play the joint notions of technologies — institutionalised mechanisms for the operation of power — and techniques — procedures used in the operation of power. He suggests that certain technologies of power were developed in the seventeenth and eighteenth centuries which allowed a far more efficient form of power than the form prevalent in feudal societies (which functioned fundamentally through signs — signs of loyalty, rituals, ceremonies, etc.) (Foucault, 1980 (b), 125). He says that all technologies must be analysed in terms of their function: 'The problem of causes must not be dissociated from that of function: what use is [it], what function does it assure, in what strategies is it integrated' (Foucault, 1980(c), 136).

While we are on the question of technologies and techniques, it is worth a brief look at Foucault's treatment of one particular technology — that of law — as it serves as a good example of how his framework allows an easy slide into essentialism. In his discussions of law he varies between a fairly non-determinist view of power — where power could never be said to determine law — and a much more essentialist view where forms of power use law for their own unified ends. On the one hand he tells us that law is not a 'mask for power', that power cannot be interpreted in terms of law, that law is 'neither the truth of power nor its alibi' (Foucault, 1980 (c), 140—141). And on the other hand he tells us that disciplinary power uses law to give it an appearance of legitimacy, to 'disguise' its 'effective exercise' (Foucault, 1980 (a), 105—106). Fine criticizes Foucault for what he sees as his failure to take a critical stance on law, for failing to understand the contradictory character of law as it relates to capitalist production and exchange (Fine, 1979, 84). But this presents law in terms of a framework of power which is just as unified and unifying as any essentialist framework. It is better to see law as having no unified form and therefore no unified status in terms of power analysis. This is a point Richard Phillipps makes decisively in an essay on the notion of 'rule of law'. He argues, offering several examples, that law operates as discrete procedures whose characteristics cannot be known in a general sense but must be analysed at the specific points of their operation. He does, as he says, 'defer the donation of concrete status to the idea of the rule of law, or of law in general' (Phillipps, 1982, 57).

We learnt above that Foucault sees technologies of power as functioning within, as being integrated in, what he terms particular strategies. It is to an examination of the nature and operation of strategies that we now turn. Jeff Minson says that Foucault's use of the term strategy is not quite the same as in the 'political-cum-military' use — 'Foucault's notion of a strategy denotes a regularly reproduced *pattern of effects, including the (re-) drawing up of e.g. reformative plans*' (Minson, 1980, 11, his emphasis). One example of a strategy in operation which Foucault offers is that of the continuance of the 'bourgeois strategy'.

The bourgeoisie is perfectly well aware that a new constitution or legislature will not suffice to assure its hegemony; it

realises that it has to invent a new technology ensuring
the irrigation by effects of power of the whole social body
down to its smallest particles. And it was by such means
that the bourgeoisie not only made a revolution but
succeeded in establishing a social hegemony which it has
never relinquished (Foucault, 1980 (d), 156).

This example highlights a major problem with Foucault's notion
of strategy. His treatment of this notion reinforces the essentialist
tendencies of his analytical framework for it forces us to understand power relations as completely unified – in the above example
they are unified around the classically essentialist economic
category 'bourgeoisie' (a term which, it must be stressed, does not
always signal essentialism). Minson points out that a strategy is
both the identification *and* unification of relations of power in
operation (Minson, 1980, 10, my emphasis). Of course the unification of relations, or practices, does not necessarily involve the
invocation of an essence (whether the unification is theorized as a
strategy or not). It is possible to theorize the unity of a particular
set of relations or practices without invoking an essence. But it is
only possible to do so within particular sites. Once this process
moves beyond specific sites, as it does in Foucault's case, it becomes false unification. It then necessarily involves the invocation
of an essence which is used as the principle which unifies the relations or practices beyond their specific sites, beyond their
specific conditions of existence.

I do not think that because of this weakness the notion of
strategy should be abandoned. Within the framework of power
analysis I am arguing for in this paper the notion of strategy has
no unifying function. It becomes, along with the notions of
technology and techniques, limited to the operation of specific
policies in specific sites. I will say no more about this at this
stage and look instead at another problem with Foucault's conception of strategies.

Foucault argues that strategies do not have subjects, being
formed instead around subject-less objectives. For example:

the moralisation of the working class wasn't imposed by
Guizot, through his schools legislation, nor by Dupin through
his books. It wasn't imposed by the employers' union
either. And yet it was accomplished, because it met the
urgent need to master a vagabond, floating labor force.
So the objective existed and the strategy was developed, with
ever-growing coherence, but without it being necessary to
attribute to it a subject (Foucault, 1980 (f), 204).

My objection to this argument (leaving aside any objections about the over-unification — again around a category of economic class — contained in it) is not to the notion that strategies are formed around objectives or to the notion that they do not have subjects. My objection is to the implication contained in the way these notions are presented. Strategies are indeed formed around objectives, but these objectives are specific objectives limited to the operation of specific policies, not global objectives such as the domination of classes. (I will argue later that global strategies exist only in specific sites and achieve their global status because they reproduce or repeat a large number of other strategies.)

As well, while strategies cannot be said to have subjects who or which possess and operate them, this is not because they develop without subjects, as Foucault suggests here. Rather, it is because the subjects associated with them are produced and/or reproduced or repeated in specific sites just as strategies themselves are produced and/or reproduced or repeated in specific sites. I will now discuss the relationship between power and subjects in detail.

Foucault, as we have seen, argues strongly that power in its modern form functions so efficiently by working on individuals. For Foucault though these individuals are not individuals in any conventional sense so much as 'bodies'. This idea is often summarized by the term 'bio-politics'. As Hodges and Hussain describe it:

> Biopolitics refers to the policies which started to appear in
> European countries from the mid-18th century onwards
> and were, as Foucault puts it, centred on the body —
> the species and the biological processes which supported
> it — for example, population growth, birth and death
> rates, the state of health of the population, nutrition,
> dwellings etc. In other words the policies which directly
> impinged on individuals conceived as physical bodies and the
> space of personal existence (Hodges and Hussain, 1979, 88).

The notion of bodies as the target of power then, is part of Foucault's attempt to avoid the liberal conception of individuals as unconstrained, creative essences. More than that, as Hodges and Hussain suggest, this notion is central to his attempt to avoid 'the cleavage between the social, economic and political, on the one hand, and the personal and psychological on the other' (Hodges and Hussain, 1979, 88). So the direct subjects of power are not individuals — individuals can only be said to be 'implicated' in power:

> Biopolitics . . . bears not directly on 'individuals' but on
> the fecundity, hygiene and moral health of national

populations. It implicates individuals and 'private
family' by imposing disciplinary norms in pursuit of
biopolitical objectives (e.g. 'national efficiency' in the U.K.)
making the latter matters of e.g. parental or pedagogical
responsibility (Minson, 1980, 3).

But this does not really make clear how subjects of power are
formed. While we can easily agree with Foucault and Minson that
the direct subjects of power are not individuals, the notion of
bodies, even though it helps in understanding power in terms of
specific policies, does not really provide us with an adequate
understanding of the formation of subjects in relations of power.

The first point to make concerning this issue is that the process
of subject formation in power is not a conscious one — 'What I
want to show is how power relations can materially penetrate
the body in depth, without depending even on the mediation of
the subject's own representation' (Foucault, 1980 (e), 186). As
for how power does form subjects Foucault gives one of his
strongest hints when he says of 'individuals': 'In fact it is already
one of the prime effects of power that certain bodies, certain
gestures, certain discourses, certain desires come to be identified
and constituted as individuals' (Foucault, 1980 (a), 98). As
Minson points out this formulation displaces the concept of the
human subject 'on to the terrain of social practices under investigation' (Minson, 1980, 31). It tells us that power produces subjects
in a social domain, but it does not tell us specifically how. Hodges
and Hussain offer a clue — 'For Foucault correction and normalisation are central to the relations of power in the society in which
we live . . . Power relations create those who are to be subjected
to them' (Hodges and Hussain, 1979, 108). Power for Foucault
produces subjects through a process of 'correction and normalisation'. Subjects are 'gradually, progressively, really and materially
constituted through a multiplicity of organisms, forces, energies,
materials, desires, thoughts etc', a process or series of processes
which add up to 'on-going subjugation' (Foucault, 1980 (a), 97).

There are two major problems with this treatment of the formation of subjects of power. It is both too general and too negative.
As I said above subjects are produced and/or reproduced or repeated in specific sites. There is no general process, whether it is
called normalization or something else, in which subjects can be
said to be produced in relation to a unified essence called power.
And in suggesting as he does here that subjects are produced in
subjugation, produced as subjects of the essence of power,
Foucault is promoting one of the major misconceptions of power
which he urges people to avoid—negative power: seeing power only

in terms of a sovereign figure who or which always prohibits or says no (Foucault, 1979 (a), 60; 1980 (c), 140; and 1980 (e), 187). I think these criticisms point not just to a weakness in Foucault's understanding of the production of subjects but also, and probably more importantly, to weaknesses in the concept of subject itself. This concept should be abandoned for two reasons. Firstly because of its negativity — because it suggests that subjects are always subjected to something or someone rather than being produced in specific sites with no inherent status in regard to a strategy or technology or other 'subject'. And secondly it should be abandoned because it carries the implication that the process of subjection works on independently existing entities, such as individuals, people, etc, rather than producing these categories within it.

This is not to argue that the analytical tasks which the concept subject is used to carry out should no longer be carried out. For instance, power analysis must be able to identify the forces involved in any site of power relations. This is clearly a task where the concept subject is used extensively. What it is is to argue that we need to understand the formation of what we now call subjects in a different way.

Minson goes a considerable way towards doing so when he suggests that the constitution of subjects through the operation of specific relations of power is best understood as the construction of 'personal' categories (which are 'limited' and 'non-given') such as 'the human person, the child, mother, father, sexual identities etc.' (Minson, 1980, 29). So in talking of the constitution of subjects we are not talking about the subjectivization of human persons who exist outside this process. We are hereby displacing the notion that

. . . power is wielded on people, whose relations to nature
are just as much the source of their 'reality' as the
power relations within which they move. People
already exist — 'as a manifestation of a form of "nature"
[Marx] — before they can be subjected to modes
of regulation and control (Fine, 1979, 92).

We are displacing the notion that subjects are already formed in the essence 'nature', or in any other essence — 'Foucault's supernatural conception of power leads him to forget that the disciplines are imposed on subjects . . . already individuated and forced into mutual antagonism by relations of capitalist production' (Fine, 1979, 92). We are objecting to any notion of the subject as 'unified and existing prior to its . . . construction'; we are suggesting that 'the subject as it appears in "society" does not assume a unified form, rather social agents are fragmented and scattered across

various sites . . . Not all of these are consistent with each other'
(Phillipps, 1982, 53). We are suggesting that what is often referred
to as the construction of individual subjects is better seen as the
construction of people. Minson clarifies this idea by offering the
example of the construction of the child.

> The child, qua product of 'social' policies, is a category
> defined in terms of a variety of moral and physical
> dangers or insecurities from the standpoint of 'biopolitics'
> and ethico religious discourses . . . This child 'in
> danger' . . . is, as never before 'socially' recognized
> as a moral individual, a legal person, a psychological being,
> in a variety of knowledges, and concomitantly as a
> corporal and/or mental resource which must be conserved
> and harnessed (Minson, 1980, 29).

This substitution of the production of persons for the production
of subjects clearly overcomes the two weaknesses of the concept
of the subject I pointed to above — its negativity and its implication
in the notion of independently existing human persons. And in
doing so it loses nothing when it comes to performing the sort
of analytical tasks discussed above. In fact it can enhance them,
as Minson shows. He says that the role of agents in particular
struggles requires consideration of the conditions of existence of
their particular personal form or category. He gives the example
of women's struggles against 'typecast domestic positions' where,
he says, it must be remembered that, 'The "powers" which attach
to such positions may well be "disadvantageous" from the standpoint of some socialist and feminist objectives, but . . . with all
their miserable consequences, these liabilities are not illusions
foisted on "brute" persons' (Minson, 1980, 30–31). In other
words, the construction of categories like 'housewife' runs counter
to the objectives of certain socialist and feminist policies and as
such tactics devised in attempting to achieve these objectives
should be directed against the construction of these categories,
against the production of these particular forms of person. Tactics
should not be devised on the assumption that the categories involved are imposed on already-existing, conscious individuals
('foisted on "brute" persons').

Before leaving the notion of the production of persons I must
address a question which has been directed at this notion. This is
the question of the 'raw materials' of this production. As Minson
asks, what is it that is 'enveloped and thereby "subjectified"
through power relations?' Minson argues that there can be no
general answer to this question, that the raw materials of persons
vary from site to site (Minson, 1980, 12). Perhaps we can strengthen

this answer by suggesting that the raw materials used to produce persons in a particular site are already existing categories of persons which are reproduced or repeated in that site. In this way the existing category of child is reproduced or repeated in sites of education and is used as a raw material to produce separate personal categories of boy and girl and pupil and slow learner and prodigy, etc., which then function separately to the category of child.

We are still left with a terminological problem here because the subjects which exist in specific power relations are not just persons. They are also companies, unions, governments, government departments, pressure groups, political parties, schools, hospitals, etc. To overcome this problem it is possible to use the term 'agents'. This term is somewhat unsatisfactory as it is usually restricted to reference to individuals. But as it can be used to refer to any of the above entities as they exist in specific sites — unions, governments etc. can be said to be agents operating in specific sites of power relations as well as women, men, children, unionists, ministers etc. — and as there seems to be no other term which would be adequate to the task at hand I will use it.

The location of power

Foucault says that power is not 'always localised in a definite number of elements', such as the state or state apparatuses or any other 'political structures' (Foucault, 1979, 59). He suggests rather, that power is everywhere — 'power is "always-already there"' . . . one is never "outside" it . . . there are no "margins" for those who break with the system to gambol in' (Foucault, 1980 (c), 141). He says power must be studied 'at the point where it is in direct and immediate relationship with that which we can provisionally call . . . its target, its field of application, there — that is to say — where it installs itself and produces its real effects' (Foucault, 1980 (a), 97.)'. We saw in the last section that for Foucault this 'target', this 'field of application' is the micro levels of 'society' — the 'smallest elements of the social body'. We saw that for him these and the process by which they are incorporated into 'ever more general mechanisms', into more global strategies, are the true object of power analysis and the true home of power. I will not cover this ground again. This section is not included to discuss Foucault's understanding of the location of power. Rather, I will use it for two other purposes: to briefly highlight the strengths of Foucault's treatment of the category of the social (or 'society'), or rather the treatment of it his work has inspired; and to outline my understanding of where power relations are located, to outline what for me should be the objects of power analysis (which will involve me challenging Foucault's proposition that some sites are incorporated into more global sites).

It is important to consider the category of the social (or 'society' because in much power analysis this category is presented as the (unchallengeable) given location of power relations. Minson argues that Foucault has shifted the ground of the 'social' so that it is no longer 'a totality "governed" by some unifying principle' but has become 'an asymptotic objective and, hence a functioning ingredient of certain disciplinary biopolitical "social" strategies' (Minson, 1980, 31); Foucault has allowed us to dispense with any notion of the social as a whole notions which Donzelot has termed 'colander' notions, presumably, Terry Counihan argues, 'on the assumption that the more content one pours into such containers, the more they leak' (Counihan, 1982, 30). We are now in a position to understand the social as a shifting category. As Counihan says, 'the social is a dispersed plurality of practices which have no constant principle or centre' (Counihan, 1982, 30). By way of an example he discusses the way in which the family has only recently come to be considered a legitimate part of the social (Counihan, 1982, 25). Another example which will help clarify this idea of a shifting category of the social is that of abortion law reform.[6] It may be thought that in analysing this site — this intersection of, *inter alia*, medical, legal and bureaucratic practices — we can link it to an independent, static category of the social. But how can we comprehend this social level independently of the specific intersection of practices involved? The social here can only be understood in terms of particular medical, legal and bureaucratic techniques and policies — the formation of policies around the notion of public health and nutrition, the formation of population profiles involving the collection of statistics, the provision of medical categories in law, etc. There is no sense in which the social informs this site; only the reverse occurs. This does not mean that the category of the social should be abandoned. It simply means that a general, meta-theory of the social cannot be involved in an analysis of sites of power relations. The term 'social' or the term 'society' must be understood only as a shorthand way of talking about specific intersections of practices. Having discussed this point I am now in a position to elaborate on my conception of the objects of power analysis, the sites of power relations.

Power relations exist only in relation to specific policies and the objectives which they encompass. These policies must not only be understood as formal, written policies. They can be said to be the objects of power analysis so long as they are operational, so long as they continue to be produced or reproduced or repeated in definite forms, with definite conditions of existence — such as in meetings, documents, procedural directions, discussions, books, films, legislation, classrooms, involving specific agents like pressure groups, political parties, government departments, law offices, planning bodies, church organisations, schools, ministers, solicitors, teachers, administrators. These operational policies — encompassing objectives concerned with whether something should or should not happen, whether something should be continued or discontinued, etc (these 'somethings', it must be stressed, are identified and evaluated within policies and this process occurs as part of the production of policies (which will be detailed later)) — are the basis of specific sites of power relations. It is around a particular operational policy that an intersection of practices can be said to exist and it is these intersections of practices around operational policies — these sites of power relations — which are the objects of power analysis.

It should be noted that by 'practices' here I mean more than institutionaly constrained actions and I mean more than something which is outside knowledge. By practices here I mean common groupings of techniques and discourses. As such practices are not essences 'practices' is the term I choose to describe an ingredient of sites of power relations without invoking the distinction between knowledge and reality. It too is an unsatisfactory term, but given my requirements I feel I have only a choice between 'discourses', defined as 'practices that systematically form the objects of which they speak' (Foucault, as quoted in Phillipps, 1982, 58), and 'practices' as defined above. I choose 'practices' simply because it seems less trapped in the reality side of the knowledge/reality distinction than 'discourses' is in the knowledge side. Perhaps an example will help to make this definition of practices clearer. Within this definition 'medical practices' does not refer just to those actions which occur within and are constrained by medical institutions (hospitals, doctors' rooms, paramedical operations, the training of doctors and paramedics, government health regulations, the operation of health funds, etc.). It also refers to the knowledge or discourses which keep these actions in place, those knowledges and discourses which are part of the conditions of existence of these actions (various medical discourses produced and reproduced in universities, books, journals, etc., legal discourses which address the category of the medical, including pieces of health legislation, discourses produced in popular magazines which define and deal with medical problems, discourses concerned with 'home remedies', etc.)

Foucault is wrong to argue that some sites of power relations, the micro sites, are incorporated into global sites, defined in terms of global strategies. This formulation suggests, very strongly, that these global sites exist as essences, which can be studied as such with the proviso that they be read as having been formed from the bottom up rather than from the top down. If we are to avoid essentialist analysis we must reject this formulation outright. Essences are essences whether we understand them as global sites which have 'invested, colonised, involuted, transformed, displaced, extended' a range of sites which constitute the 'infini- tesimal mechanisms' of the 'social body' or as entities which determine all the practices which fall within their reach. We must rather understand larger or more global sites as specific inter- sections of practices around specific operational policies which are granted the status 'global' because of the number of other sites which they reproduce or repeat (a term by which, by the way, I mean to reproduce systematically) as objects within their own boundaries. The sites repeated in this way are not incorporated, they have no necessary connection with the global sites, they exist separately, although of course they may themselves repeat some aspect of more global sites. For example, a particular company exists as a specific site — it is an intersection of, inter alia, business, bureaucratic and work practices formed around a policy concerned with the objective of producing goods or services at a profit. This particular company may be repeated, using techniques like the surveying of company records, the production of statistics on companies, discussions with company directors, in the more global site of government economic manage- ment — an intersection of, inter alia, parliamentary, legislative and bureaucratic practices formed around a policy of successfully managing the economy. The company (and its policy) is not incorporated in government (and its policy). It is repeated in government as an object within its boundaries. It has no necessary connection with government, it exists independently, although of course aspects of government policy are repeated within it using techniques concerned with the following of bureaucratic directives and specific pieces of legislation (presenting records for auditing, paying award wages, producing goods or services to a particular standard, etc.).

This formulation of the relationship between smaller and more global sites, it must be stressed, is not restricted to consideration of sites the size of those discussed in the above example (companies, national governments). It is also applicable to sites which deal with 'the world', as a totality. For instance, the World Bank, the International Monetary Fund and even the operation of various nuclear war machines which conceptualize the world as a target can (and should) be seen as sites which are granted the status 'global' or 'more global' because they repeat within their boundaries, within their constituent practices, many smaller sites (management of national economies, national banking procedures, national procedures for the funding of certain projects, 'localized' wars, the operation of international trade, the operation of international borders, etc.).

The possibility of resistance and struggle

[T] here are no relations of power without resistances; the latter are all the more real and effective because they are formed right at the point where relations of power are exercised; . . . hence like power, resistance is multiple and can be integrated in global strategies (Foucault, 1980 (c), 142).

For Foucault resistance, like power, is everywhere. But how is it formed and what exactly is its relationship to power? He offers an answer to the first part of this question by suggesting that resistance is formed and operates as part of a 'plebian quality or aspect' which resides in the 'social body' —

[There is] . . . something in the social body, in classes, groups and individuals themselves which in some sense escapes relations of power, something which is by no means a more or less docile or reactive primal matter but rather a centrifugal movement, an inverse energy, a discharge. There is certainly no such thing as 'the' plebs; there is as it were a certain plebian quality or aspect (Foucault, 1980 (c), 138).

And he offers an answer to the second part of the above question by suggesting that this 'plebian quality or aspect' operates as a 'counterstroke' to power. He says this 'quality or aspect' is

. . . everywhere in a diversity of forms and extensions, of energies and irreducibilities. This measure of plebs is not so much what stands outside relations of power as their limit, their underside, their counter-stroke, that which responds to every advance of power by a movement of disengagement. Hence it forms the motivation for every new development of networks of power (Foucault, 1980 (c), 138).

These two answers reveal a particularly essentialist understanding of resistance. It is essentialist in that it views resistance as being everywhere part of a 'plebian quality', despite the fact that it may take a 'diversity of forms', and it is essentialist in that it is formed against and relates to a unified and seemingly determining power. I will return to this criticism shortly, after a further look at Foucault's conception of resistance and how it works.

He tells us that resistance must be analysed in 'tactical and strategic terms', that we must posit 'that each offensive from one side serves as leverage for a counter offensive from the other' (Foucault, 1980 (d), 163 164). However, this point is over-shadowed by the suggestion that resistance is only truly effective at the most global level, at the point where smaller sites of resistance have been incorporated into a larger strategy. For instance, when asked if there is any point in the prisoners in a Panopticon at-tempting to take over the central tower, he replies, 'Oh yes, provided that isn't the final purpose of the operation.' He elaborates on this by asking, 'Do you think it would be much better to have the prisoners operating the Panoptic apparatus and sitting in the central tower instead of the guards?' (Foucault, 1980 (d), 164–165). This unfortunate totalizing of resistance is made even more unfortunate by the confirmation of the tendency we glimpsed above to portray resistance as totally determined by a unified power. As Minson summarizes Foucault's position, power 'produces, fixes in place and manages' resistances, making resistances into 'supports' as well as 'targets' or 'adversaries'. He goes on —

> They derive their means of struggle, their very social location
> from the prevailing form of power . . . It follows that . . .
> the successful exercise of power . . . may depend as
> much on the promotion of some kinds of resistance as on
> the effectiveness of means mobilized against them. This
> means — particularly since if resistances or forms of
> individuality are promoted by power this is to the
> detriment or exclusion of more unstabling forms — that
> *un*successes in the exercise of power cannot be simply
> registered as such. Tactical failure may be accounted in more
> than one sense, a strategic advantage (Minson, 1980,
> 9, his emphasis).

Of course this cannot be accepted — 'all means, objectives and points of resistance cannot be construed as necessarily invested in the dominant form of power . . . If [they were] . . . there could only ever be one form of power' (Minson, 1980, 23). Resistance is not determined by any essence and nor is it part of any essence, such as a 'plebian quality or aspect'. Resistance or opposition, like power relations, has no fixed or unified form and no fixed or unified location. It exists in specific sites — specific intersections of practices formed around operational policies and the objectives they encompass. Resistances are the objects of power analysis so long as the sites in which they exist continue to be reproduced or repeated in definite forms with definite conditions of existence. The policies in which they exist are always policies defined against other policies, those policies which they are resisting. But this does not mean they are determined by these other policies; it means only that the repetition of these other policies in the sites of the resistances is always one of the conditions of existence for them. For example, resistance to the recent proposal that many Australian child-care centres, currently publicly funded, be turned over to private enterprise[7] exists in a specific site, an intersection of, inter alia, educational, child-minding, welfare and feminist political practices, formed around a policy with definite conditions of existence in feminist groups, speeches to meetings, principles of welfare agencies, etc. This policy is defined against the policy of the privatisation of child-care, but it is not determined by this policy. Rather, the repetition of this policy in the site of this resistance is one of the conditions of existence of this resistance. Within this formulation we can recognise that the concepts of strategy and tactics have a role to play. But they must always be seen as restricted to particular policy objectives, not the other way round, as Foucault implies. Longer term strategies operate within a policy objective of the replacement or eradication (or fulfilment) of another policy (or that policy itself) — as in strategies within the policy objective of the replacement or eradication of the privatisation of child-care policy, like a challenge to the legality of this policy. And shorter term tactics operate within such strategies, such as tactics aimed at raising the privatisation policy as a legal issue in parliament, calling protest meetings to discuss its legality, etc.

In line with this and in line with what I said above about the relationship between smaller and larger sites of power relations, smaller sites of resistance are not incorporated into global sites or strategies of resistance. And certainly smaller sites of resistance are not meaningless or worthless or ineffective unless they are part of larger, more global sites. If smaller sites of resistance are present in larger, more global sites it is because they are reproduced or repeated there, not because they have been incorporated or because they are having their 'full potential' realised. For example the site of resistance to the privatisation of child-care may be repeated in the larger site of resistance to the privatisation of all institutions. But it is not incorporated by this larger site and nor is its effectivity

realised in this site. It exists and operates separately whether or
not it is repeated in larger sites, and its effectivity must be judged
using criteria specific to its own policy objective (although of
course its specific level of effectivity has no necessary relation to
the level of effectivity of larger sites in which it may be repeated).
Let us now turn to the question which is often seen as the central
question about resistance — that concerning the relationship between policies of resistance and the polices they are resisting:
the question of struggle.

Foucault argues that the notion of struggle is often used
inappropriately. He says it should not be a notion which refers to
general contradictions. 'This theme of struggle only really becomes
operative if one establishes concretely — in each particular case —
who is engaged in struggle, what the struggle is about, and how,
where, by what means . . . it evolves' (Foucault, 1980 (d), 164. It
seems then that for Foucault struggles are just that — struggles —
battles involving two or more specific forces each with a chance
of victory. He says analysis of struggles should have 'no built-in
tendency to show power as being at once anonymous and always
victorious' (Foucault, 1980 (d), 163). Elsewhere he emphasises this
point by discussing the possibility of struggle against the disciplinary
form of power, which as we have seen, he believes to be very
powerful indeed. He says we should be struggling to formulate
a new 'theory of right' — one which is 'antidisciplinary but at the
same time liberated from the principle of sovereignty' (Foucault,
1980 (a), 108). But in the case of the technology of discipline
there is a contradictory tendency on Foucault's part to portray
it as all-powerful, as being so powerful as to make struggle as he
describes it here impossible. He also contradicts his point that in
struggle all forces have an equal chance of victory. He suggests that
the forces in power relations are always 'unequal', that there is
always 'an above and a below', that there is always 'a difference of
potential' between forces (Foucault, 1980 (f), 201).

Fine, in opposition to these arguments of Foucault, especially
those which suggest that struggles against discipline are impossible,
argues that discipline is not as 'despotic' as Foucault makes out.
He argues that discipline is not dominated by utilitarianism and
that despite Foucault's claim that discipline is so powerful that it
is not subject to democratic control (which it has 'undermined
from within') struggles against discipline are not only possible,
they can be successful (Fine, 1979, 81, 84 and 86–87).

I do not think we need concern ourselves with the question of
whether struggles against forces of power are possible or winnable.
If we abandon the idea that power is a unified force, as I have
argued we should, then this question loses all relevance. In fact I

suggest we should do away with the notion of struggle altogether. Its use should be restricted to the practice from which it came – the analysis of military engagements. It has no place in the analysis of power relations in non-military sites, where the agents involved cannot be identified at a meta-level and must be thought of in their specificity. As we have seen these agents, which are produced or reproduced or repeated in specific intersections around specific policies, have specific forms such as solicitors, teachers, police, welfare workers, children, men, women, pressure groups, companies, political parties. They should be seen as such, not as 'forces' engaged in 'struggles'.

This de-centred conception of 'struggle' does not mean that we must also do away with notions like democracy and socialism which are often portrayed in unified terms in association with unified 'struggles'. Rather, we must rework them. Clearly we cannot understand democracy as either an essential object of study or essential means of 'struggle'. But we can understand it as policy objectives of specific sites – such as the democratisation of decision making procedures in a particular company, sporting body, school, etc. Or we can understand it as a technique which is produced or repeated in specific sites as a strategy or tactic aimed at securing a particular policy objective – such as in cases where the democratisation of procedures is part of an attempt to save a building from demolition, to prevent the sacking of certain workers, to allow certain courses to be taught in a school, etc. Or we can understand it as a technique which is produced or repeated in sites of government (more global sites) as a (more global) strategy aimed at securing the (more global) policy objective of governing populations. As part of this latter understanding we must realise that it is a multi-form technique – it may be of direct form, national/federal representative form, republican representative form, etc. To rework the notion of socialism is not quite as easy a task.

As Minson suggests the rejection of the notion of a fixed category of the social entails a complete rethink of the notion of socialism. As he says, it involves 'the repudiation of the ideal of "social" revolution' (Minson, 1980, 40). But resistances against policies of those specific sites which because of their constituent practices attract the label 'social' (and it must be remembered that these constituent practices cannot be known in a general way by means of a general theory – they can only be known in their specific form, in their specific intersection) can also be said to be 'social sites' or, by extension, 'socialist sites' or 'socialist resistances'. And the repetition or re-presentation within the more global of these sites of themselves as 'socialist policies' can be accepted because their constitution involves the repetition of the above smaller sites or 'socialist resistances'. For example, the site of resistance formed around the policy of attempting to thwart or eradicate the former Australian federal government's policy of using an Industrial Relations Bureau in the handling of industrial disputes[8] is defined against this policy, which is the basis of a site — the intersection of, inter alia, parliamentary, legal, industrial and trade union practices — which is repeated or re-presented as a social site. Therefore this site or resistance can be said to be a social site itself, or a socialist site or socialist resistance. And the Australian Labor Party (A.L.P.) can be said to be a socialist party with socialist policies insofar as it repeats or re-presents in its more global sites, in its more global policies, smaller socialist resistances such as the one outlined here. Of course the more global sites in which the A.L.P. operates include sites of government and in these sites socialism, like democracy, must be understood (as well as being understood in the sense described above in the case of the A.L.P.) as a multi-form (centralised social democracy, decentralised democratic socialism, state/bureaucratic socialism, etc.) technique produced or repeated as a strategy aimed at securing the policy objective of governing populations.

By this formulation, it must be stressed, the idea of a unified notion of socialism is rejected completely (along with the notion of a political party or any other organization as a unified socialist representative or force).[9] Also this formulation involves the rejection of the proposition that the idea that all 'struggles' are struggles against a super, unified power is a 'necessary illusion' in conducting specific resistances (a proposition put to Foucault by Alain Grosrichard (Foucault, 1980 (f), 200)[10]). Obviously, within the terms of the formulation outlined above, this idea is a hindrance to the conduct of specific resistance rather than a 'necessary illusion'. The conduct of a specific resistance, formed around a particular policy objective, will involve the consideration, in the drawing up of strategies and tactics, of the specificity (practices and agents involved) of the policy which is being resisted. It will certainly not, or certainly should not, involve the consideration of a super, unified power which has no specificity.

The nature of power

As in the section on the location of power, much of what can be said about Foucault's position on what power is has already been said. For Foucault, while power is generally multi-form, in the 'modern' period, in the period to which most of his concrete analyses refer, it is of one main form, the disciplinary form. This form has allowed power, so Foucault says, 'to gain access to the bodies of individuals, to their acts, attitudes and modes of every-day behaviour', it has been able 'to grapple with the phenomena of population, in short to undertake the administration, control and direction of the accumulation of men' (Foucault, 1980 (b), 125). We have seen that he understands power in this modern form as a process which operates from the micro — the 'smallest elements in the social body' — to the global — 'ever more general mechanisms and forms of global domination'. I have criticised this conception of power for being too all-encompassing, for being falsely unified — in short for being an essence — and for being too negative, too much concerned with control and repression. In this section I will briefly look at some of Foucault's statements on the nature of power not examined so far, I will discuss the way Foucault's understanding of the nature of power has been read by a few of his followers/critics and I will highlight what Foucault and some of his followers/critics see as the major differences be-tween his understanding of the nature of power and a particular Marxist understanding of the nature of power.

Foucault makes an interesting and hitherto undiscussed point about the nature of power when he suggests that the true nature of power in its modern form only really became visible after the events of May 1968. He says that before this time power was analysed usually in terms of either 'the Sovereign' (by 'the Right') or 'the State' (by Marxists) (and of course he sees a similarity between the two) and as a consequence 'the mechanisms of power in themselves were never analysed'. He continues

> This task could only begin after 1968 . . . among those whose
> fight was located in the fine masks of the web of power.
> This was where the concrete nature of power became
> visible . . . To put it very simply, psychiatric internment,
> the mental normalisation of individuals, and penal
> institutions have no doubt a fairly limited importance
> if one is looking for their economic significance. On
> the other hand they are undoubtedly essential to
> the general function of power (Foucault, 1980 (b), 115—116).

While it is undoubtedly the case that the events of May 1968 in France started a transformation in the way power is theorized — a transformation which has reached many parts of the world and in which Foucault is a major figure — we should not be misled into thinking that this transformation has been completed, as Foucault implies here. The main principle behind the production of this paper is that this transformation should never be closed, should never be seen as completed.

Another interesting point about Foucault's treatment of the nature of power is his use of military analogies. He uses such analogies as if they are ideal for describing power. For instance he says that power is a 'war-like relation' as well as being the fruit of war, that which is 'won like a battle and lost in just the same way' (Foucault, 1979 (a), 60). Elsewhere, he goes into more detail:

> One is driven to ask this basic question: isn't power simply
> a form of war-like domination? Shouldn't one therefore
> conceive all problems of power in terms of relations of war?
>   . . . A whole range of problems emerge here. Who
> wages war against whom? Is it between two classes or more?
> Is it a war of all against all? . . . What is the relevance
> of concepts of tactics and strategy for analysing structures
> and political processes? What is the essence and mode of
> transformation of power? All these questions need to
> be explored. In any case it's astonishing to see how easily
> and self-evidently people talk of war-like relations of
> power . . . without ever making clear whether some form
> of war is meant, and if so what form (Foucault,
> 1980 (b), 123).

Foucault is right to suggest that military analogies are used far too freely. But he is wrong to argue for their use at all. As I argued above in the case of the notion of struggle, power relations are not the same as military relations. Power relations exist in specific sites, they involve agents who or which are produced or repeated in specific form in these specific sites - they are not about a grand or even local 'war' in which 'forces' 'do battle' or 'engage in struggles'.

In his critique of Foucault's conception of power Fine suggests that while Foucault's understanding of power seems to include careful consideration of the specificity of the disciplinary form of power, he in fact fails to appreciate or consider the specific form of that which is really at the root of disciplinary power — 'on the one hand, a growth in the quantity and scale of organisation and production; and on the other side, by the economic requirement for a rational and useful ordering.' For example, Fine claims, 'we are presented with no analyses of capital, that distinguishes it from   the means of production in general', and also he fails 'to separate analytically the character of co-operation in general, from that of capitalist co-operation' (Fine, 1979, 88—89). I have argued consistently that Foucault's position on the nature of power is far too general, that in constructing power as an

essence he fails to provide a framework which will allow consideration of objects of analysis in their specificity, as they have to
be looked at solely in terms of the maintenance of a particular
form of control, a particular form of power. But this does not
mean I agree with Fine. One of the starting points of an attempt
to construct a truly non-essentialist framework for power analysis
is of course the realisation that economistic frameworks have
stood in the way of non-essentialist analysis for quite some time.
So there is no point in rejecting Foucault's essentialist understanding of power only to turn or return, as Fine does, to another
essentialist understanding — that which sees the specificity of forms
of power only in terms of economic imperatives.

Meaghan Morris and Paul Patton, who can be said to be much
more sympathetic to Foucault's project than Fine, argue that
Foucault's conception of the nature of power is especially superior
in its treatment of 'global forms of domination'. They say Foucault
is able to go 'behind the seemingly natural object, in order to bring
to light the particular combination of discursive and non-discursive
practices which give it its distinctive historical existence'. They
offer the example of Foucault's treatment of the 'modern state':

> while the central locus of power in society undoubtedly
> involves a certain co-ordination of the more lowly
> techniques and power relations, it cannot be deduced from
> these. It functions also on a different register; its
> principle concern is the governance of larger multiplicities:
> territories or populations. The birth of the modern state,
> Foucault suggests is to be sought in the history of
> a certain art of governing populations (Morris
> and Patton, 1979, 9).

This passage not only repeats the knowledge/reality distinction
(in the form discursive/non-discursive) — or at least seems to
repeat it; to be fair to Morris and Patton they may not be equating
the term 'non-discursive' with reality but only using this term to
refer to non-regularized configurations, like informal conversations,
which do not as yet warrant the label 'discourse'. It also repeats
both the negative and essentialist features of Foucault's understanding of power. It talks of power in terms of global domination
and despite the gesture towards a suggestion that smaller sites of
power relations are not necessarily related to more global sites it
undoubtedly constructs the more global sites, especially the state,
as unified essences which are 'above' and incorporate 'more lowly'
sites. As I have argued at several points more global sites do not
exist 'above' smaller sites and incorporate them; they exist
independently of and use specific techniques to reproduce or

repeat these smaller sites within their boundaries. All we need say about the state is that rather than being a unified essence with a definite form (and I must stress that I am levelling this criticism only at Morris and Patton's treatment of the state (in the above passage); there are of course a multitude of theories of the state and it would be absurd to attempt a single critique which addressed them all), the state is only a category which can be used to repeat or represent several specific practices – government practices, semi-government practices, bureaucratic practices, etc. – as a grouping in specific sites. In this way a site around the policy of managing the economy, or a site around the policy of regulating broadcasting to a particular standard, involving the representation of the practices of several government departments, semi-government agencies, advisory bodies etc. may be said to be the state. But this is all the state is, it does not mean that these practices constitute a fixed, separately existing category of the state. They can only be said to constitute the state if and when they are repeated as a grouping in specific sites. In being only this the state is certainly not an always-important object of analysis – something it can only be when it is constructed as an essence. So whether Foucault produces a 'better' or 'worse' account of the state is only really important in terms of criteria produced within any essentialist framework which so constructs the state.

In another essay Patton says that Foucault's treatment of the nature of power shows 'the global effects of the judicial-penal system in the social field, or, more particularly, the way the 'carcereal archipelago' serves the 'bourgeoisie'. Also he claims that

> . . . his [Foucault's] position is a materialist one *par*
> *excellence* since it goes beyond, or behind, those categories
> in terms of which we have been accustomed to think the
> operations and effects of power (ideology, economic relations
> or political classes, for example) to base itself on the
> material support of all of these: the body (Patton, 1979,
> 115–117).

Again we have an extremely essentialist reading of Foucault. Patton proposes the body as the essence of Foucault's framework, an essence which always supports power relations and is always the base of 'economic relations', 'ideology' and 'classes'. He is concerned to show that Foucault's framework can produce analyses which meet criteria constructed and repeated in economistic frameworks – analyses which explain the dominance of the 'bourgeoisie' and which are always on the 'right' side of the knowledge/reality distinction (this time in the form idealism/materialism). As I suggested above in the case of the criterion concerned with accounts of the state these criteria should be abandoned not treated as meta-criteria.

Foucault clearly sees his treatment of power as having overcome the weaknesses of the understanding of power in terms of a unified Sovereign and as such sees it as having overcome the weaknesses of certain Marxist understandings of power. This is a theme taken up on Foucault's behalf by several writers. For example:

— When all the recent complications of Marxist
political theory are taken into account, the figure of
the ruling class can still be discerned insistently playing
the same unifying function . . . as the various
incarnations of political forms, Princes, Sovereigns,
Legislators, etc. play in classical political theory. [Marxism
cannot] . . . except at the cost of theoretical
indeterminacy, refuse the assumption of the homogeneity
of political power (Minson, 1980, 6).
— . . . despite all the sophistication and complications
in Marxist theory over the last decade, one can still
easily discern the familiar pyramid like image of the social
body with the ruling class at the top and the workers
at the bottom (Counihan, 1982, 31).

As well, Marxists (and 'neo-Marxists') have been accused of only partially learning the 'lessons' Foucault's work on power offers. They are said to

. . . attempt to appropriate the historical analyses of power
mechanisms in order to bolster the marxist science of
history, while rejecting straw-man versions of
those parts of the anlayses which might subvert their
schemas (Morris and Patton, 1979, 8).

Of course many people have defended Marxist positions against what they see as Foucault's attack. As we have seen, Fine is a good example. He thinks Foucault has interpreted Marx's theory of power 'too mechanically', that Marx's theory of power is more 'historically constrained' than Foucault understands (Fine, 1979, 77—78). I have already criticised Fine for substituting one form of essentialism for another. So I will say no more about this defence of Marxism here. As for the Foucault-inspired criticisms of Marxism looked at above, I think two things must be said. The first is that these criticisms falsely unify Marxism. Like theories of the state, there are many Marxisms and to attempt a single critique which addresses them all is to fall into an essentialist trap. The second thing that must be said is that we should be aiming for a continuing transformation of the way power is theorized. We

should not be knocking down existing houses of power analysis
only to replace them with new ones, in the name of Foucault or
anyone else, especially if the new houses are constructed largely
of glass.

Towards a new framework for power analysis

Again I must start a section by pointing out that much material
which comes under the section heading has already, by necessity
I would suggest, been raised in one form or another. I have discussed in varying degrees of detail, the following aspects of the
framework of power analysis I am arguing for in this paper: power
relations exist only in specific sites formed by an intersection of
practices around specific operational policies; there is no one unified site or sites of power relations such as the social or the state
and all such categories must be defined as specific groupings of
practices which are repeated or represented in specific sites;
strategies, tactics, techniques and technologies of power relations
do not exist in or operate as meta-sites of power, incorporating
smaller sites — they repeat the smaller sites within their boundaries
and the smaller sites repeat them, or aspects of them, within
them; no distinction can be made in power analysis between
knowledge and reality; the agents who or which operate in specific
sites of power relations are produced or repeated within these
sites, they do not exist and operate in an essentialist, unified
form; the agents who or which operate in specific sites of power
relations may be persons, types of persons (e.g. ministers, teachers,
police officers, lawyers etc.) or groups or companies or trade
unions or governments etc; the agents who or which operate in
specific sites of power relations are not subjects in the sense that
they are subjected to a force because power relations do not
operate as or through a unified force or essence; resistance is not
determined by any essence, it exists and operates in specific sites
formed as intersections of practices around specific operational
policies; the relationship between smaller and more global sites
of resistance is the same as that between all smaller and more
global sites of power relations; resistances must be analysed in
their specific settings and this means abandoning the notion of
struggle and completely redefining any diversifying notions like
democracy and socialism; this 'new' framework for power analyses
is part of an on-going transformation of the process of power
analysis, not its new house. In this section I will discuss in more
detail the nature of power relations within the framework I am
arguing for (and in doing so I will make clear my debt to Minson

in building up this framework) and will detail the way sites of power relations are actually formed.

The central passage in Minson's critique of Foucault's conception of power is a critique of the concept of power itself.

> I submit that the concept of power lacks any explanatory
> force or theoretical significance. Nothing can be
> explained in terms of power because on any understanding,
> one thing (be it political subject, economic structure
> or whatever) must be attributed to the unconditional
> capacity to dominate another. Rendering power as an
> attribute with a causal efficacy means that the
> outcomes of (power) struggles must be either deducible
> in advance from the power attributes of the forces or relations
> involved, or else beyond calculation altogether,
> inexplicable (Minson, 1980, 24).

Of course I agree with Minson that to conceive power as an attribute is necessarily essentialist, but I do not think this means we should abandon the notion of power altogether. Rather, we have to theorize it as a particular type of relation, a task which is aided considerably by a suggestion of Minson's.

> Instead, 'powers' might be conceived as *differential
> advantages* (or disadvantages) regarding the possibility of
> social agents being successful in realizing certain objectives,
> particularly, wherever the compliance and support of
> other agents is a prerequisite. It is not necessary to construct
> those differential advantages and disadvantages, such as
> popular aspirations, morale, responsibilities, principles, rights
> or virtues as essential human or subjective factors belonging
> to a moral domain. Rather it is possible to treat these
> phenomena of the moral or personal life as always determined
> by the specific discourses and social relations in which they
> are formed and where they exercise definite, albeit
> limited effects (Minson, 1980, 24, his emphasis).

Power relations, as we have already seen, exist in specific sites formed by an intersection of practices around a particular operational policy. We can now see that power relations are, more precisely, relations of advantage/disadvantage in terms of objectives within particular operational policies (and only in terms of the objectives within particular operational policies — 'advantage' and 'disadvantage' are not the two arms of some newly formed essence). So, to continue with one of our earlier examples, an anlaysis of the site of the privatisation of child-care services has to see this site as a site of relations of advantage/disadvantage in terms of the achievement of this privatisation. And of course the agents involved in this site — governments, parents, children, child-care workers, private profit-making child-care agencies, etc. — along with their aspirations, morale, responsibilities, principles, rights etc., have to be seen as products of this site, products of the intersection of governmental, educational, work, welfare, parental and legal practices which constitute this site. (Of course this analysis, like all power analyses, is a specific assessment of a specific site at a specific time. Power analysis should always be an on-going process.)

The obvious question which must be answered when looking at the way sites of power relations are formed is that which asks from *what* are these sites formed. What are the raw materials of sites of power relations? To simply point out that they are formed around particular policies is obviously not good enough. Policies and their objectives, and hence the sites of power relations which are formed around them, are produced using already existing sites as raw materials (in much the same way as new agent-forms are produced). A site is reproduced or repeated with slight variations in the intersection of practices which constitutes it. When these variations can no longer be accommodated within the policy in which they are situated, a new policy is produced to accomodate this new intersection. This production is carried out by the agents involved in the site which cannot accommodate the variation of practices within it, but because they themselves are the products of this site-under-stress this production cannot be said to be determined by them; it is not a wholly subjective production process. An example should help to make this point clear and will serve as a conclusion to the paper.

The intersection of work practices, legal practices, bureaucratic practices, management practices, government practices, trade union practices, etc. which make up the site of modern industrial relations, which is formed around the policy of producing goods or services in as harmonious an environment as possible (a policy with definite conditions of existence in boardroom discussions, company documents, union documents, procedures of and directives from departments of industrial relations, etc.) has spawned many new sites. It has continued to be reproduced or repeated, but at times under such stress that many new policies have been produced using it (or smaller sites which it, as a global site, repeats) as raw materials and which are usually produced as resistances against it (or against one of the smaller sites which are repeated within it). One such new site which has recently been produced in this way is that around the policy of opposition to sexual harassment at work.[11] The policy of producing goods or services in as harmonious an environment as possible has continually repeated within it the policy of treating women in a particular (sexist) way (a policy formed around the intersection of domestic practices, sexual practices, medical practices, biological scientific practices, etc., with definite conditions of existence in domestic procedures, medical procedures, books, magazines, films, television commercials, etc.). However, variations in the constituent practices of this site of harmonious work relations — variations concerned with the changing role of women in many of the practices involved — could (and can) no longer be accommodated within this site, with its continual repetition of sexist policies. The new site of opposition to sexual harassment has been produced by agents within the harmonious work relations site. These agents are mostly those constituted within the harmonious work relations site as 'women workers' and repeated in the new site in this form as well as in the newly produced agent-forms 'victims of sexual harassment' or 'targets of sexual harassment', at the same time as other agents constituted in the harmonious work relations site as 'managers' or 'bosses' or 'fellow workers' are repeated in the new site in these forms as well as in the newly produced agent-form 'harassers'. The new site has as its conditions of existence not just the written policies of groups like the Women's Electoral Lobby, Australian Union of Students, Victorian Teachers' Union, other unions and the A.L.P.'s 'Status of Women' Committee but also representations of the 'women's movement' in newspapers, magazines, journals, films, books, plays, discussions, etc. So far in Australia, unlike the U.S.A., the conditions of existence of this site do not include specific pieces of legislation, although they do include some specific regulations, such as the regulations governing employment in the federal Public Service. (To have opposition to sexual harassment inscribed in legislation must be seen at this stage as a strategy within this site.)

Sociology Research Group
in Cultural and Educational
Studies,
Department of Education,
University of Melbourne,
Parkville.
Victoria 3052
Australia

* I would like to thank Peter Botsman, Terry Counihan, Lesley Johnson, Noel King, Dave McNeill, Geoff Whitty and Peter Williams for their comments and suggestions on earlier drafts of this article.

Notes

1 In the preface to the book of essays by Foucault which they edited, Meaghan Morris and Paul Patton described his analytical framework in the following terms: 'Nothing less than a new conception of philosophical work is involved: one whose method is that of wide ranging historical analysis, and whose orientation is given along the triple axis of truth, power and struggle' (Morris and Patton, 1979, 8).

2 Most of the interviews and lectures I will be considering are collected in the extremely useful book, *Power/Knowledge*, edited by Colin Gordon.

3 Ross Harley and Jon Roper summarize the advantages to be gained by not aiming for a general theory. They point out that not to do so '. . . opens up fields of analysis for specific intervention and work. These fields may well overlap, but we reject the possibility of providing *one* field which exists as the key to unlock all the others (Harley and Roper, 1982, 127–128, their emphasis)'. They go on to show, in the novel and entertaining form of a video script, the problems associated with existing attempts to provide a general theory of sexuality.

4 Foucault sometimes refers to the fact that power works through the smallest elements of the social body by using the term 'microphysics of power', a term which Valencia-Villa (1981, 362) says describes 'the endless and changeable and proliferating dynamics of power relationships'.

5 It should be noted that Foucault has suggested that this is not *always* the way power works. In his 1980 (f) (199- 200, my emphasis) for example, Foucault says, after pointing out that 'generally speaking' power works from the bottom up, 'But there are *always* also movements in the opposite direction, whereby strategies which co-ordinate relations of power produce new effects and advance into hitherto unaffected domains.' I believe this inconsistency is another example of Foucault's tendency to construct power as an essence which has a particular direction.

6 This example was suggested to me by Ian Hunter.

7 This issue is discussed in more detail by Counihan (1982, 19–21).

8 This issue is discussed in more detail by Mitchell (1979).

9 In making this point I am agreeing with Minson's argument that there is a pressing need to 'reconsider current relations of political parties and programmes to specific "social" struggles; and in particular whether the movements of women, blacks, prisoners, anti-psychiatry and so on are necessarily furthered by thus being as easily subsumed as they currently are within party-political programmes' (Minson, 1980, 40).

10 Foucault, unfortunately, does not reply as someone else asks a question before he can and the conversation changes direction.

11 I have chosen this example not because it is in any way a special example, but because at the time of writing the site of opposition to sexual harassment at work received something of a fillip in Victoria. Reports were published and broadcast of an attempt by a minister in the state Labor government to kiss and hug a woman opposition M.P. and, following this, a statement was released under the names of nine women members of the government condemning the opposition M.P. concerned for failing 'to distinguish between sexual harassment and warm, human friendly behaviour' (*The Age*, 21/10/82, p.1).

In formulating the details of this example I owe a debt to Jenny Macklin and Helen Bannister.

References

The Age, 21/10/82.

Counihan, T. (1982), 'Minding the Family, Donzelot and his Critics', in Botsman, P. (ed.), *Theoretical Strategies (Local Consumption*, Series 2).

Fine, B. (1979), 'Struggles Against Discipline: The Theory and Politics of Michel Foucault', *Capital And Class*, No. 9.

Foucault, M. (1979(a)), 'Power and Norm: Notes', in Morris, M. and Patton, P. (eds), *Michel Foucault: Power, Truth, Strategy*, Ferral Publications, Sydney.

Foucault, M. (1979(b)), 'What is an Author?' *Screen*, Vol. 20, No. 1.

Foucault, M. (1980(a)), 'Two Lectures: Lecture Two', in Gordon, C. (ed.), *Power/ Knowledge: Michel Foucault*, Pantheon Books, New York.

Foucault, M. (1980(b)), 'Truth and Power', in Gordon, C. (ed.), ibid.

Foucault, M. (1980(c)), 'Power and Strategies', in Gordon, C. (ed.), ibid.

Foucault, M. (1980(d)), 'The Eye of Power', in Gordon, C. (ed.), ibid.

Foucault, M. (1980(e)), 'The History of Sexuality', in Gordon, C. (ed.), ibid.

Foucault, M. (1980(f)), 'The Confession of the Flesh', in Gordon, C. (ed.), ibid.

Foucault, M. (1980(g)), 'Questions on Geography', in Gordon, C. (ed.), ibid.

Harley, R. and Roper, J. (1982), 'Here Comes the Night (Introduction and Video Script)', in Botsman, P. (ed.), op. cit.

Hindess, B. (1977), 'The Concept of Class in Marxist Theory and Marxist Politics', in Bloomfield, J. (ed.), *Class, Hegemony And Party*, Lawrence and Wisehart, London.

Hindess, B. and Hirst, P. (1975), *Pre-Capitalist Modes of Production*, Routledge and Kegan Paul, London.

Hodges, J. and Hussain, A. (1979), 'La Police des Families', *Ideology And Consciousness*, No. 5.

Minson, J. (1980), 'Strategies for Socialists? Foucault's conception of power', *Economy And Society*, Vol. 9, No. 1.

Mitchell, R. (1979), 'Industrial Relations Under a Conservative Government: The Coalition's Labour Law Programme 1975 to 1978', *The Journal of Industrial Relations*, December.

Morris, M. and Patton, P. (1979), 'Preface', in Morris, M. and Patton, P. (eds), op. cit.

Patton, P. (1979), 'Of Power and Prisons', in Morris, M. and Patton, P. (eds), op. cit.

Phillipps, R. (1982), 'Law Rules O.K.?', in Botsman, P. (ed.), op. cit.

Valencia-Villa, H. (1981), 'Foucault and the Law: An Antijuridical Jurisprudence?', *Phillipine Law Jurnal*, Vol. 56.